A CAUTIONARY TALE

▼▼▼▼▼▼

FOOD FIRST

Food First Development Studies

Peter M. Rosset, series editor

A CAUTIONARY TALE

Failed
U.S. Development Policy
in Central America

Michael E. Conroy
Douglas L. Murray
Peter M. Rosset

LYNNE
RIENNER
PUBLISHERS

BOULDER
LONDON

Published in the United States of America in 1996 by
Lynne Rienner Publishers, Inc.
1800 30th Street, Boulder, Colorado 80301

and in the United Kingdom by
Lynne Rienner Publishers, Inc.
3 Henrietta Street, Covent Garden, London WC2E 8LU

Library of Congress Cataloging-in-Publication Data
Conroy, Michael E.
    A cautionary tale: failed U.S. development policy in Central
    America / Michael Conroy, Douglas Murray and Peter Rosset.
    p.   cm.—(Food First Development Studies)
    Includes bibliographical references and index.
    ISBN 1-55587-630-7 (alk. paper)
    1. Produce trade—Government policy—Central America. 2. Exports—
Government policy—Central America. 3. Agriculture—Economic
aspects—Central America. 4. Economic assistance, American—Central
America. 5. United States. Agency for International Development.
I. Murray, Douglas L., 1947–   II. Rosset, Peter. III. Title.
HD9014.C462C66 1996
338.9'17308—dc20   95-26189
                                                              CIP

British Cataloguing in Publication Data
A Cataloguing in Publication record for this book
is available from the British Library.

Printed and bound in the United States of America

        The paper used in this publication meets the requirements
    ∞   of the American National Standard for Permanence of
        Paper for Printed Library Materials Z39.48-1984.

    5   4   3   2   1

*We dedicate this work to Myrna Mack Chang,
who was murdered while conducting research
for an early stage of the project
that eventually became this book.*

*May your spirit live on in the
struggle for justice in Guatemala.*

CONTENTS

▼▼▼▼▼▼▼▼

TABLES AND FIGURES

▼▼▼▼▼▼▼

▼ **Tables**

ix

▼ Figures

FOREWORD

▼▼▼▼▼▼▼

Don Marcelo Xuc

I am a representative of the Farmer's Improvement Committee [COPROA], a group that includes fifty-four *campesinos* from the Patzún area. . . . I want to share with this workshop our experiences working with nontraditional products.

Before the arrival of nontraditional crops, our community was dedicated to the production of our sacred corn, hard beans, our local peas, potatoes, and wheat. We used natural fertilizers, covering the ground with compost and animal manure. We didn't use insecticides because we didn't face pests that damaged our crops.

The products we harvested were good; the population was healthy. The costs of the tools and the products we needed were within the reach of most people. We focused on working the land, marketing, and construction. Our women were dedicated to family care, artesanry, and caring for our animals. The daily wage we received was Q1.50 [quetzals, the Guatemalan currency], and it was enough to cover the necessities of the family. In those days the life of our communities was marked by happiness, respect, and collaboration. Those were happy times, and we had time to get together and meet at the community level.

Broccoli growing was introduced around 1978. At that time there were two cooperatives in our town, the Cooperativa el Agro and the Cooperativa

---

Translators' note: Don Marcelo Xuc is a fifty-five-year-old representative of a Guatemalan indigenous farmers' group. He delivered these comments at a conference on nontraditional agricultural exports, sponsored by the World Resources Institute, in Antigua, Guatemala, on September 21, 1993. His remarks were translated by the authors.

San Bernardino. The ALCOSA export company invited two representatives of each cooperative to participate in a workshop on export products in Chimaltenango. These leaders, very enthusiastic about the benefits farmers were going to obtain, returned to convince their communities. They began to raise consciousness in their communities, focusing on the yields of our traditional products, the time it took us to grow them, and the prices we received. They talked to us of the advantages of production for export, with products that took less time to grow, and of the prices we were going to receive.

At first they gave us some advantages. They provided fertilizers on credit and seeds at a good price. Technical assistance was covered by the company, and they took the trouble to teach us the cultivation and care of these products. They started us using fertilizers and fungicides. Through BANDESA [the national development bank] they gave us loans at 7 percent annual interest.

Since our lands were in parcels too small to respond to the needs of the production they wanted, they formed us into groups with the goal of uniting thirty to fifty *cuerdas* [two to four hectares] as a minimum. And seeing the initial results, which were rather favorable, we small producers began to reduce our production of corn, beans, and wheat in order to increase the production of broccoli.

After broccoli came cauliflower, then brussels sprouts; in 1982 snow peas, in 1990 string beans and sweet green peas; and last year the production of mini vegetables. Seeing the increase in production, the export companies began to bring their installations to the town. Some of our townspeople with greater economic resources began to open stores for the sale of fertilizers and fungicides, and some began to work as intermediaries and as transporters of the products.

We now have to say that only some 5 percent of our population has benefited from the production of nontraditional products, and the other 95 percent has been impoverished by them. We are living under worse conditions than those we had before these products were introduced. Let me give some examples, from our experience, that reinforce what I'm saying.

At the start, we received U.S.$13.00 per quintal [hundredweight] of broccoli, when the quetzal was at Q1 per dollar. Presently we are receiving Q50.00 per quintal, or approximately U.S.$8.63. Fifteen years have gone by and our product has declined in price 40 percent, rather than rising.

Our dependence on fertilizers, insecticides, and other agricultural inputs has increased. The quality of fertilizers and insecticides has dropped. If we needed fifteen pounds of fertilizer for a cuerda before, now we need 150 pounds. And the same happens with the poisons: from half a scoop before, we now need three scoops, depending on the type of product.

The costs of the agricultural inputs and of the tools have gone up considerably. They change depending on the movement of the dollar [with respect to the quetzal]. When we turn our products over to the company, they deduct at least 10 percent for blemished fruit, and more if we can't get the quality that the company wants. The prices and rents for land have gone up. . . . The number of workdays has gone up, and we don't get a fair price for our product. The cost of transport has gone up considerably. When we attempt to protest the deductions from our payments, they threaten that they won't take any of our harvest. What can we do with our product when it has cost us time and money to get it to the company? The intermediaries, transporters, and businesspeople have enriched themselves, and the producers have become impoverished. There are now more sicknesses we didn't have before: arthritis, gastritis, respiratory illnesses, and others. Our children and our wives also suffer as a consequence of the poisons and the type of work that we now do. Our family life has been affected. . . . There is little time left for taking care of our kids, and they now have to go and work with us. Our spouses have to leave our houses unattended in order to help us, and they no longer work in artesanry and care of the family animals, which used to be a help to the family's income.

Now there's no time for community life. We are worried about taking care of our crops, and we even have to sacrifice our Sundays. We don't have time to get together and worry about our neighbors. Each one of us, focused on his own, is more individualistic, not interested in the other.

We are losing our respect for and our valuation of Mother Earth. We see her as an instrument, even getting to the point of anger if she doesn't give us the product that we need to hand over.

When we turn in our products we don't receive payment in cash. Sometimes we wait up to two months, and on some occasions payment has been delayed up to six months, without any consideration for our needs. The treatment that we receive from the employees and the managers of the companies is very bad. There is no respect for us, as though we were begging from them or like they were doing us a big favor accepting our products. We are conditioned to what the company requests. We are losing our liberty; if there is a failure in the crop, they blame us.

The interest rates on loans have gone up. Now BANDESA charges 24 percent annual interest and they won't lend less than Q10,000 [about U.S.$2,000 in 1993]. The companies don't fulfil their promises. Even when we have written promises from the truckers who are going to transport our products, they let us down.

As you can see, it is the law of the strongest. The weak are condemned to die.

ACKNOWLEDGMENTS

▼▼▼▼▼▼▼▼

Many thanks to those without whose help this work would have been impossible. Our research was generously supported by several institutions and many collaborators. The Ford Foundation Office for Mexico and Central America provided the initial financial support through a grant to the University of Texas at Austin. The Guatemala portion of the project grew to a larger, deeper analysis of nontraditional agricultural exports with additional funding from the John D. and Catherine T. MacArthur Foundation and the Pew Charitable Trust to PACCA (Policy Alternatives for the Caribbean and Central America) in Washington, D.C., under the direction of Robert Stark, and to AVANCSO (Asociación para el Avance de las Ciencias Sociales) in Guatemala. Small additional grants came from the Central American office of Greenpeace Latin America to enhance the ecological dimensions of the work, and local resources were contributed by each of the collaborating institutions. Individual research support was provided to Douglas L. Murray by the John D. and Catherine T. MacArthur Foundation Program on Peace and International Cooperation, and by the Fulbright Central American Republics Research Program. Peter M. Rosset was supported for the research period by CATIE (Centro Agronómico Tropical de Investigación y Enseñanza) and by the Fulbright Senior Lectureship Program. The chance for him to write was provided by the University of Texas at Austin, the University of California at Berkeley, and Stanford University. The Institute for Food and Development Policy (Food First) sponsored the final compilation and preparation of the book under his direction.

Sandra Kinghorn of ICADS (Institute for Central American Development Studies) in Costa Rica was a critical early collaborator. Much of the on-site research was undertaken by Central American institutions as part of a regional project coordinated through the University of Texas. Each institution published country-specific results cited throughout this book. In Costa Rica, collaborative research was undertaken by CECADE (Centro de Capacitación para el Desarrollo) under the direction of William Reuben, Alvaro Rivas Villatoro, and María Dalva Trivelato. In Guatemala the project was sponsored by AVANCSO, under the direction of Myrna Mack Chang and Edgar Gutiérrez, with the assistance of Fernando Vargas, Rubio Caballeros, and Luis Arriola. In El Salvador, collaborative research was undertaken by PREIS (Programa Regional de Investigación sobre El Salvador) under the direction of Breny Cuenca and Roberto Codas. In Honduras, work on the project was undertaken at POSCAE (Posgrado Centroamericano en Economía y Planificación) at the National Autonomous University of Honduras, directed by Hugo Noé Pino with the collaboration of Rodulio Perdomo. In Nicaragua the project was supported by Mario R. López and Irene Guevara O. of the National Autonomous University of Nicaragua, through the Centro de Investigaciones Económicas y Sociales and the Department of Agricultural Economics. Helda Morales, Ronaldo Pérez, and Charles MacVean of the Universidad del Valle in Guatemala undertook a crucial piece of contract research on the environmental impact of nontraditional export crops in the Guatemalan *Altiplano*.

In this book we both synthesize and extrapolate from country-specific results, providing analysis that generalizes from those experiences. The viewpoints we express escape the subtle constraints on criticism of USAID (United States Agency for International Development) felt by members of all of the country research teams, constraints rooted in the political power and research-funding dominance of USAID in their respective countries. This is, we believe, the more complete picture that they could not publish. Nevertheless, this book does not in any way speak for the researchers noted above.

The following people contributed intellectually to the gestation of this book through their conversations with the authors, and we thank them deeply: Carlos Campos, Greg Vunderink, David Kaimowitz, Alicia Korten, Lori Ann Thrupp, Polly Hoppin, Elizabeth Katz, Susan Stonich, Margaret Reeves, Jorge Simán, Brad Barham, Michael Carter, Robert Rice, John Vandermeer, Ivette Perfecto, Terry Karl, Miguel Altieri, Elisabeth Wood, Rob McConnell, Maarten Immink, John Lamb, Dale Krigsvold, Wayne Williams, Mario Pareja, Kristen Nelson, Michael Watts, Bill Friedland, Laura Raynolds, Joseph Collins, Mary Clark, Tom Thacher, Lisa Nelson, Bea Bezmalinovic, John Gershman, the Grupo COSECHA in San José, Costa Rica (you know who you are), and the many Central American farmers who patiently allowed themselves to be interviewed. An anonymous reviewer provided many useful suggestions. We thank Rich Ann Roche, Dereka Rushbrook, and David Drucker in Austin and Jaana Remes and Aaron Strain at Stanford University for research assistance. María Elena Martínez-Torres and Stephanie Tarnoff at Food First provided editorial assistance.

Finally, however, this book is the sole and exclusive product of the authors: we assume full responsibility for any errors of commission or omission that may appear in its pages.

A CAUTIONARY TALE

▼▼▼▼▼▼

▼▼▼▼▼▼▼▼▼▼▼▼▼▼▼▼▼▼▼▼▼▼▼▼▼▼▼▼▼▼▼▼

1

CENTRAL AMERICA'S LOST DECADE AND NONTRADITIONAL AGRICULTURAL EXPORT STRATEGY

A cornerstone of U.S. economic development policy for Central America and the Caribbean in the 1980s and early 1990s, implemented by the U.S. Agency for International Development (USAID), was the promotion of non-traditional agricultural exports (NTAEs) from the region and their shipment worldwide, but especially to the United States. NTAEs consisted of melons, strawberries, broccoli, cauliflower, snow peas, squash, and other perishable farm products, often shipped fresh directly to supermarkets in the United States, on which much of the hope for economic recovery in Central America came to be placed. For us, the authors, they represented the fruits of Central America's social, political, economic, and ecological crisis of the same era, a desperate plunge into globally oriented production that may have, in fact, deepened the crisis for most of the small-scale, poor farmers who were enticed to plant them. The promotion of nontraditionals was an expensive policy gamble, whose dubious payoff we evaluate in this cautionary tale.

The NTAE policy was implemented vigorously in all the Central American countries, including Nicaragua after the return of USAID in 1990.[1] It involved creating ambitious programs of production research, tailoring loan programs, assisting the development of brokering links with U.S. importing firms, and a wide range of other costly subsidies. Hundreds of millions of dollars were granted and loaned to Central Americans to enhance this process, and it remained an important component of the policies of all Central American governments in the early 1990s. These policies led, in some cases, to impressive increases in production and exports of some products, from some countries, under some circumstances. Yet for many if not most of the region's poor rural majority, the policy failed to provide any improvement in the dismal living conditions that led to more than a decade of armed conflict.

1

Central America's search for new exports was a response to the region's debt crisis, declining exports, and, we argue, a prohibition on USAID to assist the region with the competitive development of either its traditional exports (cotton, cattle, sugar, coffee, and bananas) or of the basic grains that form the mainstay of the diet of most of its population. NTAEs were visualized as an ideal way to take advantage of Central America's geographic proximity to U.S. markets, to encourage the production of crops that might be grown by poor farmers, and to diversify the region's export structures away from traditional products. But there is strong evidence that, even in successful cases, there are negative effects worthy of greater consideration. There is evidence that NTAEs have tended to undermine small farmers' economic position, drawing them into increased debt and sometimes leading to significant land concentration. At the same time, the viability of traditional corn and bean cultivation has been undercut by trade policies, leaving the rural poor without the peasant safety net of basic grain production for the domestic market and their own consumption. There are still other questions about the role of multinational corporations in directing and controlling NTAE production, about serious abuses of national sovereignty by development agencies like USAID in their mad dash to implement these policies at any cost, and about the ecological and health consequences of heavily pesticide-dependent new crops.

The developmental edifice built upon this cornerstone is beginning to show serious cracks. We believe that this development strategy embodies serious inherent design defects. In fact, it is unlikely to facilitate either the short-term reduction of rural poverty or the long-term sustained, diversified, and equitable development that its designers predicted.

This book is the culmination of three years of research by the authors on these themes, in collaboration with five research teams, one in each of the principal Central American nations: Costa Rica, El Salvador, Guatemala, Honduras, and Nicaragua.[2] We document and analyze fundamental failures in the NTAE strategies. The failures display a fascinating intermingling of social, economic, and ecological problems, combined with the fundamental nature of production strategies, international industry structure, and the role of an international assistance agency in promoting a process that visibly impoverishes a large proportion of the families it purportedly seeks to benefit.

▼ **Central America's "Lost Decade"**

The 1980s will undoubtedly be recorded in Central American history as the worst decade experienced in the twentieth century. After twenty years of impressive economic progress during the 1960s and 1970s, the 1980s brought to these nations insurrection, revolution, civil war, an exploding debt crisis, falling income levels, brutal structural adjustment, a severe deterioration in physical capital and social infrastructure, and worsening health and education levels that pushed the majority of the region back to living standards last seen in the 1960s. It mattered little that some countries, like Costa Rica, were not directly involved in the worst of the political instability. Shared global images of the region meant shared social and economic fates. It was within this context that NTAE strategies were promoted. It is in this context that one must understand the headlong plunge into experimentation with nontraditional production.

▼   Basic Characteristics of the Region

The five Central American nations on which we focus are small, with relatively open economies. The total population of the region in 1990 was 26.3 million, only slightly larger than that of the state of California (see Figure 1.1). Guatemala is the largest country, with more than 35 percent of the population, and Costa Rica the smallest, with under 3 million people. The aggregate economic size of the five countries, measured by total gross domestic product (GDP) in 1990, was less than U.S.$25 billion, about the same as that of an intermediate-sized city in the United States in that year. Figure 1.2 displays the relative economic size of each country. Guatemala accounts for a little more than 33 percent of regional output, with El Salvador and Costa Rica each at slightly more than 20 percent, although El Salvador has nearly twice the population. Nicaragua, after the deepest economic decline in the region, had the smallest economy in 1990, with total annual output at only $2.5 billion. It is important to remember the small magnitude of each economy when we begin to look at the relative size and importance of NTAEs.

▼   Growth Experiences of the 1960s and 1970s

Central America enjoyed relatively unprecedented economic growth during the 1960s and 1970s. Data from the Inter-American Development Bank (IDB), shown in Table 1.1, illustrate both the encouraging growth of these two decades and the collapse experienced in the 1980s. All of the countries of the region achieved roughly 2.4 percent real per capita growth per year during the 1960s, and several repeated the performance in the 1970s. This was a period of rapid industrialization and economic integration within the Central American Common Market (CACM). Although the overall region enjoyed two decades of rapid growth, there is no promise in those data that

Figure 1.1   Central America, 1990 Population (in millions)

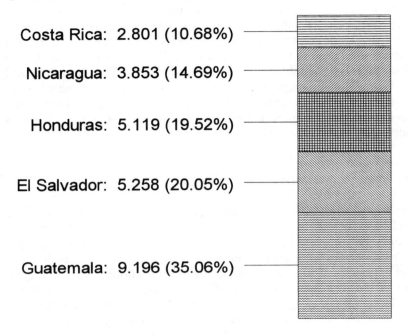

Costa Rica: 2.801 (10.68%)

Nicaragua: 3.853 (14.69%)

Honduras: 5.119 (19.52%)

El Salvador: 5.258 (20.05%)

Guatemala: 9.196 (35.06%)

Source: World Bank (1993).

the benefits of that growth were distributed widely within each. The 1978–1979 insurrection and civil war in Nicaragua, and the onset of civil war in El Salvador in 1980, lessened the decade-long performance for each, as is reflected in Table 1.1. But their economic performance during the years preceding the onset of crisis was not dissimilar from that of Latin America as a whole.

The collapse of all these economies during the 1980s, as well as throughout most of Latin America, led the IDB to describe these years as Latin America's Lost Decade (IDB 1989). From 1980 to 1988 the decline in real income for these five Central American nations averaged more than 16 percent per capita. This was more than twice the decline for Latin America as a whole. The pattern over the decade differed in each country, as we shall see below; this means that the data in Table 1.1, comparing an arbitrary starting and ending point, are somewhat misleading, for they do not necessarily

Figure 1.2   Central America, 1990 GDP (in billions of U.S.$)

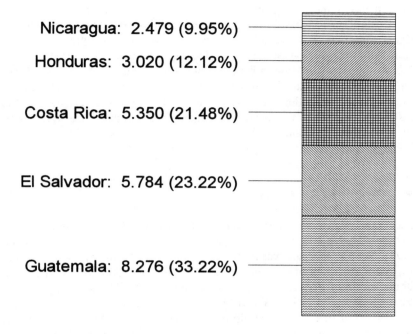

Nicaragua: 2.479 (9.95%)

Honduras: 3.020 (12.12%)

Costa Rica: 5.350 (21.48%)

El Salvador: 5.784 (23.22%)

Guatemala: 8.276 (33.22%)

Source: World Bank (1993).

Table 1.1   Central American Growth and Stagnation, 1960–1988

	Real per capita GDP (1988 dollars)				Change (%)		
	1960	1970	1980	1988	1960–1970	1970–1980	1980–1988
Costa Rica	1,435	1,825	2,394	2,235	27.2	31.2	−6.6
El Salvador	832	1,032	1,125	955	24.0	9.0	−15.1
Guatemala	1,100	1,420	1,866	1,502	29.1	31.4	−19.5
Honduras	619	782	954	851	26.3	22.0	−10.8
Nicaragua	1,055	1,495	1,147	819	41.7	−23.3	−28.6
Latin American Region	1,374	1,802	2,512	2,336	31.1	39.4	-7.0

Source: IDB News (October–November 1989).

capture either the high or the low point of each nation's problems at that time. But several characteristics of the Central American economies, and their change in the 1980s, can be seen clearly from the table.

Costa Rica's standard of living throughout this period was considerably higher than that of its neighbors; in fact, it was roughly equivalent to the Latin American regionwide average. Honduras and El Salvador shared the dubious honor of the lowest standard of living, measured by real GDP per capita, well below half that of Costa Rica. The intermediate levels seen in Nicaragua in the earlier years were lost by the end of the period, after the destruction caused by the insurrection against the Somoza dynasty, followed by five years of contra war against the Sandinistas, a U.S. economic embargo, and war-related hyperinflation (Conroy 1990).

▼   Origins of the Crisis

There is an extensive historiography on the origins of Latin America's Lost Decade (Fagen 1987; Pérez-Brignoli 1989; Miller 1992; Hansen-Kuhn 1993). Central America was struck especially hard by the global crises that trapped Latin America as a whole. Rapidly rising oil prices, after the Organization of Petroleum Exporting Countries (OPEC) cartel began coordinated activity in 1973, affected the Central American nations particularly because all of them imported virtually all their hydrocarbons. The wave of international borrowing that permitted some continued growth in the region during the last half of the 1970s ended abruptly at the start of the 1980s when first Brazil, then Mexico announced that they would not be able to continue repayment on their outstanding debt. As world financial markets recoiled in general from Latin America, they fled even more precipitously from Central America, especially after the 1979 triumph of the Sandinista Revolution in Nicaragua and the 1980 outbreak of civil war in El Salvador. At the same time, hikes in global interest rates doubled and tripled the burden of debt contracted in the 1970s, forcing all of the countries of the region to further increase their debt by effectively borrowing more each year simply to cover the interest payments on prior debt that they could not redeem.

The impact of this combination of conditions on each of the five countries is illustrated in Figures 1.3a–e, which show both relative growth in the 1970s and the differing patterns of decline in real income per capita after the onset of the Central American crisis. The differences in depth and timing of the respective economic declines can be seen there, as well as the comparable economic impact of natural disasters, such as Hurricane Fifi in 1974.

Central America's rapid growth in the 1960s and 1970s was based upon a set of policies developed and advocated by the U.N. Economic Commission for Latin America (later ECLAC). By closing themselves off

Figure 1.3a   Costa Rica's Lost Decade (GDP per capita, constant 1987 colones in thousands)

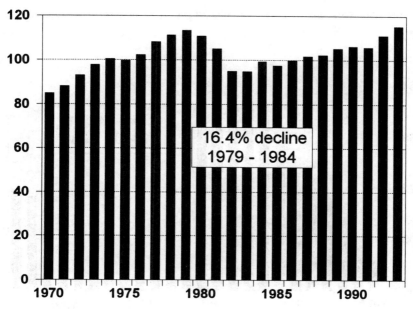

16.4% decline
1979 - 1984

Source: World Bank (1994).

Figure 1.3b   El Salvador's Lost Decade (GDP per capita, constant 1987 colones)

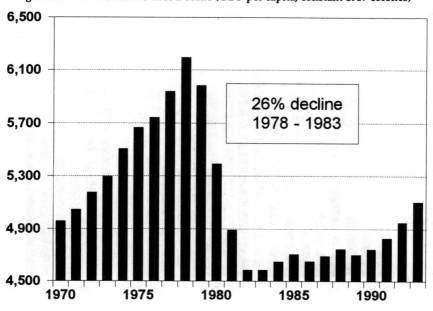

26% decline
1978 - 1983

Source: World Bank (1994).

Figure 1.3c   Guatemala's Lost Decade (GDP per capita, constant 1987 quetzals)

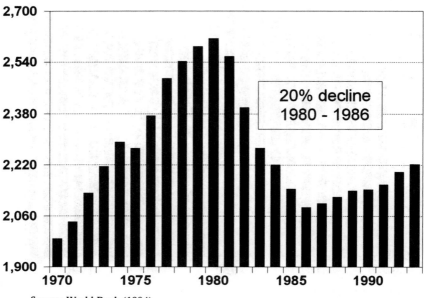

Source: World Bank (1994).

Figure 1.3d   Honduras's Lost Decade (GDP per capita, constant 1987 lempiras)

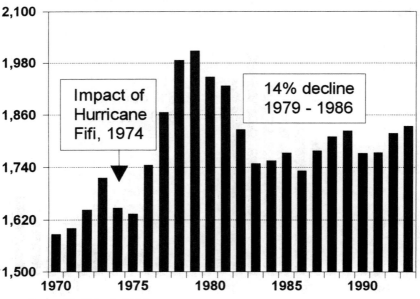

Source: World Bank (1994).

Figure 1.3e   Nicaragua's Lost Decade (GDP per capita, constant 1987 cordobas)

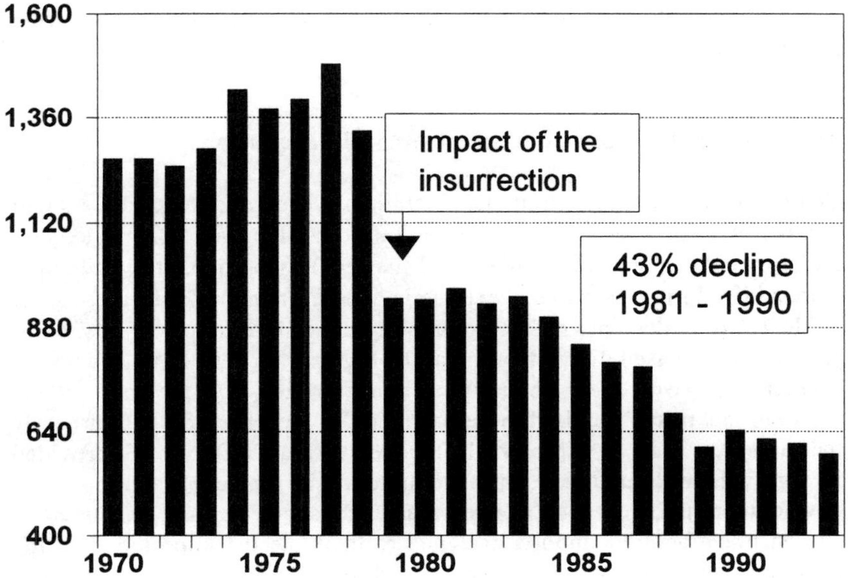

Source: World Bank (1994).

somewhat from international competition, the Central American nations implemented import-substituting industrialization, creating competitive space for local investment that did, in fact, lead to substantial increases in the production of local manufactured goods, increases in industrial employment, and rapid overall economic growth. The limitations of small protected markets were offset partially by the creation and expansion of the CACM (Bulmer-Thomas 1987), though loopholes in the tariff barriers still allowed multinational corporations to reap the lion's share of the benefits.

Why did this model fail in the 1980s? The Kissinger Commission, appointed by President Ronald Reagan, asserted in 1984 that the failure was linked to the "superimposition" of a small amount of growth upon a society characterized by fundamental and abject poverty for the vast majority of the population (Kissinger Commission 1984). The Sanford Commission, organized by U.S. Senator Terry Sanford (Dem., N.C.), reached the same conclusion, arguing that, "despite periods of strong economic growth, the gains from that growth were distributed extremely inequitably" (ICCARD 1989). Moreover, it noted, "economic growth failed to translate into political and economic decision-making power for the majority," and "the political repression that predominated in most of the region sparked vigorous, wide-spread public frustration" (p. 15). There were also, however, more directly economic explanations for the virtual collapse of these economies during this period.

▼ Regional Export Concentration and Stagnation

Central American export trade has historically been dominated by a small number of basic agricultural commodities. Coffee and banana exports underpinned regional economies until the 1950s. Cotton, cattle, and sugar were added during the wave of economic expansion in the 1950s and 1960s. Table 1.2 provides data on the commodity concentration of exports, com-paring the increased diversification at the high point of the CACM with the dramatically worsened commodity concentration by the mid-1980s. International prices for all of these commodities have been falling for nearly half a century. The CACM, which flourished from 1960 to 1975, provided new growth opportunities that proved more fragile than expected. Industrial development policies, such as overvalued exchange rates and selective tar-iffs on manufactured imports designed to facilitate the importation of the machinery and intermediate goods needed for locally oriented manufactur-ing growth, tended to discriminate against agricultural exports (Bulmer-Thomas 1987). In Table 1.2, for example, we can see that Central America's exports have been heavily concentrated in agricultural commodities. Costa

Table 1.2   Central American Commodity Export Concentration (percentage of export earnings)

		Coffee	Cotton	Beef	Sugar	Bananas	Top Ten
Costa Rica	1972–1976	25.5	0.0	7.7	5.8	24.8	63.8
	1981–1985	27.6	0.0	5.6	2.4	24.2	59.8
	1986	31.2	0.0	5.5	1.1	17.1	54.9
El Salvador	1972–1976	41.9	10.7	0.0	8.3	0.0	60.9
	1981–1985	58.2	5.6	0.0	3.5	0.0	67.3
	1986	81.3	5.4	0.0	3.0	0.0	89.7
Guatemala	1972–1976	29.8	11.3	0.0	11.1	0.0	52.2
	1981–1985	30.8	7.6	0.0	5.4	0.0	43.8
	1986	40.4	6.9	0.0	4.5	0.0	51.8
Honduras	1972–1976	18.5	0.0	6.7	0.0	26.2	51.4
	1981–1985	22.4	0.0	4.4	0.0	30.2	57.0
	1986	28.2	0.0	3.0	0.0	39.0	70.2
Nicaragua	1972–1976	15.9	26.8	9.3	7.5	0.0	59.5
	1981–1985	31.1	26.3	6.1	5.3	0.0	68.8
	1986	46.6	31.1	10.0	3.6	0.0	91.3

Source: IDB (1987).

Rica was the only nation in the region that did not increase its disproportionate dependence on agricultural exports after the collapse of the CACM in the late 1970s. El Salvador and Nicaragua, on the other hand, were drawing 90 percent or more of their export earnings from these few commodities by 1986; and El Salvador earned more than 80 percent from just one, coffee.

Figure 1.4 illustrates the dramatic stagnation in the region's total exports under these conditions. The failure of export agriculture, precisely as the region was becoming more dependent upon it, was one of the most critical sources of economic decline during the 1980s. A more proximate cause of economic decline, however, was the total impact of the debt crisis. For even if the region's exports had continued growing, the proportion of those exports required to repay both debts contracted in the 1970s and the expanding debt of the 1980s would have led to devastating net financial transfers out of the region. And it was that debt crisis that led lenders to impose the draconian structural adjustment policies that reinforced the economic decline.

Figure 1.4   Stagnation of Primary Central American Export Commodities (excluding fuels, millions of U.S.$)

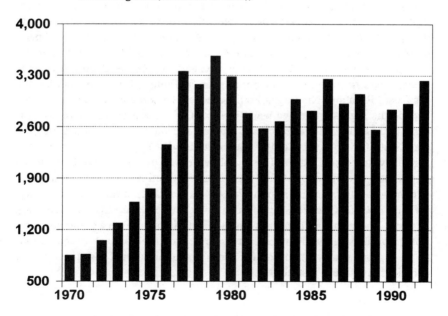

Source: World Bank (1994).

▼ The Debt Crisis

Central America's total external debt prior to 1970 never exceeded $800 million for the region as a whole. By the 1980s it had expanded more than ten times to $8.5 billion, reflecting patterns seen throughout Latin America during the 1970s (see Table 1.3). By 1990 it tripled again to $23 billion.

Table 1.3   Central American Total External Debt, 1970–1990 (millions of U.S.$)

	1970	1975	1980	1985	1990
Costa Rica	246	684	2,744	4,401	3,772
El Salvador	183	412	911	1,854	2,132
Guatemala	120	243	1,166	2,653	2,777
Honduras	109	379	1,470	2,728	3,525
Nicaragua	155	611	2,176	5,728	10,623
Central America	813	2,330	8,467	17,365	22,829

Source: World Bank (1993).

The true burden of that debt was felt in the proportion of export earnings that had to be dedicated to simple debt repayment during the 1980s. In the early 1970s debt repayments in Central America (both interest and principal payments), as in most of Latin America, averaged less than 15 percent of export earnings (ECLAC 1983). By the early 1980s the Central American average had risen to 21.2 percent, as seen in Table 1.4, but the debt burden for Costa Rica and Nicaragua both exceeded 30 percent. By the end of the decade the regional average was 51 percent, all countries were over 40 percent, and Nicaragua had reached 73 percent. That meant that more than 50 cents out of every export dollar was being used simply to pay old debt, and primarily interest at that. This intolerable set of conditions became an important part of international agencies' motivation for seeking ways to expand exports from the region. For it was felt that, in the absence of significant debt forgiveness, this burden could be reduced only by expanding exports. The resulting export promotion activities became a principal component of the structural adjustment strategies required of each of the nations in the region, as a precondition for additional international assistance of any sort, including debt restructuring.

▼ Structural Adjustment Policies in Central America

There is no doubt that Central America's economic conditions were unsustainable during and at the end of the lost decade of the 1980s. Some form of

Table 1.4   Central American Debt Burden (principal and interest payments as percent of exports of goods)

	1980–1981	1988–1989
Costa Rica	32.4	45.0
El Salvador	7.9	44.8
Guatemala	6.3	42.6
Honduras	21.6	48.5
Nicaragua	38.0	73.3
Central American average	21.2	50.8

Source: IDB (1990).

dramatic change in the region's economies was undoubtedly needed. Thus the debate over structural adjustment in Central America should focus on whether the specific measures required by the international financial institutions were the most appropriate and whether they deepened the crisis, rather than alleviating it.

The Central American economies, prostrate before their creditors, torn by war, capital flight, massive refugee movements, and falling export earnings, found little or no basis for resisting the prescription dictated by the international and bilateral financial institutions. The USAID formula for recovery was export expansion through the subsidized development of nontraditional exports, both agricultural and manufacturing. Behind those policies, however, there also lay a formula for massive restructuring of the region's economies along neoliberal lines dictated by the International Monetary Fund (IMF) and the World Bank. Beginning in 1983, each of the Central American economies accepted the policies and programs required by those agencies, and by USAID, as preconditions for new loans or the restructuring of interest rates and payment schedules on their old loans. Nicaragua was the last to accede, after the 1990 change of government, even though the Sandinistas attempted some stabilization measures in 1988 and 1989 without receiving the significant new external assistance that had been promised (Conroy 1990).

Structural adjustment, as practiced in Central America during the 1980s, contained most of the classic components incorporated by its designers for use in other parts of the world, notably government austerity measures, trade liberalization, currency devaluation, and privatization.

Government budget deficits were considered one of the principal evils leading up to this period, bringing on inflation that undercut export competitiveness. Cutbacks in government spending, including massive reductions in government employment, were one of the first measures required of each nation. For reasons dictated by the political conditions in each country, this rarely meant reductions in military spending; rather, it almost always meant significant reductions in social spending, for health and education, as well as reductions in the size and scope of other government services. Government support for agriculture, especially credit and technical assistance, was one of the critical victims of this process, until USAID and other agencies began replacing it piecemeal with specialized programs designed to promote nontraditional agriculture (see Chapters 2 and 3).

The high-growth decades of the 1960s and 1970s were associated with heavy levels of protectionism behind which local industries grew. These policies, however, were anathema to the international financial institutions and to USAID. Each of the countries was required to reduce its import tariffs, encouraging massive inflows of cheaper imports, formally in the interest of providing lower-cost products to consumers and industry alike, but in practice competitively undercutting local industry. The most tangible effect was the massive elimination of those industrial jobs that had grown through production for the CACM. Costa Rica and Guatemala, the two nations that achieved the highest levels of industrialization under CACM, were the hardest hit. Basic grains producers throughout the region were also devastated as grain imports almost doubled by the end of the decade (see Figure 1.5). This proved to be a critical factor in the evolution of NTAEs, for farmers who had historically produced basic grains were now forced to seek alternative crops. The net impact of trade liberalization can be seen in Figure 1.6, which displays the regionwide balance of trade during the decade when structural adjustment measures were implemented. The trade deficit more than doubled as imports flooded local markets and local export production stagnated. The much heralded expansion of nontraditional exports did little to counter this phenomenon, for they proved to be export products requiring massive new imports of supporting inputs, including seeds, agricultural chemicals, and equipment.

Currency devaluation was required of every country, although it was a measure stalwartly resisted by several. Devaluation was expected to increase the demand for the region's exports, reduce the dollar cost of wages, and consequently make the region more attractive to foreign investors. But currency devaluations were of considerably less benefit for nontraditional agriculture, for they increased the costs of all agricultural inputs not manufactured domestically and discouraged the expansion of domestic manufacture of those that could be.

That Central American governments sell off those industries and services they had developed in earlier years to fill needs unmet by the private sector was an explicit requirement forced upon the region, and welcomed by wealthy local and foreign investors. In perhaps the most acute case, the USAID mission gave the Honduran government a list of state firms and agencies, specifying the order and deadlines for their sale if promised economic assistance were going to be disbursed (Michael E. Conroy, personal

Figure 1.5   Imports of Basic Grains, All Central America

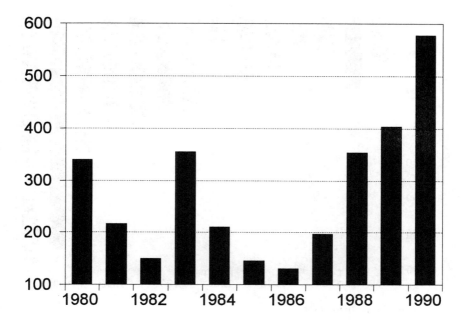

Source: ECLAC (1992).

communication 1993). In Chapter 3 we focus on how USAID designed, financed, and implemented the creation of privately controlled "parallel states" to replace government agencies.

These policies have transformed the economies of Central America in ways that are only now, in the mid-1990s, being totally felt. There have, certainly, been some benefits associated with increased efficiency, reduced government deficits, and reduced rates of inflation in some countries. What is equally apparent, however, is that Central America emerged from the decade of structural adjustment far more impoverished than it was when it entered, far more indebted, and with far fewer obvious development prospects than it had enjoyed in any previous decade. It is in this context that the gamble on NTAEs must be seen.

Figure 1.6   Central American Trade Imbalance (regional total, millions of current U.S.$)

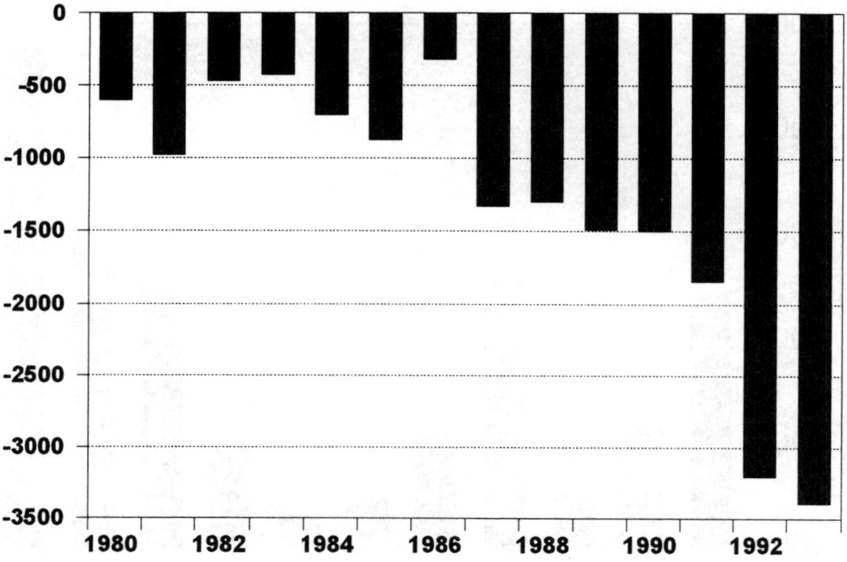

Source: World Bank (1994).

▼ The Case for an NTAE Strategy

Given the history of Central America through the mid-1980s, what strategy might have been capable of improving the conditions in which the majority of Central America's poor rural population lives? The case for an NTAE strategy begins with that question. Although there have been many proponents of increased exports, structural adjustment, liberalization of imports, and other characteristics of the economic policies adopted by most Central American governments since the mid-1980s, there has been no more important proponent of NTAEs as a core strategy for the region than USAID. USAID was the single most important donor to Central America throughout the 1980s; it was also the only donor whose programs, as we see below, were constrained by its government to a very narrow range of agricultural options.

If one wishes to understand the single-mindedness with which USAID policies favoring NTAEs have been implemented in Central America, we believe that it is important to understand the diligence with which the intellectual case for this strategy was developed within the agency. The following analysis, therefore, has been developed primarily from official USAID documents and from studies by agency staff and consultants. We also believe, however, that it is critical to understand the theoretical shortcomings of the model, even before looking at the practical problems of implementation discussed in later chapters.

USAID viewed Central America as having exceptional potential for the development of alternative, less traditional exports. Its climatic diversity, from tropical lowlands to cool highlands, suggested that a much wider variety of crops could be produced. Experiments in the region in the late 1970s with alternative products had indicated potential for greater levels of income per hectare from crops such as melons grown for export, especially when compared with basic grains produced for the domestic market.

The alternative export crops that were suggested included cool-weather vegetables such as broccoli, snow peas, and cauliflower; fruits ranging from citrus to blackberries, raspberries, and strawberries; cut flowers and ornamental plants; hot-climate fruits and vegetables such as cantaloupe and honeydew melons, cucumbers, tomatoes, miniature squashes, and watermelons; and tree crops such as cocoa, macadamia nuts, apples, pears, and peaches.

These alternative crops offered many theoretical advantages. They could be grown on small or irregular plots; rotated easily across seasons in some areas; and were more labor-intensive than some of the traditional exports, such as cattle and cotton. And they appeared to require fewer imported inputs. Many of these features, it was claimed, would benefit and even favor the region's poor rural majority of peasant farmers. Furthermore, the potential for the development of food-processing industries, both for export of frozen foods and for shipment of canned foods to local markets, was considerable. It was assumed that the trend in U.S. and European markets toward increased consumption of fresh foods would continue, and that Central America would ship to those markets during winter months and other "windows of opportunity" (Barham et al. 1992). One USAID analyst wrote:

> [These] horticultural exports have good potential for further expansion, despite protectionist pressures in the United States. They also are labor intensive, can be grown efficiently by small farmers, and have a relatively low import intensity. Thus they provide more backward linkages and multiplier effects (as well as forward linkages into processing) than most manufacturing and assembly operations [Zuvekas 1988:14].

▼ **The Drive to Diversify Exports**

Two reasons explain the earlier decline in exports from the region as a whole, according to the USAID analysis: falling prices for the principal traditional exports (coffee, cotton, cattle, sugar, and bananas); and the collapse of the CACM because of political turmoil. Traditional products accounted for more than 63 percent of the total exports from the region in 1980; half of it came from coffee alone, which brought in $1.7 billion that year. When coffee prices plummeted in 1981, it cost the region nearly 10 percent of its total export earnings (Zuvekas 1988).

In one of the clearest and most concise statements of the problem, USAID analysts in Costa Rica made the following points about the dilemma posed by the country's traditional development model:

> Historically the country has relied on agriculture, the main economic engine, to provide a major portion of foreign exchange earnings. Specifically, four traditional export products (coffee, bananas, sugar, beef) provide over 50 percent of export revenue and were the basis for past economic growth.
>
> However, these products can no longer be looked to for sustained economic growth. Costa Rica's foreign exchange earnings are tied to a great extent to these traditional products which are subject to conditions beyond the country's ability to control. For example, although the 1985 coffee freeze in Brazil will result in a temporary bonanza for Costa Rica, once Brazil returns to prior production levels the world coffee supply situation will stabilize and an expansion of Costa Rican plantings will only continue to contribute to a weakening of world prices. Increased employment opportunities in the traditional crops are also bleak.
>
> The decline in markets for bananas and sugar have reduced employment. Coffee and beef remain at stable levels of employment, but will generate no additional jobs related to these products. Consequently, the traditional exports cannot contribute significantly to future economic growth nor are they likely to contribute to sustainable increases in foreign exchange earnings [USAID/Costa Rica 1986:ii–iii].

As the data in Table 1.5 illustrate, the prices of Central America's traditional exports have indeed fallen consistently since 1980 and, with the exception of bananas, in 1993 were at levels well below those of the worst

Table 1.5 Price Indices of Central American Traditional Exports

	1980	1981	1982	1983	1984	1985	1986	1987
Bananas	100.0	107.0	99.9	114.4	98.5	101.4	105.4	100.5
Beef	100.0	89.6	86.6	88.4	82.4	78.0	75.9	86.4
Coffee	100.0	83.1	90.6	85.4	93.5	94.4	125.0	72.8
Cotton	100.0	89.6	77.4	89.7	86.3	63.9	51.1	79.8
Sugar								
World market	100.0	58.9	29.3	29.5	18.1	14.1	21.1	23.6
U.S. import price	100.0	65.7	66.3	73.4	72.4	67.8	69.8	72.7

Source: IMF International Financial Statistics, as cited in Zuvekas (1988).

years of the crisis. This confirms the need to diversify Central America's export base away from traditional products.

The concept *diversification of exports* is used widely, and loosely, to mean the introduction of any "new" or different export product (Conroy 1989). By that definition of diversification, nontraditional exports are almost necessarily diversifying. Nontraditional exports are defined, most simply, as any exports other than the five traditional Central American exports: coffee, cotton, cattle, sugar, and bananas. It is more complete to define them as one of three types: (1) products not previously produced at all; (2) products previously produced for domestic consumption but now being produced for export; and (3) products now being shipped to a new market (Barham et al. 1992). The first is most closely associated with the simple definition of diversification; the second relates to diversification of export earnings, but not necessarily to diversification of the economic structure of a country. And the last class of nontraditionals may involve diversification of markets but may also mean further expansion and specialization in the production of a traditional agricultural export product.

USAID literature in the 1980s consistently used the term *diversification* in its loosest construct: the introduction and export of a product that previously was not being produced or exported (Lack et al. 1989). Diversification became synonymous with depending on new products for the export stimulus that small, open economies, such as those of Central America, must have in order to grow.

▼   Defining and Measuring NTAEs for Central America

There are several definitions regularly used to describe nontraditional exports from Central America. The most general USAID definition includes all manufactured exports plus fruit, vegetable, spices, and plant exports, less banana exports (USAID 1991). NTAEs, then, would consist of fruits, vegetables, plants, and spices, excluding banana exports. A more comprehensive definition is provided by the Inter-American Institute for Cooperation on Agriculture (IICA), which offers a definition that also includes tobacco, root crops (such as cassava), sesame seed, vegetable oils, almonds, and other nuts. IICA also classifies cardamom exported from Guatemala as a traditional export from that country, excluding it from estimates of NTAEs. For our purposes, there is also a much narrower, alternative definition that is useful: simply all fruits and vegetables, less bananas. This definition is particularly important if one wishes to focus on those fresh fruits and vegetables that receive little or no further processing before reaching the final consumer and for which questions of pesticide residues are an important issue. Figure 1.7 illustrates the extent to which Costa Rican NTAEs varied from

Figure 1.7   Costa Rican NTAEs to the World

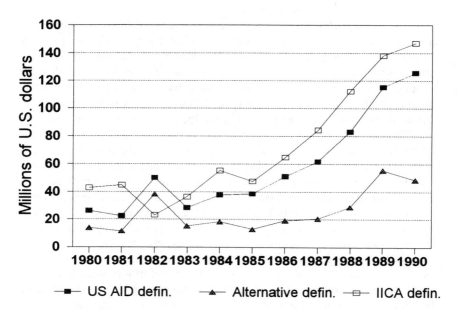

Source: USDA (1992).
    Note: USAID definition = fruits, vegetables, flowers, spices, no bananas; alternative definition = fruits, vegetables, no bananas; IICA definition = fruits, vegetables, flowers, spices, others, less bananas.

1980 to 1990 under each of the different definitions. With the exception of an unexplained anomaly in 1982, all three definitions track relatively closely.[3]

Nontraditional exports from Central America responded to extensive promotion by USAID and to high levels of subsidies, experiencing rapid rates of growth in the 1980s. From an average level of approximately $45 million in 1975 and $130 million in 1980, NTAEs rose to $250 million by 1990, under the USAID definition, a compound annual growth rate of nearly 30 percent over the fifteen-year period and more than 10 percent during the 1980s.

Under the more inclusive IICA definition (available only for 1980–1990), total NTAEs from Central America grew less rapidly, from a level of $178 million in 1980 to a total of $315 million by 1990, an average annual rate of growth for the 1980s of 6 percent (Kaimowitz 1991). Table 1.6 shows the distribution across countries of these regional totals.

Table 1.6   Central American NTAEs to the World (IICA definition; millions of U.S.$)

	1980	1985	1989
Costa Rica	42.7	47.6	138.0
El Salvador	13.1	15.8	11.4
Guatemala	72.7	74.8	106.1
Honduras	41.9	60.3	53.5
Nicaragua	7.2	11.5	6.3
Central America	177.6	210.0	315.3

Source: Kaimowitz (1991).

Guatemala had the early lead in NTAEs at the start of the decade, with more than $72 million, 41 percent of the regional total. Honduras and Costa Rica had virtually identical levels, at approximately $42 million each. At that time Guatemala's NTAEs consisted of tobacco, flowers, sesame seed, and potatoes, in descending order of importance. Costa Rica exported mostly rice and prepared fruit products at that time, and Honduras concentrated on tobacco, pineapple, and prepared fruit products (Kaimowitz 1991). El Salvador and Nicaragua were minor players. By 1989 Costa Rica was the region's leading producer of nontraditional exports, exporting almost as much as the regional total in 1980 and 44 percent of the 1989 regional total. Fully 62 percent of those expanded exports consisted of flowers, ornamental plants, and pineapples, products that were virtually absent from Costa Rica's 1980 export profile. In 1989 Guatemala was still the second most important nontraditional producer in Central America, but broccoli, snow peas, and melons had become a $20 million annual export industry, while flowers and tobacco had grown very slowly over the decade. Honduran exports in 1989 now emphasized melons (35% of the total), in addition to pineapples.

The composition of regional NTAEs, overall, is shown in Table 1.7. Fresh fruits (34.8%) and flowers and ornamental plants (20.8%) dominated the profile, with pineapples and melons most important among the former. Fresh vegetables, especially snow peas and broccoli, amounted to 9.6 percent of the total. The programs implemented during the decade had, in fact, changed both the magnitude and the composition of the region's nontraditional exports.

▼   A Preliminary Critique of the USAID Analysis

Our fundamental critique of USAID-promoted NTAE strategies focuses on their impacts upon farmers, especially small-scale poor farmers; upon the nature and structure of government programs in the region; and upon the

Table 1.7 Commodity Composition of NTAEs from Central America, 1989

	Millions of dollars	Percentage
Fresh fruits	102.5	32.5
Pineapples	51.0	
Melons	31.9	
Fresh vegetables	28.3	9.0
Snow peas	8.2	
Broccoli	4.1	
Chayote squash	5.2	
Root crops	16.8	5.3
Yucca	8.0	
Flowers, plants, etc.	61.2	19.4
Miscellaneous	106.5	33.8
Sesame seed	27.5	
Tobacco	21.7	
African palm oil	7.0	
Cocoa	5.7	
Plantains	5.8	
Other	38.8	
Total	315.3	100.0

Source: Kaimowitz (1991).

environment. But there are also conceptual shortcomings in the model, even as articulated by its proponents, that must be seen from the outset.

The first problem is one of critical oversimplification of the dichotomy between traditional and nontraditional production. Lumping all previous exports into one category—to be deemphasized—and choosing to support promotion of virtually any and all others, with no reservations on marketability, carries an implicit assumption that there is more homogeneity within the two groups than across them and that virtually any NTAE expansion would be superior to increased exports of traditionals. This fallacy is especially obvious in the case of coffee, whose production and marketing structure is considerably different from that of, say, bananas, in part because coffee is not a perishable product. Bananas, on the other hand, have production and marketing characteristics much more similar to the nontraditionals than to other traditionals. Emphasis upon new and nontraditional export production implicitly disparages all other production, whether or not comparable analyses of export potential and economic effect have been made.

The auspicious growth rates of exports of nontraditionals, furthermore, build upon very small bases and are therefore artificially high. The absolute value of exports of nontraditional agricultural products from Central America remains an extremely small proportion of total exports of each country, even under conditions of very low prices for traditional export products. NTAEs (under the USAID definition) accounted for no more than 7 percent of total commodity exports by the end of the decade, and only slightly more by the end of 1991. That may be a doubling of the share of nontraditionals between 1983 and 1990, but the total value remains a very small proportion of total exports.

It was explicitly noted in the justification for nontraditional exports that expanded production in Central America of traditionals, such as coffee, would worsen global supply problems and lead to lower prices. It was never shown, conversely, that the robustness of markets for nontraditionals from Central America was significantly greater. On the contrary, the rapid expansion of nontraditional agricultural production for shipment to a limited number of markets from a large number of explicitly competing countries tends to be associated with very large short-term and seasonal fluctuations in prices. These may be far more dangerous to long-term export stability than the periodic fluctuations in prices for traditional exports, such as coffee, cotton, sugar, and frozen beef.

Why, one might ask, does USAID not promote the transfer of technology and stimulate increases in employment and productivity in domestically oriented food crops, lessening the needs of these countries to import basic grains? The answer is as straightforward as it is troubling. USAID is prohibited from supporting the development of any agricultural production abroad that will compete with U.S. agricultural commodity exports. The Bumpers Amendment to the Foreign Assistance Act of 1961 (USAID's fundamental charter), enacted on July 2, 1986, provides that

> none of the funds appropriated by this or any other Act to carry out . . . the Foreign Assistance Act of 1961 shall be available for any testing or breeding feasibility study, variety improvement or introduction, consultancy, publication, conference, or training in connection with the growth of production in a foreign country of an *agricultural commodity for export which would compete with a similar commodity grown or produced in the United States* [emphasis added].

How, then, does USAID promote the production of melons, pineapples, squash, broccoli, snow peas, root crops, and so on? The amendment exempts "activities designed to increase food security in developing countries" but only where such activities "will not have a significant impact on the export of agricultural commodities of the United States." The legal dictum has been implemented within USAID by its Policy Determination 15 (PD-15), which states in part that "AID does not intend to support production of agricultural commodities for export that are likely to have a significant impact on competing U.S. exports." And USAID, in a miracle of convoluted reasoning, suggests that increased nontraditional exports will lead to a greater ability to import food, thus improving food security.

It is disturbing to recognize how much USAID in this argument differs from the conclusions of most other major studies of the region, which recommend concrete programs of expanded local production of basic grains and other commodities for food security. USAID's espousal of NTAEs may, in fact, be dictated by the fact that it cannot support production of food crops because Central America is a major importer of U.S. grain! How, then, does USAID justify its support for cut flowers and ornamental plants, even though there is widespread production of competing flowers and plants in the United States, and for fruits and vegetables that are also produced in abundance in the United States? The key, according to a USAID staff member and a consultant, who asked to remain anonymous, is the extent to which producers of competing products wield the political muscle in Washington needed to call on the law to block USAID assistance. Producers of basic grains, beef, and sugar wield that power effectively; producers of fruits, vegetables, and other nontraditionals perhaps do not. U.S. cut flower producers are an intermediate case, at first unable to block assistance to Costa Rican growers but later succeeding in imposing trade sanctions (Thacher 1990; Rosset 1991b).

For whatever reasons, whether a well-intended conviction that NTAEs offered Central America its best hope for an improved future or whether NTAEs provided a best set of alternatives under the constrained circumstances, these strategies were the hallmark of USAID activity in Central America during the 1980s. Their comprehensive impacts upon the region's political, social, economic, and ecological conditions are the focal point for the rest of this book.

▼ Notes

1. The development of NTAEs was also one of the most vigorous forms of agricultural diversification pursued by the Nicaraguan Ministry of Agricultural Development and Agrarian Reform (MIDINRA) during 1988–1989. Nicaragua dramatically expanded its plantings and exports of pineapples, melons, citrus products, and avocados, even before USAID's return.

2. Centro de Capacitación para el Desarrollo (CECADE), Costa Rica; Asociación para el Avance de las Ciencias Sociales (AVANCSO), Guatemala; Programa Regional de Investigación sobre El Salvador (PREIS); Regional Program in Political Economy, Honduras; Department of Agricultural Economics, Universidad Nacional Autónoma de Nicaragua. We thank them immeasurably for their contributions, which they have published independently in each country.

3. The other basis for almost inevitable variation in estimates from different sources is the nature of the prices used for exports. Data taken from individual government export records are generally based on FOB (free on board) pricing, meaning the value declared by the exporter at the point of shipment. There is ample evidence that for a variety of reasons these data may be biased downward (Dornbusch 1990). Internationally comparable export data, such as the UN data used here to illustrate the other two definitions, are more generally listed CIF, i.e., including production costs, insurance, and freight to the point of entry into the importing country. U.S. import data, furthermore, are generally quoted on the basis of customs value

declarations, which are, like FOB data, biased downward for the purpose of evading duties. There is no reliable, uniform, fully comparable alternative that would eliminate the differences in data series on the same export phenomenon.

2

CULTIVATING INEQUITY:
NONTRADITIONAL AGRICULTURAL
EXPORTS AND THE RURAL POOR

One of the central concerns of our research on NTAE strategy was to determine its impact on the rural poor in Central America. The rural poor are either landless agricultural laborers or peasant farmers who have historically tended to produce foodstuffs for their own consumption and/or for the domestic market. Peasants have traditionally grown basic grains (primarily corn and beans) and, if they were somewhat better off, vegetables such as tomatoes, peppers, cabbage, and potatoes. They tended to sell their vegetables to intermediaries who then resold them in urban markets. In the case of corn and beans, the part they did not consume within the home they tended to sell to a government marketing board, which frequently offered a minimum price guarantee, or to other intermediaries in the private sector.

It is our belief, and that of respected development economists such as Alain de Janvry (1981) and Jeffrey Sachs (1987), that the sort of inequity and poverty the peasantry must face actually blocks true development. The rural masses are so poor that they have little purchasing power. They thus do not constitute an important market for domestic industry. This in turn means that domestic markets are too small to stimulate much economic activity, so production is largely directed toward foreign markets and urban elites. As a consequence the level of demand in the economy is too narrow to sustain broadly based, effective development. This creates a high degree of dependence on foreign markets and a lack of structural incentives that would encourage ruling elites to promote better living standards for the poor. In short, poverty becomes a vicious circle that is itself an obstacle to development.

NTAE strategy was originally presented by local government agencies and outside donors such as USAID as a poverty reduction program, designed in part to break the low-income cycle in the countryside. Since basic grain prices were too low to permit producers to escape from poverty, it was argued, higher-value alternatives were needed for peasant farmers. Since nontraditionals sell for higher prices than corn and beans, and in many cases are more labor intensive, NTAEs were considered a better option for the poor. And, as we have seen, considerable resources were devoted to creating an agroexport "boom" based on nontraditionals. A key question for this chapter, then, is to what extent this agroexport boom has differed from previous booms throughout Central American history, in terms of its impact on the poor.

▼ A History of Crises: Export Agriculture and the Rural Poor

There is a long history in Central America linking crisis, social instability, and conflict with the impact of export agriculture on the poor. Time and time again the introduction and boom of a new export crop has driven peasant farmers off their lands. Each such wave has been followed by a period of intense rural strife, gradually subsiding as the new landless move to the cities or to the agricultural frontier.

During the rapid growth of coffee in the last century diverse legal and extralegal methods were used to remove small producers of basic grains from prime lands (Biderman 1982; Barry 1987; Seligson 1980). As a result, contemporary distributional maps of coffee and corn production in El Salvador are like photographic negatives of one another, with corn grown in a ring of marginal lands surrounding the coffee areas (Durham 1979). The expansion of coffee in the late nineteenth century and the resulting landlessness led directly to one of Central America's historical periods of agrarian violence (Avery 1985).

The cotton boom in the 1950s and 1960s similarly drove small farmers off their lands, this time through economic mechanisms more than physical coercion (Williams 1986; Paige 1984; Núñez 1978). Once again, social unrest and violence, instability and insurgency, were a secondary yield of the characteristics of the agricultural export boom (Flora 1987). A U.S. Department of State bulletin summarized it aptly: "Over time . . . cotton displaced campesinos and their subsistence crops [and] was increasingly seen to enrich the upper classes while it disadvantaged the rural poor. . . . [This] combination of displacement and increased disparity of incomes . . . played a significant part in the susceptibility of Central American states to political destabilization" (Avery 1985).

▼ Are NTAEs Merely More of the Same?

In the specific case of contemporary NTAEs it seems logical to expect that many of the same mechanisms by which previous export booms accentuated inequity would be operative today. Each of Central America's traditional exports was itself a nontraditional when first introduced, and many were promoted with equal vigor. The only significant difference might be that the current set of export crops can be produced on small plots of land, and, because they are labor intensive, there may be diseconomies of scale (see, e.g., von Braun et al. 1989:29). In other words, these crops may favor small farmers over larger ones.

Rosset (1991b) developed a series of hypotheses, or criteria, by which to judge who is favored by the promotion of NTAEs. He suggested that the key resources needed for economically successful farming—for anyone from peasants to corporations—are land, credit, favorable prices relative to costs, accessible technology, technical assistance, and a favorable position in the market. To evaluate the true impact of NTAE strategy on poor farmers, we must focus on the distributional effects of these resources in the context of nontraditionals. In other words, we wish to know to what extent each factor acts as an economy of scale favoring those who are already better off, or a diseconomy of scale favoring the smaller farmer over the larger. Although each resource alone may lack the weight to be a driving force in changing patterns of land tenure and social welfare, the combined effect of many such factors could indeed be a sharp acceleration of the process of social differentiation,[1] that is, an increase in relative inequality as some producers are enriched while others are further impoverished (de Janvry 1981). We would expect some participants in NTAE strategy to be winners, able to increase the size of their landholdings (von Braun et al. 1989), while others lose access to their lands and livelihoods.

The rural poor in Central America have had three options in the context of the NTAE boom: (1) they could continue to produce basic foodstuffs, never venturing into nontraditionals; (2) they could attempt a complete switch to nontraditionals; or (3) they could follow a mixed strategy, leaving some portion of their land in basic grains while experimenting with NTAE production on the rest. They have been faced with both the economic climate for production of food for domestic consumption, as it has been modified by structural adjustment, and the climate for nontraditionals created through NTAE promotion. In this chapter, therefore, we examine both nontraditional production and basic grain production.

The evidence presented in this chapter supports several arguments. First, the rapid expansion of nontraditional agricultural production has occurred under conditions that are especially difficult for small, poor farmers in Central America. These conditions include sharp decreases in agricultural credit for planting basic grains, the mainstay of the smaller, poorer farmers; conditions for obtaining credit for nontraditional production that are strongly biased toward larger-scale, wealthier farmers; and evolution of marketing conditions for nontraditional production that bias prices, market access, and influence toward larger-scale producers.

In Chapter 4 we discuss the way in which the very nature of the nontraditional export industry is also biased against Central American small-scale producers, leaving them with most of the risk and very little of the value-added in the total production and distribution of their products.

Reviewing both our own data and those available in the literature, it becomes apparent that the experiences of the peasantry under structural adjustment and NTAE strategy have varied considerably from country to country, among regions within countries, and across crops within regions. In some cases there have even been considerable differences between farmers growing the same crop in different towns in the same region (see, e.g., Barham et al. 1992). Nevertheless, certain broad generalizations emerge, which we analyze below through a series of illustrative case studies. First, Costa Rica provides a special case for a number of reasons. Costa Rica has encountered greater overall success with nontraditionals, and producers in Costa Rica have operated under a more draconian structural adjustment process. Second, Guatemala shows different patterns between the highland areas, inhabited by indigenous people, and the seasonal lowlands, inhabited by ladinos. Third, in El Salvador and Honduras NTAEs have to date never really reached the same level of national importance, unless you consider shrimp mariculture an "agricultural" activity (as do Stonich et al. 1994). Nevertheless they provide evidence of notable failures. We take these cases in order, after a brief consideration of the situation faced by producers of basic grains in each country.

▼ Patterns of Basic Grain Production in the 1980s

Central American basic grain production in the 1980s was marked by several interrelated characteristics. First, basic grain production decreased sharply for the region as a whole. Second, it decreased most rapidly in those countries that experienced the most rapid increase in NTAE production, Costa Rica and Guatemala. And third, it appears that the basic grain production that did occur was increasingly concentrated in a smaller number of large farms. That is, small-scale farmers were forced out.

Figures 2.1a–c illustrate regionwide trends for the production of corn, beans, and rice. Corn production per capita fell by 14 percent from an average of nearly 1,100 pounds per capita in the first three years of the decade to an average level below 950 pounds per capita during 1986–1989. Bean production fell by nearly 25 percent over the decade, from an average of more than 115 pounds per capita in the early years to less than 90 pounds per capita in the last three. And rice production declined by more than 15 percent, from levels of 90 pounds per capita at the start of the decade to slightly more than 75 pounds per capita at the end.

Figure 2.1a   Central American Corn Production

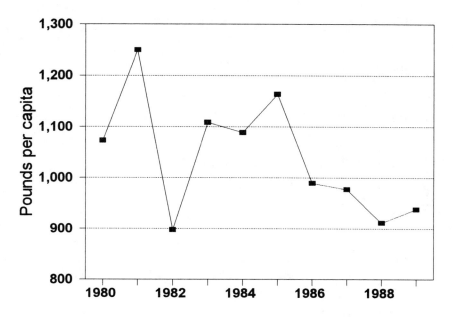

Source: USDA (1992).

Figure 2.1b   Central American Bean Production

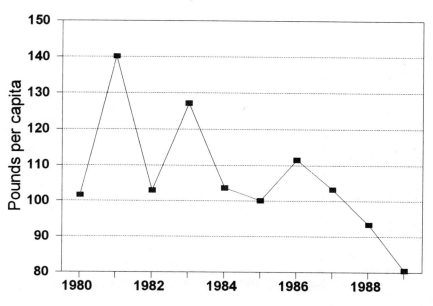

Source: USDA (1992).

Figure 2.1c   Central American Rice Production

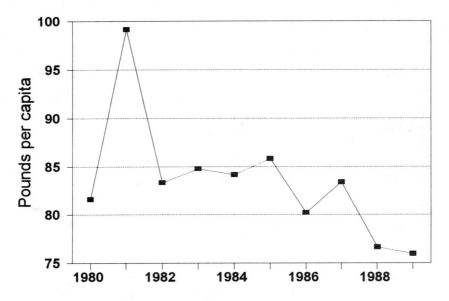

Source: USDA (1992).

Figure 2.1d   Wheat Plantings in Guatemala

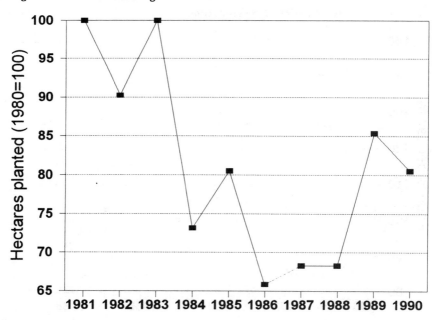

Source: FAO *Yearbooks* (1981–1990).

In Figure 2.1d we present the trends in area planted to wheat in Guatemala, the region's most important wheat producer. Wheat is grown primarily in the temperate climate of the Guatemalan *Altiplano,* where it has been produced almost exclusively by indigenous farmers for hundreds of years.

How can we explain these patterns, and what do they mean for the rural poor in each country? In both Costa Rica and Guatemala the sharp drop-off in basic grain production can be linked directly to a drop in credit available for basic grain production. This is illustrated in Figure 2.2. Agricultural credit for the planting of corn, beans, and rice fell by 70 percent in Costa Rica in just five years, from 1983 to 1987. In Guatemala it fell by 40 percent from the 1983 level, after an unusually strong one-time increase in 1984. In Costa Rica there was also a sharp decline in support prices for corn and beans. Support prices fell by 20 percent for corn and by 25 percent for beans from the 1984/85 harvest year to the 1987/88 harvest (Vermeer 1989).

Reductions in credit and support prices were caused by reductions in the government budget required as part of the structural adjustment programs in

Figure 2.2   Credit Crunch for Basic Grains: Total Farmer Credit for Corn, Beans, and Rice (1983 = 100)

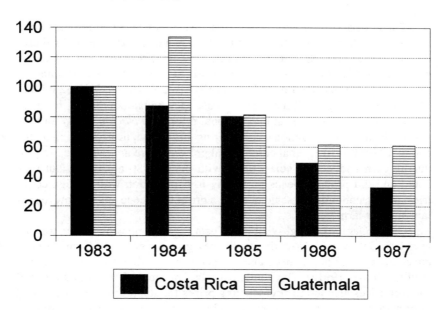

Sources: Vermeer (1989) and Banco de Guatemala.

each country (Hansen-Kuhn 1993). They also probably reflect some effect of the aggressive campaign mounted in Costa Rica to convince small farmers to switch from basic grains to nontraditionals (Rosset 1991b).

There is strong evidence from Costa Rica on the concentration of production in basic grains. Table 2.1 illustrates the fact that there was far greater concentration in the production of all three basic grains by the end of the decade than there had been when the credit crunch began and reductions in price supports were implemented. The number of farms producing corn decreased by 33 percent, the number of bean farms by 67 percent, and the number of rice farms by an astounding 95 percent.

Table 2.1   Number of Farms Producing Basic Grains in Costa Rica, 1984 and 1989

	1984	1989	Change (percentage)
Corn	29,000	18,500	−33
Beans	26,000	8,500	−67
Rice	15,000	700	−95

Source: Based on Korten (1992).

The pattern of U.S. food aid to Costa Rica may be an additional explanation for both the concentration of production and the declines in total production. Between 1982 and 1987 Public Law 480 (PL-480) food donations, which totaled $117 million, consisted mostly of wheat (which substitutes for corn in the local diet), corn, and rice (CENAP et al. 1988). Only $2 million of beans were shipped. Meanwhile, Costa Rica began purchasing beans in 1988 on the world market at international prices (*La Nación* 1988). In fact, Costa Rican bean production soared during this period, nearly tripling by the end of 1989. It is likely that commercial growers were not interested in producing corn and rice in competition with the PL-480 donations, but they could and did produce beans profitably in competition with foreign countries, using economies of scale to make a profit at price levels too low to sustain smaller farmers.

Carlos Campos, a high-visibility Costa Rican campesino leader, told us, in a 1987 interview, "Now the credit they give for corn and beans doesn't cover the cost of production, and the price we get doesn't even cover the credit" (Rosset 1991a). The combined effect of reduced credit and reduced support prices also led to skyrocketing prices for staples in Costa Rica. Not only were the rural poor confronted with their diminished capacity to produce their own food, but by 1987 it was from four to six times more expensive for them to buy corn, beans, rice, and bread than it had been at the start of the decade (see Table 2.2).

Table 2.2   Index of Retail Prices for Staples in Costa Rica (1980 = 100)

	Bread	Rice	Tortillas	Beans
1980	100	100	100	100
1981	144	166	143	102
1982	281	379	294	388
1983	343	517	249	398
1984	358	535	350	453
1985	372	541	416	514
1986	434	616	430	608
1987	469	653	450	625

Source: Based on Korten (1992).

Costa Rica experienced peasant protests in 1987 and 1988 of unprecedented scale and intensity. Highways were blocked, entire towns were taken and declared liberated zones, government officials were held hostage, and marchers battled with baton-wielding civil guardsmen (Rosset 1991b; Anderson 1991; Vunderink 1990–1991). Several observers were moved to comment on the apparent "Central Americanization" and "Salvadorization" of relatively peaceful Costa Rica (Rosset 1991b). Peasant protesters explicitly denounced what they felt to be an intolerable situation created by the conjuncture of three factors: cutbacks of supports for basic grains; food donations that flooded the domestic market; and the promotion of NTAEs, in which they felt they could not compete.

Similar levels of protest never materialized in the other countries, probably reflecting less-severe declines in the profitability of basic grains as well as political environments in which protest was less acceptable to the governments and more dangerous to the protesters themselves. As the structural adjustment processes and NTAE promotion programs were somewhat staggered in time after those of Costa Rica, it may also be that the startling signs of social unrest in Costa Rica deterred other nations from similarly draconian measures.

▼ The Case of NTAEs in Costa Rica

"I take good advantage of my land, I plant tuber crops," says Don Jorge Zúñiga Zamora, owner of an eight-hectare farm in Guácimo. Like Don Jorge, many farmers are now with the Agriculture of Change. Join the Agriculture of Change! The change that we all need.
—*Paid advertisement placed by the Costa Rican Ministry of Agriculture in* La Nación, *May 19, 1988*

Such advertisements helped induce many peasant farmers in Costa Rica to change which crops they grew. In many cases they switched completely from producing basic grains like corn and beans for the domestic market to nontraditional export crops such as melons, squash, tubers, cocoa, and broccoli. The rates of growth in production of these products were spectacular, as illustrated in Table 2.3. These advertisements were part of a USAID-funded campaign to promote Agriculture of Change, or Agricultura de Cambio, as NTAE strategy is called in Costa Rica. Understanding the experience of farmers in these programs is critical to grasping why so many Central American farmers have been willing to gamble on nontraditional crops and why so many of the smaller, poorer farmers have abandoned them after suffering terrible losses.

Table 2.3   Rate of Growth in Area Planted to NTAE Crops in Costa Rica, 1984–1988

	Change (percentage increase)
Pineapple	642
Strawberries	558
Roots and tubers	468
Melons	378
Papaya	374
Ginger	251
Macadamia nuts	213
Flowers	191
Squash	164
Ornamental plants	159
Black pepper	146
Ferns	111
Cacao	104

Source: Based on Korten (1992).

The story of USAID Project 515-T034 at El Indio land settlement in Don Jorge's district of Guácimo offers a particularly ironic example of what happened all too often (Rosset 1991b). The $2.9 million project included a program to work with the poorest farmers in the area, those who produced yellow corn on tiny plots of land. This program consisted of credit, technical assistance, and marketing expertise aimed at helping the farmers switch to cocoa, along with tuber crops and *ayote* squash for the growing U.S. Latino market.

During the first season (1983/84) project personnel selected twenty outstanding farmers to begin production of ayote. They were provided with credit, a full-time extensionist, certified disease-free seed imported from Miami, and a purchase contract with an export company. The first year was an outstanding success. Farmers growing the new crop earned up to forty times more per hectare than their corn-growing neighbors. The second year, however, it seems that the project provided neither seed nor a marketing contract, and the extensionist was no longer full-time. Nevertheless, based on the previous year's results, about one hundred local farmers decided to plant ayote. That year prices dropped in the United States in response to new competition from other countries with lower production costs. The farmers also suffered heavy disease losses because of the poor-quality seed they used, and most were unable to find a buyer for their meager production. Fully 50 percent defaulted on their credit. The following year forty hardy individuals persisted, and all defaulted (Rosset 1991b, Nelson 1988).

Thus ended a typical cycle in Central American nontraditional agricultural production. Early adopters made what appeared to be windfall profits, only to have the number of producers jump dramatically, ending with most of the farmers heavily indebted and suffering losses. This seems to be a common pattern with peasant participation in nontraditionals. In this case, as in many others, the buyers ended up signing contracts in later years with large growers, forgoing the problems associated with peasant production.

Various forms of bias against small farmers hurt the Guácimo farmers. Interviews with exporters revealed a marketing economy of scale.[2] For the packers and exporters, it is easier to offer contracts to a few large producers, with better quality control, than to pay the costs of contracting with dozens of small farmers who, they believe, often grow an inferior product. There was also a technological economy of scale. After the first year small farmers had no access to certified seed or adequate technical assistance, problems not faced by large commercial growers. Finally, Costa Rica as a country faced a macrolevel marketing economy of scale: it could not compete with the lower production costs in the Philippines (Rosset 1991b).

The negative experience of the Guácimo farmers with NTAEs is not an isolated case. Throughout Costa Rica a combination of factors conspired to limit peasant success with nontraditionals while reducing their options for continued basic grain production; this despite the impressive overall increases in the production of nontraditionals the country as a whole experienced.

Rising Rents and Land Values

Many peasants are not legal owners of the land they farm. They are often renters, sharecroppers, or simply squatters. When a new and potentially high-return alternative is introduced into a region where these land tenure patterns are common, the opportunity costs associated with traditional peasant land use rise. As the opportunity cost of land rises, access for low-return traditional activities decreases. Landlords can earn more by renting their land to those who grow higher-value crops, or they may produce these new crops themselves. Thus land values and rents rise while sharecropping opportunities become scarce.

If rising land values are accompanied by declining profitability of traditional activities, then even landowning peasants may be displaced. As it becomes no longer possible to live off traditional production, and if the start-up capital necessary for export production is beyond their means, then campesinos may be left no alternative but to sell their lands at the more attractive prices. Former landholders thus join the ranks of the landless laborers or migrate to the cities.

Since no Central American country has conducted an agricultural census since the onset of NTAE strategy, it is difficult or impossible to acquire unequivocal data on changing land tenure patterns. However, some anecdotal evidence does exist. Guanacaste Province in the northwest corner of Costa Rica is a seasonally dry area known historically for its wealthy cattlemen and its dirt-poor peasant producers of corn, beans, and dryland rice. During the 1980s it was heavily targeted for the promotion of NTAEs, and wealthy investors moved in to take advantage of the new opportunities. Corporations like Laechner & Saenz—a holding company that owns the Costa Rican dealerships of Xerox, IBM, Apple, Chevrolet, and Isuzu—and United Brands, the banana company, began developing extensive plantations of melons, mangoes, miniature papayas, *guanábana,* irrigated cacao, and other nontraditionals. According to Carlos Campos and other peasant leaders, "the campesinos were lining up in droves to sell their lands in Guanacaste." In the face of rising land prices, they said, combined with the impossibility of continuing to make a living on basic grains, and with insufficient capital to invest in nontraditionals, they were taking the option of selling out for the most they could get. Some claimed that local unemployment figures in the region rose as high as 50 percent during this period (Rosset 1991b).

Capital and Credit: Barriers to Entry

Obtaining sufficient capital is always a key obstacle for peasant producers. The viability of each potential crop in a series of options open to a peasant producer who has access to land is determined in great part by access to the necessary start-up capital and operating expenses involved. Start-up capital functions as a barrier to entry for small-scale producers. Those who cannot obtain the necessary funds simply cannot participate. It is thus an either/or condition; either you can or you can't raise the funds. While credit for ongoing operations is also dichotomous in that sense (i.e., some may be able to obtain while others cannot), there also appears to be a scale factor affecting availability of credit, especially credit for NTAEs. Those who are better off have access to greater sums and/or more-favorable interest rates. Traditionally, basic grains have been favored with preferential interest rates for small farmers, but as we see below that is rapidly changing.

Though a significant (but unknown) proportion of basic grains has always been produced with credit in Central America, the consideration of capital and credit is particularly important with nontraditionals, as they are very costly to produce. Data from Guatemala are presented in Figure 2.3. It is true, of course, that the value of the product varies as well. But the initial cost barrier for small, poor farmers in snow pea production is nearly fifteen times the cost of planting basic grains. The initial cost barrier for the other four nontraditional export crops, all annuals, is more than five times greater than that of basic grains.

Figure 2.3   Production Costs of NTAEs (U.S.$ per manzana [0.7 ha], 1987)

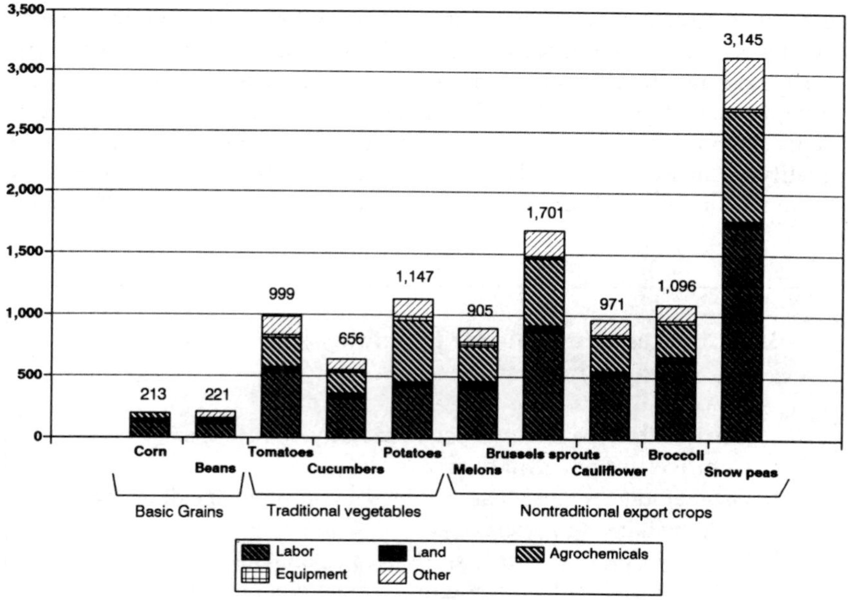

Source: Banco de Guatemala (1986).

Data from Costa Rica reinforce the Guatemalan evidence and add considerations that enter when the crop is not an annual, but rather must be supported for years before a full harvest is reaped. Bezmalinovic and coauthors (1987:16–17) reviewed the capital requirements of the different multiyear crops officially classified as NTAEs. They found that these ranged from a low of 169,093 colones per hectare for cardamom (U.S.$2,700 at the 1987 exchange rate) to a high of 85.5 million colones per hectare (U.S.$1.3 million) for macadamia. More than 97 percent of the agricultural population of Costa Rica earned less than 180,000 colones annually. By comparison, production costs under traditional cropping systems (*frijol tapado* and *maíz con espeque*) varied from 11,342 to 13,765 colones per hectare (U.S.$180–220) for beans and from 30,525 to 33,309 colones per hectare (U.S.$490–530) for corn (Reuben Soto 1989:220); in the same range found in Guatemala.

For the poorest of farmers even qualifying for credit may be next to impossible. Box 2.1 lists the full set of requirements that must be fulfilled by a Costa Rican farmer who solicits credit from the national banking system, including the special credits provided for NTAEs. Each may present difficulties for the poor. The requirement of a land title, for example, probably excludes a great many farmers. Seligson (1980:1) cites estimates that no title exists for 25 percent of farms in Costa Rica. This figure rises to 91 percent in remote areas of the country. It is unlikely that wealthy absentee landlords would travel to a bank and wait for a meeting with the loan officer to approve the loan agreement for the tenant farmers or sharecroppers farming their land. Even if the farmer qualifies for credit, the amount still depends upon an analysis of his or her assets and production plan, thus disqualifying many from the large loans necessary for nontraditionals. For these reasons Costa Rican peasant organizations denounced as "hollow,"

Box 2.1   Requirements for Obtaining Agricultural Credit in Costa Rica

1. Certificate of payment of social security contributions
2. Certificate of payment of taxes
3. Official letter stating that one does not have outstanding debts with the banking system
4. Property title of the farm, to be used as collateral
5. In the case of renters, a notarized rental contract, and the landowner must personally meet with the loan officer to approve the credit agreement
6. The loan must be cosigned by two guarantors, both of whom must demonstrate that they are not in default on any loans from the banking system

Source: CENAP et al. (1988).

under the prevailing circumstances, government promises to provide them with more credit for NTAEs (CENAP et al. 1988).

Normal financial channels' credit and capital requirements are significant barriers to entry for peasant farmers, especially given the high capital costs of entering nontraditional production. But there is a characteristic way for these producers to enter into the NTAE gamble: packers and exporters who offer "private" credit—often in the form of fertilizer, seeds, and pesticides—to farmers to produce under contract. This is particularly true for those crops where marketing is dominated by transnational corporations (see Chapter 4 of this book; and Glover and Kusterer 1990). USAID-funded programs also frequently allot special sums to be distributed through normal channels to small farmers, with easier conditions (see, e.g., von Braun et al. 1989; Nelson 1988).

Is there a bias toward larger producers even among those farmers who do obtain credit, whether through banks or from other sources? The surveys we conducted among melon farmers in Costa Rica as well as in Guatemala, El Salvador, and Honduras included information on credit obtained.[3] Statistical profiles of these farmers, by country and size class, can be found in the appendix (Table A.1). We found that small farmers tended to pay significantly higher rates of interest on their loans for production of melons, the only crop for which we had cross-national comparisons. Of the 147 who responded to questions about interest rates, those who cultivated less than 3.5 *manzanas* of melons (1 manzana = 0.7 hectares or 1.8 acres) paid on the average almost 2 percent higher rates of annual interest than those who farm larger areas (Rosset 1991a, 1992a).

Costa Rica did, in fact, make available many millions of dollars to promote NTAEs (see Figure 2.4), but funds have by and large not been readily available to the poor. In summary, then, the overall panorama in terms of credit was one of cutbacks for basic grains, on the one hand, and abundant credit for NTAEs on the other. The abundance for NTAEs was relative, as the ease of access, and even the interest rates, tended to favor large producers.

Incentives for NTAEs: Subsidies for the Rich

While neoliberal ideology and structural adjustment led to a slashing of subsidies to the poor, a vast array of subsidized incentives was created for producers and exporters of nontraditionals (see Table 2.4). These range from a variety of tax breaks and credits to easy access to foreign exchange and the elimination of the red tape associated with export permits. Two kinds of biases against small producers limit access by small farmers to these incentives. The first type offers incentives to direct exporters and importers of inputs. Subsidies to exporters include reduction of export taxes, while those

Figure 2.4   Total Credit Allocations to Principal NTAE Crops (Costa Rica State Banking System, 1985–1987)

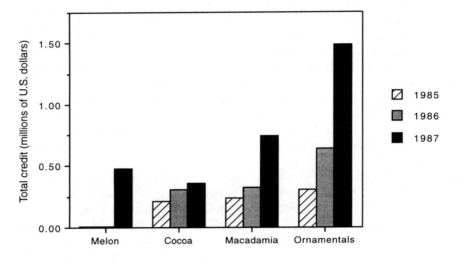

Source: Based on Vermeer (1989:76) using IMF exchange rates.

Table 2.4   Incentives for Exporters and/or Producers of NTAEs

	Guatemala	El Salvador	Honduras	Costa Rica
Fiscal				
Export tax reduction or exemption	x	x	x	x
Exemption from taxes on imported inputs	x	x		x
Income-tax reduction	x	x		x
Accelerated depreciation				x
Credit bonds against future taxes		Up to 30% of FOB value	Up to 15% of FOB value	Up to 20% of FOB value
Foreign Exchange				
Preferential access to foreign exchange		x	x	x
Freely negotiated rate for some foreign exchange needs			x	
Preferential exchange rates		x	x	
Special foreign currency accounts		x		
Other				
One-stop service to expedite export paperwork *(ventanilla única)*	x	x	x	x
Special rates for use of ports				x

Sources: Compiled from de la Ossa and Alonso (1990), Codas (1991), Perdomo and Pino (1991, 1992), Banco Central de Costa Rica (1988).

to producers who import their own inputs include exemption from import taxes. Yet only the largest producers or companies are involved in direct export or import. The second type includes those subsidies that explicitly prohibit access by small producers through size-dependent stipulations. For example, Costa Rica has a plan through which producers of nontraditionals have expedited, preferential access to foreign exchange for the import of inputs. Yet the program is limited to those companies whose exports totaled at least $500,000 the previous year (Banco Central de Costa Rica 1988).

Other forms of subsidies received by exporters of nontraditionals are made possible by the USAID financing of parallel state institutions (discussed in Chapter 3). Export promotion offices are maintained in destination ports, high-priced marketing and production experts are brought in to give seminars and make recommendations, specialists put sellers in contact with buyers—all at no charge to the exporters. It is thus ironic that while the main argument against the continued promotion of peasant agriculture has been that it is inefficient and dependent on subsidies, the nontraditional industry rests on subsidies that go far beyond anything available to producers of basic foodstuffs.

The Market: A Question of Bargaining Position

The marketplace presents risks, beyond price fluctuations, to all farmers. The smaller the farmer's scale of production, the weaker his or her bargaining power, and the greater the vulnerability to exploitation by intermediaries. A wealthy grower who provides a substantial proportion of the produce bought by a seller may be in a good position to bargain for higher prices, while a peasant who supplies only a tiny fraction may have no say at all.

Because of their relative powerlessness in the marketplace, small farmers who switch from basic grains to nontraditionals may face a price bias relative to scale. In our survey of melon producers we asked them what prices they received for their produce. In Guatemala, El Salvador, and Honduras we found that farm size, measured in manzanas, was a significant determinant of price. Every additional manzana that a farmer had planted in melons translated into a 1 percent higher price for produce (Rosset 1991a). In other words, an additional ten manzanas meant a 20 percent premium received. The situation was worse in Costa Rica, where each additional manzana translated into a 6 percent increase.

A farmer who produces a crop for local consumption has a certain degree of control over the market. He or she may be at the mercy of middlemen, yet these intermediaries are largely local people as well. Thus, at the very least, a face-to-face complaint and resolution of a conflict is a possibility. In some cases farmers may travel to market and sell their produce themselves, avoiding intermediaries and exerting as much control as a seller can exert. If the crop is not a perishable—if it is dry corn or beans, for example—then the farmer can choose not to sell, storing the product until prices improve. In the worst of cases basic grains are something that the farmer and his or her family can consume themselves. With nontraditionals that is not the case. This led Costa Rican farmers to chant "we eat beans, we don't eat flowers," in a 1987 march protesting favorable treatment for nontraditionals like cut flowers.

Most nontraditionals offer the worst possible marketing scenario for the small farmer. They are perishable crops that are not consumed locally but are often bought by anonymous brokers in a foreign country. To illustrate the precariousness of this situation, consider the Coopetierrablanca cooperative in Costa Rica, which for years has been one of the region's most successful small-farmer co-ops, specializing in vegetables for the domestic market. Interviews with members of this cooperative, conducted by students of one of the authors in 1987, revealed a strongly negative experience when they attempted to produce broccoli for export. Their story is one that was repeated to us in each of the countries in the region.

In 1985 co-op farmers were offered written contracts by a U.S. company (they remembered the name as "Food Pro") to produce broccoli to be shipped frozen to the United States. Many members set aside land and planted broccoli, but when harvest time came nobody from Food Pro showed up to purchase their produce. A check with the U.S.–Costa Rican Chamber of Commerce revealed no company by that name, and a visit to the consulate proved equally fruitless. In the end, the produce was fed to the pigs, for there is little or no market locally for broccoli. Larger-scale producers or producer associations, with a more sophisticated knowledge of the market and better contacts, would be less likely to fall into such a situation.

Technical Assistance

Most farmers require some form of agricultural extension or technical assistance to effectively produce their crops. This is particularly true for new crops with which farmers are not familiar. But even peasant producers of corn and beans require assistance. This may seem counterintuitive to some readers, since Central American peasants have produced these crops for untold generations, and since local cultures are rich with knowledge of traditional farming systems. But historically the richest and most fertile soils were farmed by peasant producers, while today they have access only to the most marginal soils and steepest slopes. Indigenous knowledge generated over centuries of corn production in the fertile lowlands often proves quite useless when applied to the thin, eroded, and rocky soils of the hillsides of Central America (Thrupp 1989; Rosset et al. 1994).

Changing patterns of access to technical assistance can exert a strong influence on the success or failure of different classes of agricultural enterprises. It is in this light that the following experience is of interest. While working on a project with the Costa Rican Ministry of Agriculture from 1987 to 1989, one of the authors became aware of a trend in the assignment of extension agents by crop and region. National co-workers would complain that after many years of work with corn, or beans, or tomatoes, they had suddenly been reassigned to miniature papayas or strawberries for export. They were upset, as this meant learning a lot of new information about new crops. It also meant giving up long-standing relations with groups of farmers, and establishing new ones with new farmers. It often meant working in a new region. Clearly the ministry's limited budget could not support a massive push toward NTAEs without cutbacks in traditional areas. Access to technical assistance was severely reduced and restricted for the poorest farmers, the basic grain producers.

In Chapter 3, Tables 3.2 and 3.3 show how government expenditures on the generation and transfer of agricultural technology declined during the 1980s. Furthermore, what activities remain in the ministries of agriculture are financed more and more by sources other than government revenues. What this means in practice is that low levels of USAID and development bank funding are sufficient to capture the activities of financially strapped government departments and redirect them toward nontraditionals. This leaves few options for peasants and producers of domestic food crops.

Knowledge and Technology

Those small farmers who do attempt to enter the NTAE game are confronted with technology that favors larger producers and transnationals. Many nontraditional crops require considerable technological sophistication, relative to traditional production, as they are either new to the region, require special care at harvest because of their perishability, or are being produced to meet the more demanding cosmetic quality standards of foreign consumers (Thrupp et al. 1995). Because the technology and often the crops themselves are new, the risk of crop failure due to insect pests, disease, or inadequate agronomic practices is much higher than for traditional crops produced for traditional markets. Under these circumstances access to technology is also biased against small-scale producers.

There is an extensive literature on the socioeconomic consequences of the technology involved in new crops or new varieties of old crops (see various chapters in Carroll et al. 1990). Cases range from processing tomatoes in the midwestern United States (Rosset and Vandermeer 1986a) to traditional export crops in Latin America (Burbach and Flynn 1980; Avery 1985). Many studies have focused on the economies of scale inherent in the high-yielding grain varieties of the Green Revolution (see, e.g., Deo and Swanson

1990; Perelman 1977; Cleaver 1972). These varieties were actually high-response rather than high-yield; that is, they responded well to costly inputs such as fertilizer, pesticides, and irrigation. In the absence of sufficient quantities of these inputs, however, yields were inferior to those obtained with traditional varieties. Among those farmers who adopted the new varieties, under great competitive pressure, there was a variable rate of success. Those who could afford more inputs benefited disproportionately, while those who could not suffered, often eventually losing their land. Those who persisted with their traditional varieties were also driven out of business as the higher yields obtained by the wealthier farmers caused prices to drop below the break-even point for traditional production.

For NTAEs the required technology is not only input-intensive but also knowledge-intensive. Because many nontraditionals are Temperate Zone crops, the principal knowledge base for their production is found in the North, rather than in tropical countries. As many are sold as fresh produce for U.S. and European consumers, cosmetic standards mean that they must be pest- and blemish-free, and health regulations limit acceptable levels of pesticide residues (see Chapter 5). This means that pest management and agronomic practices are delicate in nature, with little room for error. Successful larger producers rely on foreign consultants for technical assistance (Thacher 1990), something clearly not available to most peasant producers.

Compounding the technical complexities of growing nontraditionals is the fact that they are often produced under novel conditions. As temperate crops, many nontraditionals are not adapted to the far greater pest and disease pressure found in the Tropics. The Coopetierrablanca cooperative discussed above offers an excellent example of what that can mean for poor farmers, once again with broccoli. In the 1986/87 growing season another export company arranged with co-op members to produce broccoli, a Temperate Zone crop, for export to the United States. The stipulated quality norm to meet U.S. standards was that there be no more than one larva of the diamondback moth per broccoli head. The diamondback is a worldwide pest of cole (cabbage family) crops and is highly resistant to pesticides. It also has much greater population levels in the Tropics than in the Temperate Zone (see Talekar and Griggs 1986 for a literature review). A tropical entomologist would tell you that only one larva per head is virtually impossible, even if one were to spray several times a week.

A Costa Rican entomologist was hired by the export company to determine the ideal spray interval necessary to guarantee the desired quality, but found that there was no such interval even theoretically possible (G. Abarca, University of Costa Rica, personal communication). Nevertheless the farmers had to bear the brunt of the losses: 60–70 percent of the produce was rejected at the packing shed and was again eaten by the pigs. Many farmers defaulted on their loans.[4] It should be clear that this situation is not necessarily damaging for the packers. They do not lose the 60–70 percent of rejected produce because they purchase only that which is perfect. (The distribution of risk between growers, packers, and exporters is discussed in more detail in Chapter 4.)

Large corporate growers in Mexico have overcome the diamondback moth problem using state-of-the-art integrated pest management technology. It is based on the deployment of technicians in the fields who monitor pest populations, entering the data into notebook computers containing mathematical simulation models of pest populations. These models tell the technicians when to spray what dosage of which product to maximize the quality of the produce. Central American peasant farmers, even those organized in relatively successful cooperatives, have great difficulty competing where such cutting-edge technology is required. Regardless of these deterrents, USAID persists in promoting broccoli as an alternative for small growers in the region.

Quality control is a new problem for small farmers not accustomed to the exigencies of foreign markets. It favors those producers familiar with the market or able to hire foreign consultants. Quality restrictions are a problem both with temperate crops like broccoli, transplanted to the region, and for tropical crops like tubers that are now being promoted for export. Although peasants may have grown tubers, like cassava, for their entire lives, it has in the past been for family consumption and/or local markets with much lower standards for appearance, pesticide residues, and insect presence and damage. In extreme cases peasant participation may be reduced to zero as a result of these pressures. One USAID evaluation of NTAEs concludes in the case of papayas that "these difficulties will restrict the product to larger, more sophisticated growers." The authors of the evaluation felt that these problems were such that only the participation of a transnational with its technical expertise could overcome them. (In this case the overriding concern was for presence of the Mediterranean fruit fly.) For that reason they argued that "USAID assistance rightly involved supporting a joint venture between PINDECO [a U.S.-owned transnational] and CAAP [the Costa Rican government agency]" (Bolton and Manion 1989:52).

Despite the technological disadvantages illustrated by cases like this, it may eventually be shown that NTAE crops of local tropical origin are more appropriate than temperate crops. Technology should be more readily available for their production and processing, and the pest and disease problems could be less severe for plants of local origin. If true, this would have strong policy implications for the types of crops that should be promoted for small farmers in the future.

When we view from afar the experience of small farmers in Costa Rica during the 1980s, it is not surprising that the decade saw unprecedented rural strife. On the one hand the cutbacks that accompanied structural adjustment combined with U.S. food aid to undermine the historical basis for the survival of the peasant sector; while on the other great efforts were made to lure peasants into nontraditionals. Unfortunately, those relatively few small farmers who attempted the changeover found themselves overmatched in competition with wealthy local investors and foreign corporations, facing unfavorable economies of scale at every turn. The result has been the further concentration of agriculture and the creation of an explosive social situation (Vunderink 1990–1991; Anderson 1991).

▼ Guatemala: Altiplano Versus the Seasonal Lowlands

Guatemala is second in the region only to Costa Rica in the degree to which NTAEs took off during the latter part of the 1980s and the early 1990s. The two principal areas of NTAE expansion within Guatemala are quite different from one another. The Altiplano is a highland area of broken terrain, with a humid, temperate climate, where the growing seasons are limited by frost, much as in the United States. Together with similar areas in Mexico, it is a potentially important site for the production of what are called winter vegetables—Temperate Zone crops like broccoli and snow peas that cannot be produced in the United States during the winter, creating a significant demand for imports during those months. The Guatemalan and Mexican highlands are ideally situated geographically and climatologically to supply this demand. Furthermore, low labor costs both in farming and in processing make it possible to compete year-round in the U.S. frozen vegetable market. Because of the broken nature of the terrain, however, it is difficult for large growers to operate in the Altiplano—there simply are not enough flat pieces of land that can be irrigated near transportation to make it possible to grow substantial quantities of produce on large tracts, thus opening the door for peasants to participate in NTAEs with less competition from larger producers.

In the lowlands near the Pacific coast and in the eastern portion of the country, however, the situation is quite different, more closely resembling that of Guanacaste in Costa Rica. It is a hot, seasonally dry region, with large tracts of flat, irrigated land. Historically the Pacific lowlands were dominated by cotton, sugarcane, and cattle, while the eastern lowlands saw primarily cattle, basic grains, and vegetables for domestic consumption as well as for export to other Central American countries. We chose the eastern province of Zacapa for our study, where the Fragua Valley has seen the most intense production of cantaloupe and honeydew melons for the U.S. winter market.

Ladino Melon Growers in the Fragua Valley

Compared to melon growers in other Central American countries, those in the Fragua Valley own somewhat less land on the average, though like their foreign counterparts they have tended to risk more than half of this land in the relatively chancy production of melons (see the Appendix, Table A.2, for producer profiles). Guatemala was the first country in the region where melon production expanded rapidly, and this is reflected in a longer average number of years' experience with the crop. As in the other Central American countries, small melon growers have faced direct competition from large national and transnational growers. In the Fragua Valley peasant cooperatives sell to packing sheds owned by transnationals like Chiquita Brands, or by independent foreign and domestic investors. At the same time they compete with larger growers, both entrepreneurs and those transnationals like Del Monte that prefer to grow their own rather than haggle with individual growers (Murray 1992). They face the same biases against small-scale producers as their other Central American counterparts in terms of access to credit and incentives and in terms of the price they receive for their produce (Rosset 1991a). And the result has been the same. Small-scale growers have had a far greater tendency to drop out of melon production. And the melon industry in Guatemala is becoming increasingly concentrated among a small number of larger local and foreign corporate farms.

A typical example is the Cooperativa Agrícola de Servicios Varios de Usumatlán, known as the CASVU cooperative, in the town of Usumatlán in the Fragua Valley (Murray 1992). In 1987 Chiquita Brands purchased Básico, a small foreign-owned packing operation in the valley, and began giving out contracts to small and medium-sized local growers. That year small farmers in the town planted forty manzanas of melons, and most apparently had good success. The next year more land was planted, and once again the harvest was successful. But in 1989, the third year, despite three hundred manzanas with good yields, the farmers suffered heavy losses, as Chiquita rejected 50 percent of the production on the grounds of inferior quality, double the rate of previous years. According to Chiquita, it was just a bad year in terms of melon quality. The farmers claimed that production had exceeded packing capacity, leading the company to invent the quality issue. Regardless of the truth of the matter, the experience motivated the small growers to band together, and they founded the CASVU co-op.

The co-op farmers' goal was to market their melons independently, freeing themselves from what they felt were Chiquita Brands' unfair practices. They obtained credit from a state bank, and they signed a contract with Alpine, a U.S. fruit broker and grower, to export their produce. In late 1990, the first year with Alpine, seventeen members of CASVU planted thirty-seven manzanas of melons. Fourteen of them made profits ranging from

U.S.$300 to $11,000 each, while three lost from $60 to $1,000 (note the large variation in profits and losses among neighbors). There are two possible melon-cropping cycles in the Fragua Valley. Given the relative success of the first planting, twenty-four members planted a total of seventy-four manzanas in the early 1991 cycle. Of these, fifteen made profits ranging from $500 to $7,000, while nine had losses that ranged from $100 to almost $4,000. Some of the biggest winners of the first year became losers the second year, while others saw their profits drop substantially. The biggest winner the second year had not even planted melons the year before. For these small growers (no one had planted more than three manzanas in either year), planting melons was like buying a very expensive lottery ticket. Production costs in Guatemala average about $1,000 per manzana for melons, a huge amount of money for a land-poor peasant. The potential gains were impressive, but so was the potential to end up heavily indebted. In the second growing cycle of 1991 only nine hardy souls decided to take the risk. It turned out to be a 100 percent loss. Alpine informed them that their shipment had arrived in port in unacceptable condition, all of the melons either overripe or rotten. No one in the CASVU co-op now plants melons. And the majority still carry heavy debt burdens left over from their experiences with Alpine and Chiquita. This has meant a tremendous human cost to the co-op members (see Box 2.2).

Chiquita Brands now works only with larger growers, and it is rumored to be trying to sell its packing shed and move out of the Fragua Valley altogether. Chiquita Brands employees told the authors that they have new projects from Hermosillo, Mexico, to Guanacaste, Costa Rica, and are considering a new site near the airport in San Salvador. As in the case of ayote squash in Costa Rica, the experience of small farmers with nontraditionals followed a short-term boom/bust cycle that left them worse off than before.

Broccoli and the Indigenous Peoples of the Altiplano

In contrast to the ladinos who inhabit the melon-growing lowlands, the majority of the peasant farmers in the Altiplano are descendants of the Mayas who once ruled most of what today is Guatemala and southeastern Mexico. To this day Spanish remains their second language. The cycles of expulsions and land concentration that began with the conquest have pushed them into the mountains and valleys of the highlands, where they live in conditions of extreme poverty. Here, Guatemalan and foreign companies have set up packing operations and frozen food plants to export broccoli, cauliflower, brussels sprouts, and snow peas to the United States. These are all crops that thrive in the cold climate of the highlands. As explained earlier, physical conditions prohibit the widespread presence of large growers in the Altiplano, though they do have a limited presence on the scattered larger patches of prime farmland.

**Box 2.2   Trapped in the Melon Patch:
The Saga of Don Manuel**

Major changes in the lives of small farmers have come with the introduction of nontraditional crops. The story of Manuel, his wife María, and their three children, as told to anthropologist Beatriz Manz and one of the authors during a 1992 visit to Guatemala, is indicative of the experience of many who have played the high-stakes game of nontraditional agriculture.

Manuel became successful in the 1970s and early 1980s growing tomatoes for a local processing plant and tobacco for a Guatemalan cigarette company. He was able to buy a pickup truck, and he became a man of some importance in his small, rural farming community. Then the whitefly came and wiped out the tomato industry throughout the valley. Don Manuel was unable to pay back his loans to the tobacco company. He had to find a new crop, and a new company with which to contract.

With a loan from a bank in Guatemala City, Manuel turned to melon farming and signed a contract with the transnational corporation, Chiquita Brands. The first year's melon harvest went well and Manuel earned a profit of U.S.$13,000. He built a modest little house for his family. He went to the bank and borrowed more money to expand his production in the following year. But half the second-year harvest was considered low quality by Chiquita, and Manuel was paid only half as much as the previous year.

Feeling he had been swindled, Manuel, along with other members of the local cooperative, contracted with a broker in Miami for sale of their third year's harvest. But the broker notified Don Manuel and the others, weeks after they had shipped their harvest, that the entire shipment had been rejected. Manuel and the others earned nothing. Manuel found himself U.S.$15,000 in debt.

María says she worries for Manuel. He is a proud man and has been unable to sleep for months. He is tormented with anxiety over how he is going to pay off this debt and provide for his family. Land rent has doubled in the last four years, leaving Manuel and the others with few options other than continuing the melon gamble in order to pay their debts and feed their families. If he can just get that one good harvest, Manuel laments, he can get out of this trap once and for all. And so he looks to the next melon season for his salvation.

He has turned to taking tranquilizers to escape his sleepless torment. María sadly observes, "He has so many drugs, our house is like a pharmacy." He has taken to dreaming of the United States, where a cousin has migrated and is now earning $9.00 an hour. He even paid a lawyer a great deal of money for a passport. Then he could not get a visa.

María has taken out a loan to finance the next melon cycle. Manuel can no longer get credit. This time the house is their collateral. The truck, she says, will be the last thing to go because they can still make something transporting goods to market. María works seven days a week, often until midnight, cutting hair, making and selling popsicles, taking in sewing and ironing. She is the sole source of income for the family. Meanwhile, Manuel looks to the coming melon season. Maybe this will be the one.

The production in the Altiplano of nontraditionals for export began in the departments of Sacatepéquez and Chimaltenango, probably because of their proximity to Guatemala City export facilities, but has in recent years spread westward through parts of Sololá, Quetzaltenango, and other departments. Great successes with small farmers were initially reported in Sacatepéquez (see, e.g., von Braun et al. 1989), but little has been written on the areas of expansion. We decided, therefore, to concentrate our efforts on the newer zones, and chose the village of Pixabaj, Sololá, to survey farmers. Pixabaj is in one of the early areas to which NTAEs spread as they moved out from Chimaltenango. Broccoli and cauliflower are the main nontraditionals in the area, and we report here on our survey of broccoli producers. (See Tables A.3 and A.4 of the appendix for profiles of broccoli producers in Pixabaj and melon growers in the Fragua Valley.)

The most striking difference between the ladinos of La Fragua and the Mayas of Pixabaj is the average size of their landholdings: fifteen versus one manzana, respectively. This reflects the overall difference in the standard of living between the ladino and indigenous parts of Guatemala. Another difference is that the average melon grower risked the majority (61 percent) of his land in nontraditionals, while the typical broccoli farmer used only 11 percent. We feel that this represents a significant difference between ladino and indigenous peasants—one that we have been repeatedly struck by. Whereas ladinos from Guatemala to Costa Rica seem to be gamblers, risking most everything on a new alternative, the indigenous peasants seem to be conservative and risk-averse, testing new crops on tiny parcels to see how well they do. If they don't like them, they quickly abandon them—witness the two years of average experience with broccoli (which had been in the area for at least ten years), versus the almost eight years that the average ladino had stuck with melons (see Appendix, Table A.4).

Other striking differences between the Fragua Valley and Pixabaj include the previous use to which the land now used for nontraditionals had been put. In La Fragua only 50 percent came out of basic grains, compared to 100 percent in Pixabaj. The broccoli producers, despite their much smaller farm size, were more than twice as likely to employ family labor in production. They were also far more likely to have had their produce rejected because of poor quality (100 percent had this experience vs. 16 percent of the melon growers), or to have lost a crop due to the lack of a buyer (94 percent vs. 18 percent). In general there was little variation in their experiences across their limited size categories (see Appendix, Table A.4), especially when compared to Central American melon growers (see Appendix, Table A.1).

There seems to a distinct pattern for these growers. We found repeatedly, both in the survey data and in field interviews, that they experiment one to three years with a small portion of their land in a particular nontraditional crop, and a large proportion of them then abandon it after negative experiences. This was confirmed for us by an interview with the technical manager of Alimentos Congelados, S.A. (ALCOSA) for broccoli in the Altiplano (Rosset 1992b). ALCOSA is a U.S.-owned company that exports frozen vegetables produced by small farmers under contract. He estimated that there are some eighteen thousand farmers in the Altiplano who among them plant some ten thousand manzanas of broccoli each year. Nine companies buy their produce, six of which are Guatemalan and three of which are foreign. ALCOSA alone has three thousand farmers under contract each year. He said that the principal factor that limits broccoli production in the region is a shortage of farmers willing to grow it. Broccoli moves in a wave across the highlands, being produced for several years in a given township until most people there are unwilling to keep growing it and then moving on to ever more remote villages in search of fresh growers. He spoke of ferocious competition between companies, as *coyotes* (buyers) from one often try to hijack broccoli under contract to another, buying it in the field before the first company's truck arrives. Nevertheless this has not translated into higher prices for the growers, perhaps because of the continuous supply of new villages to which exporters can introduce the crop.

Continuing our research, we moved a little farther out from Pixabaj to the township of Santa Lucía, where broccoli has been present for no more than five years. Through extensive interviews we were able to document forty-seven experiences with broccoli by local peasant farmers, and three by larger, independent or corporate growers. All forty-seven small growers reported bad experiences with the crop, and twenty-nine had already abandoned its production (Rosset 1992b). Totaling all of their experiences, they reported net losses in 53 percent of the cropping cycles. The main reasons they cited for their losses were rejections because of quality, pest damage, low prices with high costs, and drought, in that order. Ten growers reported that the export companies sometimes paid them up to nine months late, and that this had helped force them out of the broccoli business. The eighteen who continue to grow broccoli are all members of one cooperative, and they had accumulated a huge debt to the local credit union because of their losses during the previous five broccoli-growing seasons (1–2 per year). They had just paid off 50 percent of that debt by selling the rights to cut down trees on their communal forest lands. We concluded that it was likely that within the year not one small farmer would be left growing broccoli in the area—yet another example of the typical life cycle of peasant participation in nontraditionals.

Of the three large growers, one company had abandoned the area after being hit by a drought its very first year. Of the remaining two, one was a local man of wealth with thirty manzanas in broccoli, and the other was a company owned by wealthy cotton growers that had forty-seven manzanas. In both cases they seemed to be doing quite well, complaining only of disciplinary problems with the local labor force, whom they paid from U.S.$2.50 to $3.00 per day to the men, and $2.00 per day to the women. Their yields were in the same range as those reported by the peasant producers, and their costs were higher, as they used far more agrochemicals in addition to hired labor. Their better profit margin was attributable to two factors: a far lower rate of rejections based on quality; and a higher price received from the buyers. One of the larger growers confirmed that the buyer gave him a higher price because of the lower overhead involved in buying a large quantity from a single grower. The manager of the other large operation said that his company's strategy is to take a couple of years to "learn a new crop" without worrying about profit and loss, expecting that by the third year it would be making profits. This corresponds with what USAID consultant Kerry Byrnes (1989, 1991) has called the ability to "weather the school of hard knocks." In other words, in order to be successful in nontraditionals, a farmer must have the economic wherewithal to survive initial years with losses before he begins to turn a profit. This is clearly not possible, however, for the region's poor. As far as they go, a few have won the lottery through a fortuitous combination of good yields and good quality that happened to correspond with good prices, leading to a strengthened relationship with a buyer. These are the peasants whom one now sees with a pickup truck or a new roof on the house. But our work shows that the vast majority of those who experimented with broccoli are worse off than before.

NTAE Success Stories: Cuatro Pinos *and ALCOSA*

Our experiences with broccoli in the Altiplano contrast sharply with other reports in the literature. Barham and associates (1992) used an econometric model based on current data to develop predicted land acquisition trajectories for small and large producers in the Altiplano over a hypothetical thirty-year period. According to their analysis, small farmers who adopted nontraditionals during the boom phase would stand to increase their landholdings the most, while small and large nonadopters would stand to lose the most. In between these extremes, large farmers who adopted preboom and midboom would also increase their holdings. If correct, their projections would imply on the one hand significant benefits for some small farmers, and on the other substantial social differentiation with clear losers. Unfortunately, the more positive projections from their model require a several-decade-long boom phase, while we have found no evidence that booms in peasant cash crop production last more than two to ten years at best.

Another set of authors are those who extol the success of the Cuatro Pinos cooperative in the township of Santiago Sacatepéquez in Chimaltenango, one of the pioneers of peasant participation in NTAEs. The members of this USAID-funded co-op produce snow peas, cauliflower, broccoli, and parsley. They are under contract to ALCOSA. This case has been used repeatedly as an example of successful small farmer participation in NTAEs (see, e.g., Ayala Rivera and Young 1990; von Braun et al. 1989; Glover and Kusterer 1990; de Janvry et al. 1989). The authors of a USAID-sponsored evaluation of Cuatro Pinos found that participation in the cooperative, and thus in NTAEs, was correlated with higher family income, greater productivity in the same family's corn plot, and better nutritional status (von Braun et al. 1989). In their words, "this case study demonstrates that with appropriate access to resources and markets, and with effective assistance in the development of community institutions, the impoverished sectors of the Western Altiplano can substantially improve their income and welfare."

It is this evaluation that almost all of the other authors cite as evidence that Cuatro Pinos in particular, and NTAEs in general, have been a boon to the rural poor. This evaluation was carried out at a time, however, when nontraditionals were relatively new to the area; in other words, during the boom phase in the community. Shortly after the publication of the report, Rosset (1991a, b) raised serious doubts about the evenness of the benefits within a community that included both co-op members and nonmembers, and thus adopters and nonadopters of nontraditionals, as well as about the longer-term sustainability of the boom.

Some of these doubts have recently been confirmed by a follow-up evaluation conducted by the same institutions that performed the first evaluation, once again funded by USAID (IFPRI et al. 1992).[5] In fact, the quintessential example of NTAE success with the poor has proved ephemeral. Five years passed between the fieldwork performed for the first and second evaluations, and Chimaltenango had passed from the boom phase of NTAE strategy to the postboom phase. The following is a brief summary of the salient conclusions of the second report.

Community members feel that co-op membership provides a "minimal level of economic security, although there was also an awareness that the benefits are not equally distributed," and that the co-op has been able to improve education, technology transfer, and access to land. Nevertheless, there has been a "clear switch" back to traditional vegetable crop production for domestic markets, as well as a continuing tendency to grow basic grains. Farmers have abandoned nontraditionals because of price instability, preferring the somewhat more stable traditional vegetables.

Since 1989, co-op members have started to sell land. Since 1991, they report that land has become too expensive to buy, their purchasing power has decreased, and land rental is a more common option. Nevertheless, land acquisition has been more common among smaller farmers.

"Real incomes have fallen for all households between 1985 and 1991." The income differential between member and nonmember households continued to be positive, but was "sharply lower in 1991 compared to 1985" (IFPRI et al. 1992).

Thus we have two distinct patterns of NTAE experience in Guatemala: one in the lowlands where ladino peasants have taken great risks and wound up with heavy losses; and another among the indigenous people of the Altiplano where relatively little has been risked, so that while they have generally not fared well, they have controlled their losses. Our final example comes from El Salvador, which, like neighboring Honduras, has seen relative success with nontraditionals.

▼ Melons in El Salvador: Passing the Risks Down the Chain

The following is a letter we received in August 1991 from a high-level consultant retained by USAID to promote nontraditionals in the entire region. The first part is a clip from a fax that he received from El Salvador; the italics give his handwritten notations.

> The Teculutan co-op, UCOPEX, was probably ripped off by their local manager (*S.V.*) on top of receiving low returns from Prevor on their exported cantaloupes. The manager is rumored to be in hiding and is threatened with Zapata-type retribution if he shows his face.

This quote, the source of which I won't attribute, is one example of why melons get a bad name and why we at PROEXAG [a USAID NTAE support project] do not recommend them for small farmers, except in association with an experienced marketeer, and why we are leery of cooperatives.

- *Prevor has a reputation for terminal market sleaze, and got bought out by PPI [a packer/exporter], which is now under British Chapter 11 equivalent.*
- *The co-op obviously picked a dishonest manager.*
- *On top of all that, they hit a low market.*

It is ironic that PROEXAG, a USAID-created and funded project, no longer recommends melons for small farmers. USAID projects were largely responsible for the initial push toward melons among Salvadoran peasants. We see here how small farmers depend on others for the marketing expertise they do not possess themselves. If they are lucky they find an honest and "experienced marketeer," but all too often they fall prey to unscrupulous traders, whose companies may be present one day and gone the next. The note alludes to additional losses attributable to low market prices, another factor that hurts the poor disproportionately.

The year 1991 was difficult for many small-scale melon growers in El Salvador. They live in the Department of Ahuapán, largely in the municipality of San Franciso Menéndez. Typically beneficiaries of the 1980 agrarian reform, corn was originally their favored crop and is still second in importance. They plant melons, their current primary crop, on two or three manzanas of their two to five manzana farms. The great majority belong to credit and service cooperatives, though most often they farm their parcels individually. Of those we interviewed in our survey, the median education level was through the second grade (Codas 1991; see Appendix, Table A.2).

Though average yields in 1991 were well within the normal limits, at 416 boxes per manzana, low and fluctuating prices proved the bane of small farmers. Melons are grown for the U.S. winter market window from January through March when U.S. production reaches its annual low. This is when prices are expected to be most favorable. Yet we see in Figure 2.5 that for the two principal varieties grown, honeydew and cantaloupe, prices fell below costs during several critical weeks. Note that these are prices in south Florida, where the majority of the production is sold. The cost figures combine production costs with shipping and incidentals—thus the figure ostensibly shows net profitability for the exporter rather than the producer. Nevertheless, the structure of the industry is such that risks are passed down the marketing chain to the farmer, as we shall see in Chapter 4. It is likely that the lion's share of the losses shown in Figure 2.5 were born by peasant farmers rather than by exporters.

Figure 2.5   Purchase Price of Melons in South Florida Versus CIF Florida Costs for Salvadoran Melons

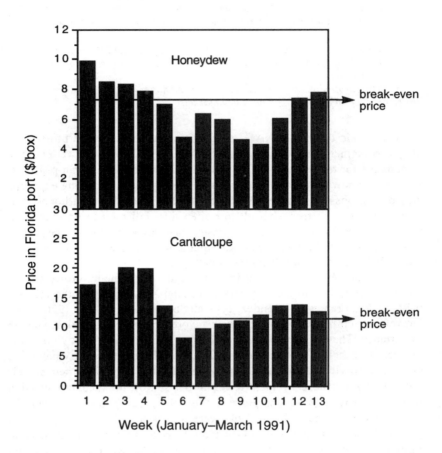

Source: Codas (1991).

This phenomenon is clearly illustrated in Table 2.5, where we estimate net profits in 1991 by farm size. We see a classic example of a bias in prices received as a function of the scale of production. Small farmers received an average price of 20.36 colones per box, with total production costs of 29.56. Meanwhile, large farmers received more than double the price (57.70 colones per box) but had only slightly higher production costs. Translated into dollars, the average small farmer lost the equivalent of U.S.$478.40 on every manzana planted, while the average large grower earned $1,446.64.

Table 2.5   Production Costs, Farm Prices, and Net Profits by Farm Size
(melon production in El Salvador, January–March 1991)

	Area of Melons Cultivated	
	< 10 mz[a] of melons	>20 mz of melons
Production, harvest and packing costs per mz[b]	10,845.00	10,960.00
Financing (20%/yr x 8 mo)	1,453.23	1,468.64
Total costs	12,298.23	12,428.64
Average yield	416 boxes	416 boxes
Cost per box	29.56	29.88
Average sale price per box	20.36	57.70
Net return per box	(9.20)	27.82
Net return per mz	(3,827.20)	11,573.12
Net return per mz in U.S.$	(478.40)	1,446.64

Source: Codas (1991) except for yield and price; these are from our survey (see Appendix).
Notes: Prices given in colones unless otherwise noted.
a. Manzana (mz) = 0.7 ha
b. Honeydew (small farmers) and cantaloupe (large farmers)

Lower than normal international prices led to the difficult situation. Many of the large growers are also exporters, which acts to buffer them against fluctuating demand and prices in several ways. They buy melons from small farmers to supplement their own production, which gives them a certain degree of flexibility. This year they apparently paid themselves acceptable prices, while losses were passed on to the peasant farmers in the form of much lower prices. At the same time they bought fewer total melons from surrounding farms. More than a third of the small growers reported that they were forced to sell between three-fourths and all of their production on the local market, for lower prices (Codas 1991).

In summary, two sorts of scale-based biases worked against the poorer melon growers in El Salvador. The huge difference in profit margins between small and large growers was most directly due to scale-related price biases, where those with more land received better prices. This was a function of a scale-related marketing bias. Large growers exerted control over the market through their dual role as producers and exporters, skewing prices and cutting the poor out of the market at the worst moment. Many small farmers, lacking influence, were forced to sell their production on the local market, where there is little demand for these export varieties. Though the 1991 problems can be blamed on an unexpected drop in prices, it is important to remember that prices for nontraditionals are always fluctuating, and dramatically so.

▼ Social Differentiation: The Sum of the Parts

We would like to know if all the biases against small producers and all the risk factors, when taken together, are of sufficient weight to change overall social and economic patterns. To answer this question we really need data for a particular crop or community taken over a sufficiently long period of time to see the changes.

Unfortunately there is little data available on NTAEs, except for the second Cuatro Pinos study, that show trends in land use over time, making it difficult to verify the occurrence of widespread social differentiation. One such data set, however, was provided by our regional survey of melon growers. We asked producers in different size classes how the area that they plant in melons had changed over the past several years. In Figure 2.6 we see a marked contrast between the two smaller size classes (< 3.5 mz, and 3.5–12 mz) and the two larger ones (12–30 mz, and > 30 mz). If we take an increase in area to indicate relative success with melons, and a decrease to indicate problems, then the patterns make sense. Farmers in the smaller two categories experienced initial success, followed by problems leading to a decline in area. Those in the larger categories experienced greater success and a steady growth in area. It is interesting to focus on the middle two size categories (3.5–12 mz and 12–30 mz). Two years ago all were in the smaller of the two categories, but in the last year they have diverged sharply, one group dramatically increasing their area while the other plummeted. Strong social differentiation has taken place among Central America's melon growers during the past few years.

▼ Conclusion: Are NTAEs Likely to
Change Central America for the Better?

We received another letter from our USAID consultant acquaintance. He had noted our concern for the risks that small farmers must assume when they switch to nontraditionals. Among these are the marketing risks that come, as in the case of ayote in Costa Rica, when USAID simultaneously promotes the same crops in different countries. Thus Costa Rican producers compete with Guatemalans, and even with Pacific Rim producers. Under these circumstances one may be undercut by another, or the market may saturate, causing prices to drop across the board and wiping out small farmers. Other problems we had mentioned included quality control, access to technology, and credit. His response is indicative of the position of USAID and international lenders, and of their near indifference to the plight of the poor:

Figure 2.6   Change over Time in Mean Area of Melons Cultivated per Farmer (Guatemala, El Salvador, Honduras, and Costa Rica, 1988–1991)

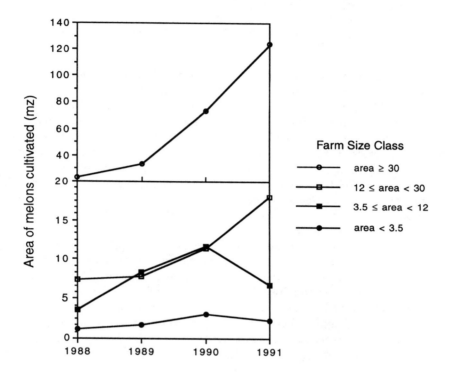

Source: Regional farmer survey conducted for this study.

Note: n = 170, 1 mz = 0.7 ha. Note change in scale on vertical axis. Repeated measures ANOVA showed significant effects of size class (P < 0.001), year (P < 0.001), and the interaction between size class and year (P < 0.001).

Because I am a believer in the benefits of free competition, I am not concerned that simultaneous support, or even promotion, of the same crops in different areas . . . will cause everyone to go broke. In the short run there will be some losers, but over time comparative advantage will prevail. The most efficient producers will remain and the total supply of low cost, high quality produce will increase, not just in the U.S. but all over the world. For an economist, this means an improvement in general welfare, both in target markets and to some extent in supplier countries.

You did express concern, of course, about the impact of agricultural diversification on the individual and collective welfare of small farmers. My team could show you many cases where they have benefited, and in a significant way. We could also show you many cases where they came up losers, usually because they got into crops that did not have a consistently attractive export market (e.g. cucumbers), or because their growing conditions did not match the production and marketing requirements of that crop; or because they lacked needed technology and know-how, or because they lacked sufficient financing, or because they listened to bad advice from local or foreign advisors.

We can analyze this letter in the context of this chapter. The "most efficient producers will remain," usually translates to "the larger producers will remain." "Many cases where [small farmers] have benefited" from NTAEs turns out to be more complicated upon closer examination. Production characteristics such as "production and marketing requirements"—quality control, in other words—"consistently attractive export market" or prices, "technology and know-how," "financing," and dependence on advice, all work to the disadvantage of the poor farmer who is locked in competition with his or her better-endowed neighbors—neighbors with more capital, better access to credit, more control over the market, and better, more expensive foreign consultants.

One might ask, furthermore, how "they got into crops" that offered poor conditions for their economic advancement. Did they spontaneously decide to grow cucumbers, or melons, or broccoli, instead of corn? Or were they lured or enticed by publicity campaigns replete with incentives, financed by foreign interests? Or did cutbacks in basic grain price supports simply leave them with no alternative? Our experience is that the answer is usually a combination of the latter two possibilities. And that is the tragedy for the rural poor that NTAE strategy has become.

In summary, then, an environment has been created by exogenous forces that is detrimental to poor farmers. Their former livelihood producing corn and beans has become increasingly difficult, while they are encouraged to experiment with new export crops. They face significant barriers to entry into these crops, however, and if they do gain entry, they face economies of scale and risks that work against them. Some few are successful, managing to increase their holdings and their income, while others face economic setbacks with insufficient economic reserves to carry them over, probably losing their land in many cases. At the same time the wealthy are well positioned to take advantage of the new opportunities opened by NTAEs, and in many cases become the winners we meet in Chapter 4. The net result is growing inequality—a growing, ever-poorer majority, and an ever-richer elite.

This situation must be viewed in the context of Central American history, throughout which inequity has been the driving force behind crisis and conflict. We have also seen how the extreme inequality in the region has effectively blocked true economic development. In this light, NTAE strategy, no matter how successful it may be for certain sectors of society, really cannot do more for Central America than the export booms that came before it, which have left the region in the lamentable state in which we find it today.

▼ Notes

1. It is perhaps worthwhile to point out that social differentiation is neither a necessary nor a sufficient condition for an increase in poverty. An increase in poverty can come about simply by means of an across-the-board decline in income. By the same token, if there is an across-the-board increase, an expanding socioeconomic pie, if you will, then a certain amount of differentiation can occur without increasing the level of absolute poverty of the poorest portion of the population. But Central America did not meet either of these criteria during the period when NTAEs were first pushed most vigorously. The Central American economies were shrinking, as we saw in Chapter 1. Under conditions of economic contraction, the social differentiation provoked by NTEAs and structural adjustment policies does indeed worsen the level of poverty of an ever larger portion of the populace. Flora (1987) made a more general form of this argument.

2. We use the term *economy of scale* in its broadest sense—any factor that, ceteris paribus, favors producers with more land, money, education, contacts, political power, over those less generously endowed. In similar fashion Gereffi and Newfarmer (1985) speak of production, pecuniary, marketing, and advertising economies of scale. This definition contrasts with the more restrictive usage employed by many agricultural economists, who refer mainly to size as a production economy of scale (see, e.g., Hayami and Ruttan 1985).

3. These data were collected by the five collaborating Central American research teams listed in the Introduction and Acknowledgments. More-detailed statistical analyses of the data can be found in Rosset (1991a, 1992a), and Rosset and Remes (1993).

4. Interviews conducted for us by María Dalva Trivelato of CECADE in August 1991 as part of the regional project coordinated by the University of Texas.

5. This report was somewhat more difficult to obtain than the earlier one, however. Whereas the first report was published and generally available, USAID suppressed the second, ordering the authors not to show it to anyone, according to a confidential source. In order for us to obtain a copy for this book, we had to enlist the support of an anonymous Clinton administration USAID official, who was determined to "end the Reagan and Bush Administration cover-ups at the Agency." It was difficult for even this official to extract the report from USAID officials in Guatemala; he was first told that it did not exist and then had to repeat several direct requests.

3

IMPLEMENTING THE STRATEGY: USAID CREATES A PARALLEL STATE

Central America's economic crisis coincided with a political transformation in the United States that included an internal and external overhaul of USAID that, after 1981, passed into the hands of Reagan-era administrators. USAID had a forceful new potential strategy for Central America, but the Reagan administration was committed to reducing the scope and functioning of government. How could Central American countries be induced to adopt the new strategy without expanding and solidifying the role of government agencies? How could the policies of structural adjustment be implemented in the face of political leaders who saw clearly its unpopularity and against resistant government bureaucracies? The solution was as ingenious as it was politically dangerous: privatize government functions into autonomous new agencies funded by USAID, responsive to USAID, and focused on the USAID agenda.

In this chapter we analyze how USAID created a new institutional framework in several Central American nations, designed to support many aspects of structural adjustment but especially focused on the promotion of nontraditional exports, both agricultural and industrial. Among the purposes of this new institutional structure were the privatization of state-owned enterprises, the liberalization of capital markets, and the creation of business-led organizations to which the functions of government agencies could be passed. The agents of change were principally USAID, the IMF, and the World Bank. These forces allied with business sectors in each country representing the interests of exporters and private banking. Other political groups within each country tended to resist these changes. The opponents mostly included social democrats and others who still believed in a strong role for the state in determining development policy. There were social and political groups concerned with improving social welfare and preserving the egalitarian aspects of state banking sectors; trade unions; and domestic industrialists oriented toward import substitution for internal markets and accustomed to preferential treatment and protectionism. Farmers' organizations, especially those who represented both large-scale and small-scale producers engaged in food crop production, also resisted.

This process began first in Costa Rica, the leading example in the region of a social welfare state that had acquired significant industrial capacity and the country that exhibited the most promise for an eventual takeoff of nontraditional exports. Costa Rica was led, at the outset of the Reagan administration, by Rodrigo Carazo, a neoliberal president openly favoring reduction of the government and the full liberalization agenda. The generally higher level of infrastructural development and educated work force created propitious conditions; if neoliberal strategies had a chance to succeed in Central America, Costa Rica offered the brightest prospects. Once the example had been set in Costa Rica, it was felt, it would then be an easy task to replicate the model in the other Central American states, with their smaller and less entrenched social welfare programs and lower levels of state intervention in the economy.

From about 1982 through the early 1990s the efforts to remake Costa Rica proceeded through phases first of resistance, then of apparent triumph, and finally of growing doubts about the social consequences of these changes. Some resistance was encountered in Honduras, as well, though substantially less. In Guatemala and El Salvador established elites rapidly embraced the new model as their own. Nevertheless, the new institutions in the latter countries have yet to achieve the level of development and organization of those in Costa Rica, in large degree because they began later, and they have been working in environments less conducive to easy success. In Costa Rica, however, the changes were so far-reaching that John Biehl, personal adviser to President Oscar Arias, denounced them as "the creation of a parallel state" (Biehl 1988:16A).

We devote the bulk of this chapter to the Costa Rican experience, emphasizing those changes with greatest impacts on agriculture, and finish with a brief assessment of the other countries. In each case we focus on USAID's role in promoting these changes. We begin with a brief historical perspective.

▼ Agriculture and the State in Central America

The expansion in size and function of the state sector was a cornerstone of Central American development in the post–World War II era. Agrarian development in particular was fostered by expanding state services in several areas, often patterned after programs and institutions developed in the United States and often responding to the U.S.-imposed requirements of the Alliance for Progress.

- Through land distribution, agrarian reform, and land titling, government programs provided greater access to land, and the security necessary to encourage expanding agricultural activity
- Through financial measures such as development bank credits, loan guarantees, and crop insurance, state policies stimulated agricultural investment and growth
- Through state grain-trading enterprises, market and price regulation, and protectionist barriers against food imports, governments provided stability to Central American producers in the face of difficult and widely fluctuating world market conditions
- Through publicly funded research and extension services, the state fostered innovation and technological development in regional food and export production

The consequent expansion of Central American development banks, ministries of agriculture, grain-trading boards, and other state services was to a great extent the creation of USAID and earlier U.S. development assistance programs.

▼ USAID's Changing View of the State: From Catalyst to Obstacle

Between World War I and the Cuban Revolution in 1959, U.S. foreign aid to Latin America was sporadic, lacking a clearly enunciated central strategy or program (Bulmer-Thomas 1987). Though total assistance over the entire period was certainly significant, and no one doubts that it contributed extensively to the development of modern infrastructure, there was little continuity of objectives and programs from year to year (Glade 1969). In the 1950s some funding was devoted to either strengthening or establishing agriculture ministries in the region (Byrnes 1992). But though there had been talk of the need for a coherent policy, it was the 1959 Cuban Revolution that really jolted the United States into action (Williams 1986). Suddenly, U.S. planners saw the threat that extreme inequality and poverty posed for stability. In the Cold War parlance of that time, it was seen as an invitation to "communist subversion." Consequently, the United States set out to promote the "reforms" of the 1960s in all of Latin America, including the Central American states.

The Alliance for Progress, announced by President John F. Kennedy in March 1961, was to be a hemispherewide, ten-year, $20 billion initiative that largely focused on modernizing the Latin American states as a means of assuring economic and political stability and growth. The Alliance for

Progress consisted of a three-pronged attack on what were perceived to be the root causes of unrest and susceptibility to subversion: the failure of the region's economies to reach the takeoff point in economic development (Rostow 1960); the lack of opportunities for the rural poor; and a weak security apparatus (Williams 1986). Economic and military aid were designed to create a powerful state in control of the development process.

U.S. assistance efforts were led by USAID and concentrated on rural development and poverty alleviation programs, export agriculture, and import-substituting industrialization under the beneficial protectionism embodied in the CACM to help overcome the limitations posed by the small size of domestic markets. During the 1960s and early 1970s USAID was the key funder in the development of a wide range of reformist government institutions. Planning of nationwide multiyear redistributive programs, including agrarian reform, were a sine qua non of most financial assistance. Agrarian institutes were created in each country to title and sometimes even distribute land; grain-marketing boards were established to provide price supports and credit programs offering limited financing to small farmers; and the acquisition and dissemination of information on new technologies was promoted through strengthened ministries of agriculture, extension services, and universities (USAID 1972; USAID/Costa Rica 1976; Barry 1987; Williams 1986; Bulmer-Thomas 1987; Biderman 1982; Seligson 1980). In the 1970s USAID became frustrated with the limited impact of agricultural ministries' research and extension activities, and funded the creation of semiautonomous institutes of agricultural technology in each country (Byrnes 1992). Among the charges given to these institutions was the technological improvement of peasant production of basic food crops.

A USAID evaluation described the objectives of U.S. assistance in agriculture during this period as targeting "the poorest of the poor" through subsidized credit for production, and "meeting basic needs" by creating or strengthening social welfare programs (Byrnes 1992). While this may overstate the benevolence of USAID programs in the 1960s and 1970s, it provides an accurate description of the way in which USAID sold itself to the U.S. Congress in the annual appropriations process. It also provides a useful contrast with the policies that emerged in the 1980s.

The reformist measures of the earlier period failed to reverse the long-standing regional trend toward uneven development, characterized by an increasingly rich elite and an ever-larger and more impoverished rural majority. Intransigent elites refused to permit reforms that would weaken their wealth and power (Williams 1986), in particular putting up near implacable resistance to land redistribution programs. Ironically, USAID's failure to overcome this resistance led to a period in Central America much like the worst post–Cuban Revolution nightmares of U.S. policymakers. The 1970s and 1980s proved to be decades of unprecedented strife and violence as each country experienced varying degrees of conflict and rebellion against the growing inequity and hardship.

▼   USAID Under Neoliberalism and Structural Adjustment

Several factors coincided in 1980 to change U.S. foreign assistance policies and ring a death knell for the same Central American reformist states that USAID had fostered in previous decades. Perhaps the most important of these factors was the advent of a Republican administration in the United States, one strongly commited to implementing neoliberal economics at home and abroad, and with the will to use all means at its disposal to do so. The Reagan administration also wished to promote an economic boom in Costa Rica in particular, as an example of capitalist success to be contrasted with what the administration helped guarantee would be "socialist" economic collapse in neighboring Nicaragua (Rosset and Vandermeer 1986b).

By this time Central America had suffered a regional economic crisis generated by the oil price hikes of 1973 and 1978 and was in the throes of the debt crisis. Notwithstanding, the Reagan administration's USAID saw the economic collapse as rather a product of market distortions and inefficiency caused by state interventionism, protectionism, and burgeoning deficits. USAID policy made a 180-degree turnaround, from seeing the state as the catalyst of development, to singling it out as the principal obstacle. An internal USAID document laid out the problems policymakers attributed to the reformist state (in this case, a critique of the Costa Rican experience), thus giving the rationale for imposing structural adjustment policies.

> Over time . . . Costa Rica moved somewhat away from a market economy and more towards a state-administered economic model as regards such variables as prices, wages, authorization to operate, and concessions for special interest groups. Social services were expanded but at the cost of heavy internal and external borrowing. Inefficient state enterprises and a significantly increased bureaucracy were created in the process. . . . White collar public sector employees, a new segment of the middle class, organized themselves into strong unions. [There were] high levels of effective industrial protection, an overvalued exchange rate, [and] subsidized interest rates. . . . Uncontrolled monetary expansion, related to attempts to maintain previous levels of public and private sector consumption, generated inflationary pressures . . . , a *de facto* moratorium on the foreign debt . . . , and a decline in the value of exports [USAID/LAC 1984:4–5].

The array of ills attributed to the state sector included protectionism, the generation of deficits, unnecessary price controls and supports, special interest group influences, expensive social services and excessive consumption, inefficient and bureaucratic state enterprises, strong unions, overvalued currency, subsidized interest rates, nonpayment of the debt, and declining exports conditioned by government-imposed obstacles. The structural adjustment policies proposed and pursued by USAID and the multilateral lenders essentially sought to dismantle the import substitution strategy and the reformist state. Protectionist barriers to imports were to be eliminated, and taxes on exports reduced. Subsidies and government budgets were to be slashed in order to reduce deficits and remove distortions. The state's guiding hand in the economy was to be replaced by the free play of market forces, supplemented by private sector institutions. As USAID's action plan for Costa Rica stated, "the basic overall structural reform which must take place . . . is a shift away from an import substitution strategy to a strategy in which the private sector is the engine for export-led growth" (USAID/Costa Rica 1986:6).

▼ The Strategy in Action: Dismantling the Costa Rican State

Costa Rica had developed, by the late 1970s, the most advanced expression of the reformist state found in Central America. Costa Rica's higher standard of living, relative tranquillity, and less-obvious differences between rich and poor have all been attributed at least partially to the social democratic policies implemented in the postwar period (Edelman and Kenan 1989). Yet during the 1980s USAID viewed "Costa Rica as a model [for change]. . . . If Costa Rica can move forward . . . it may encourage some of the other Latin American countries . . . to make similar shifts in policy and operations" (USAID/LAC 1984:14). The heavy-handedness of USAID, the World Bank, and the IMF, as they sought to force a model of structural adjustment on Costa Rica, dominates the institutional history of this era.

USAID and the multilateral lenders appear to have had two reasons for choosing to pursue the opening up of the economy to free trade, "the difficult work of non-traditional agricultural export promotion," and "getting national producers into the export arena" largely outside of the existing government structure (USAID/Costa Rica 1989). First, because of the ideology outlined above, they viewed the state as too large and too inefficient. Second, they believed that many key actors within public institutions had vested and/or ideological interests in opposing such changes. The principal tactic for overcoming resistance and assuring compliance was the use of conditionality in the formal assistance agreements signed between the donors or lenders and the recipient government. The donor or lender institutions established a set of explicit government policy reforms, institutional changes, and concrete macroeconomic targets that became requirements for the disbursement of funds. Disbursement of funds was repeatedly tied to the progress made by the local government toward implementing the required reforms.

Table 3.1 provides a classification and quantification of the covenants signed into agreements between the Costa Rican government and USAID in the annual Economic Policy and Recovery Agreements from 1982 to 1990. Between 1982 and 1990, in these agreements alone, USAID mandated a total of 357 covenants stipulating specific policy reforms. In the early years the Central Bank was targeted; later, privatization was stressed; and finally the exchange rate was floated and nontraditional exports were heavily pushed.

Table 3.1   Conditionality Covenants in Economic Policy and Recovery Agreements Between USAID and the Government of Costa Rica, 1982–1990

Policy Category Affected	1982	1983	1984	1985	1986	1987	1988	1989	1990	Total
Price structure			2	3	1	1		1	1	9
Private banking	1	3	5	1	1	2	1		3	17
Privatization (general)		1	4	6	10	5	6	6	3	41
Privatization of CODESA			4	6	10	3	2	5	3	33
CINDE		1					2			3
Foreign exchange availability	2	1	2	1	1	1	1	1	1	11
Exchange rate	2	3	2	2	2	2	2	15		30
Export promotion	1	2	2	4	1	2	12			24
Imports from United States	1	1	1	1	1	1	1	1	1	9
International capital flows			1	1		1		1	1	5
Central Bank credit	2	4	8	3	1	3	4	1	1	27
Interest rates		2	9	3	1	3	1	1		20
Credit policy		2	7	3	2	3	1	2		20
CNP (grain subsidies)			2	1			1		1	5
Employment and housing		1	2		1	1	7	8	2	22
Small business promotion	3	2								5
Private energy sector creation							1	1	1	3
IMF co-conditionality	1	2	1	1	1	1	1	1	1	10
World Bank co-conditionality									1	1
Administrative requirements		1	3	1	2	2	3	5	5	22
Other	1	3	4	2	3	5	7	7	8	40
Total	14	29	59	39	38	36	53	56	33	357

Source: Based on Sojo (1991).

The first step, however, was to weaken the old state by forcing budget cutbacks. Debt and loan negotiations with the IMF, the World Bank, and USAID were first tied to drastic cuts in state spending and the resultant reduction of government employment (Lordan 1986; "AID Provides $140 Million" 1987; Carvajal 1986; USAID/LAC 1984). Corporación Costarricence de Desarrollo, S.A. (CODESA) was the Costa Rican holding company for principal state enterprises. The National Production Council was the government grain-trading board that provided price supports for basic grain production. The explicit intent of USAID conditionality covenants can be seen in the following analysis of conditions placed on financing by the USAID Mission in San José:

> The Mission expects the dissolution, sale, or transfer of the majority of CODESA companies to be completed before the end of 1987. . . . The Mission's . . . privatization objective will focus on continuing to prevent CODESA from creating, acquiring, operating, or financing commercial activities. [The Central Bank] will establish an overall limit of financing . . . to CODESA. . . . The National Banking System will not authorize credit to the National Production Council when such credit is designed to cover . . . provision of subsidies. . . . The intent of the covenant is to reduce the . . . element of subsidized credit, . . . a limit of Central Bank expansion of credit to the economy [will be established, with] a limit on . . . the non-financial public sector [USAID 1987:34].

The requirements were unambiguous and gave the Costa Rican government no room for maneuvering if it wished to receive continued U.S. assistance. This attack on spending was accompanied by measures that hampered the government's ability to generate revenues. A key component of the export promotion strategy was the softening of disincentives to traders. Taxes on profits, exports, and imported inputs were to be reduced or eliminated, and the currency was to be devalued to make the exports more attractive on the world market. While promises of assistance were the carrot offered to induce these changes, the withholding of disbursements of already committed funds functioned as the stick. In 1984, for example, "the IMF suspended disbursements after it had determined that Costa Rica was maintaining a tax on foreign remittances," and "AID withheld disbursements . . . until corrective action was taken, i.e., a 5 percent devaluation, and legislative action to remove the tax on remittances" (USAID/LAC 1984:6).

The social democratic ideology institutionalized in the state banks made them unwilling partners to USAID's efforts to remake the nation's economy in directions that ran counter to the Costa Rican government's traditional commitment to social welfare. USAID ordained that "the Central Bank will prepare a program designed to reduce the cost of credit . . . through measures concerned with the . . . profit margins of the [state] banks" (USAID/LAC 1984:27). Thus the power of the state banks to direct national investment patterns was reduced by, among other measures, weakening their financial base through an attack on their profit margins.

These measures formed what were called the first "combined policy reform efforts of . . . the IMF, the IBRD [World Bank], and AID" (USAID/ Costa Rica 1986:6). The international agencies were severe: at any point where progress was not sufficiently rapid, reprisals were forthcoming. A USAID document noted that "the IMF suspended negotiations . . . until the [government of Costa Rica] had obtained legislative approval for stop gap measures to reduce the deficit" (USAID/LAC 1984:12). USAID's 1984 internal project paper on balance-of-payments support to Costa Rica stated that "AID reserves the right to suspend scheduled monthly disbursements in the event that the [Government of Costa Rica] is not in substantial compliance with the IMF agreement as determined by AID" (USAID/LAC 1984:6). The World Bank was equally active, as noted by María Elena Carvajal, the conservative financial commentator of Costa Rica's English-language paper the *Tico Times* (Carvajal 1986:25): "The World Bank already has issued its ultimatum on the need to bring agricultural prices down to realistic levels, which means reducing, or eventually eliminating, state subsidies. The National Production Council (CNP), the government entity responsible for establishing price supports, already has received the message and knows that cuts are in order . . . as part of the drive to cut the fiscal deficit."

The result of the policies was an across-the-board weakening of the government's ability to service its traditional clients in, among other places, the agricultural sector. Tables 3.2 and 3.3 show how the Central American Ministries of Agriculture were hit economically by structural adjustment. Though there was actually a net increase of personnel in the Costa Rican Ministry of Agriculture (MAG) between 1978 and 1988, there were sharply reduced operating funds available per agronomist. Peter Rosset worked with the MAG from 1987 to 1989 and was witness to a situation in which few professionals ever left their offices (Rosset 1991b). Either they had no vehicles, or they had a vehicle and no fuel, or there were no funds available for per diem expenses. From 1979 through 1988 the MAG's operating expenditures dropped by 65 percent relative to the overall government budget, which itself dropped 32 percent in relation to GDP.

Table 3.2   Percentage Changes in Staff and Expenditures for Agricultural Research and Extension by State Agencies, 1978–1988

	Staff[a] (S)	Expenditures[b] (E)	E/S
Costa Rica[c]	+26.4	−51.5	−61.6
El Salvador	−4.4	−63.3	−61.8
Honduras	+301.0	+120.4	−44.8
Guatemala	+79.4	+104.6	+11.1

Source: Based on Lindarte (1990:51).
Notes: a. Number of professionals.
b. In constant 1985 local currency units.
c. Research only.

Table 3.3   Changes in Ministry of Agriculture Expenditures Relative to GDP,
Agricultural GDP, and Total Government Expenditures, 1979–1988

	1979 (%)	1988 (%)	Percentage Change 1979–1988
Costa Rica			
MAG[a] expenditures[b]/government[c] expenditures	3.4	1.2	−64.7
MAG expenditures/agricultural GDP	3.8	0.9	−76.3
Agricultural GDP/total GDP	18.5	18.3	−1.1
Government expenditures/total GDP	20.3	13.9	−31.5
El Salvador			
MAG expenditures/government expenditures	8.7	4.8	−44.8
MAG expenditures/agricultural GDP	5.0	4.8	−4.0
Agricultural GDP/total GDP	26.6	12.6	−52.6
Government expenditures/total GDP	15.4	12.6	−18.2
Honduras			
MAG expenditures/government expenditures	12.4	5.0	−59.7
MAG expenditures/agricultural GDP	10.9	6.0	−44.9
Agricultural GDP/total GDP	28.0	21.7	−22.5
Government expenditures/total GDP	24.7	26.0	+5.3
Guatemala			
MAG expenditures/government expenditures	5.0	4.8	−4.0
MAG expenditures/agricultural GDP	3.3	3.6	+9.1
Agricultural GDP/total GDP	22.1	23.2	+5.0
Government expenditures/total GDP	14.7	17.5	+19.0

Source: Based on Lindarte (1990:53–54).
Notes: a. Ministry of Agriculture or equivalent.
b. Total expenditures.
c. Central government.

The ministries of agriculture in other Central American nations fared little better. In El Salvador, Honduras, and Guatemala MAG expenditures also fell as proportions of total government expenditures, even when government expenditures declined as proportions of GDP, as in El Salvador. Only Guatemala shows relatively persistent funding of the Ministry of Agriculture, and Guatemala is the Central American nation to which the smallest amount of USAID funding was allocated (other than Nicaragua under the trade and aid embargo). Furthermore, as pointed out in Chapter 2, total credit available to small farmers and support prices for corn and beans dropped sharply over much of the same period.

▼ Creation of the "Parallel State"

As state agencies were progressively weakened, new private sector institutions were created that duplicated many of their functions (Honey 1994). The key differences between these new institutions and the older ones were that the new ones were all in the private sector and catered to a different clientele, with a mix favoring larger commercial farmers and leaving out peasant farmers. The most important of these new institutions were in the private banking sector.

Costa Rica nationalized its banking system in 1948, and the Golden Era of Costa Rican economic growth in the 1960s and 1970s occurred with virtually its entire financial system in public hands. Successive Costa Rican governments utilized the state banking system as a central tool in guiding development along lines consistent with prevailing Costa Rican political preferences, which were predominantly social democratic (Edelman and Kenen 1989). The civil service cadre of the banking system to a great extent internalized social democratic ideas, and they mounted a formidable obstacle to neoliberal policies. To achieve the successful implementation of its new reform policies, USAID felt it necessary to create and strengthen a private financial sector so that it might take the lead. Private banking and finance activities were legalized under external pressure in 1978, though significant further reforms were still needed in the 1980s to make private finance institutions significant players in USAID's strategy (Reuben Soto 1988). USAID couched its plans for the finance sector in the language of efficiency.

> Credit quotas and differential interest rates, which favor some economic sectors (or people) over others, make financial intermediation in the National Banking System inefficient. . . . These inefficiencies reduce the flexibility of the system to channel adequate credit to new and more productive sectors of the economy. . . . The private banking sector, which could provide a healthy degree of competition to the state banks, suffers from unequal access to financial resources [and] there are indications that some of the private sector *Financieras* (finance companies), especially COFISA, may be in a position to use additional credit resources. . . . We propose to explore this situation and accord the problem a high priority [USAID/LAC 1984:10, 34].

The solution to the problem was to be highly irregular: making the disbursement of economic support funds conditional upon the National Assembly's passing various amendments to the national currency law (La Ley de la Moneda), the most important of which was to make it legal for foreign assistance funds to bypass the Central Bank and go directly to private banking institutions. USAID's own documents reflect the pressures that were brought to bear, at risk of "high political cost."

> Conditionality for the first Agreement has been negotiated and . . . there will be two pre-conditions to AID authorization and obligation of the first Agreement: submission by the [government of Costa Rica] of a Letter of Intent acceptable to Management of the IMF, and a revision to the

Currency Law. This revision would facilitate both making loans in Costa Rica denominated in foreign currency, and access by private banks to foreign financed Central Bank credit operations. . . . A third prior action had been contemplated, i.e. approval of a revision of the Banking Law submitted last year in satisfaction of an ESR II covenant [USAID agreement], which was designed to permit direct private bank access to Central Bank credit operations. Soundings taken . . . indicate that an unacceptably high political cost would be entailed in pushing through this measure. The [Banco Central de Costa Rica] proposes to withdraw the proposed amendment to the Banking Law, and simultaneously to include in the amendment to the currency law a provision which would enable direct access by private banks . . . where the origin of the funds is external. . . . An informal check with the private banking community indicates that the proposed change would satisfy their aspirations [USAID/LAC 1984:2].

The Costa Rican Institute for Social Studies (ICES 1987:50) interpreted this policy very directly: "They were interested in weakening the capacity of the Costa Rican state, so given to reformist deviations, to internally redistribute external financing, and in strengthening the position of the private banks as a support for the application of the policies of free business development being pushed by the Reagan administration."

USAID forced the administration of Costa Rican President Luis Alberto Monge to submit a constitutional amendment to the National Assembly that, if passed, would weaken its own power to direct the development process. The bill proved to be extremely controversial, and it was filibustered and blocked for more than sixteen months by members of Monge's party in alliance with congressional representatives from the left. Claiming that Costa Rica's postwar stability and economic growth were in large part based on control of the banking system that was nationalized by the social democratic party, Party of National Liberation (PLN) deputy Julio Jurado del Barco said that bill was "an attack against the nationalization of the banks and the very foundations of the PLN" (ICES 1987:45). PLN deputy Bernal Jiménez went on, "AID lays down conditions, pressures for changes in Costa Rican legislation, because it knows that it's the owner in this situation" (ICES 1987:46).

The United States was upset at Monge's inability to enforce party discipline in the National Assembly. In early June 1984 Ambassador Curtin Windsor said, in a local newspaper interview, that "the PLN is responsible for the future of Costa Rica. . . . If the National Assembly doesn't approve the reforms, U.S. $200 million will not enter the country." On June 28 USAID's assistant director for Costa Rica announced the retention of a U.S.$23 million disbursement, because of Monge's failure to comply with a "promise," at the same moment that the country had exhausted its foreign exchange reserves (ICES 1987:55). USAID's assistant administrator for Latin America, Marshall D. Brown, had foreseen this situation at the beginning of the year, though his conservative calculations were about two months off. In an internal planning document he had written that,

> under present conservative estimates . . . the Central Bank will exhaust its liquid Foreign Exchange Reserves in early March . . . and we expect the hard earned stabilization process to begin to unravel. . . . [AID] Mission strategy is to assure compliance with conditionality both by tranching disbursements . . . and by using the sequential nature of the Agreements and Amendments thereto to also make funds available for transfer dependent upon progress/compliance with conditionality requirements [USAID/LAC 1984:13, 16].

Tranching refers to the tactic of paying out funds in installments, each one conditional upon the Costa Ricans having taken some required action since the previous disbursement. The acute political pressure brought to bear on the Monge administration came from a combined attack by the U.S. Embassy, USAID, and right-wing elements of the private sector. The Costa Rican Chamber of Commerce (CCCR) took out an ad on July 2 in the country's major daily that was reminiscent of warnings published in Salvadoran and Guatemalan papers (ICES 1987:48):

> Some deputies are dedicating themselves to attacking and offending AID, which has been generously offering bountiful resources to our country. . . . We are faced with an emergency situation of utmost gravity that requires the firm, decided, and patriotic willingness of all who love this country, to defeat those who by their action or inaction, for personal, dastardly, or greedy reasons, wish to carry her to the brink of economic, political, and institutional collapse.

Governing party deputies took this as a thinly veiled threat. The Monge administration was also in a tight situation with the United States at this time because of the president's partial resistance to the contra war against Nicaragua. He had recently called U.S. Secretary of Defense Caspar Weinberger a liar, in public, for having falsely announced that the United States and Costa Rica would hold joint military maneuvers, and he had reiterated the Costa Rican position that it was a neutral state with respect to the Reagan administration's activities against Sandinista Nicaragua. Furthermore, the civil guard under his pro-neutrality Security Minister Ángel Solano had discovered and shut down contra bases operating in Costa Rican territory (ICES 1987).

Monge was clearly obstructing U.S. policy on several fronts. The response was not long in coming. On the fifth of August the daily newspaper *La Nación* published a sensational interview with Interior Minister Alfonso Carro, who together with Vice President Aráuz represented the right wing in Monge's coalition cabinet. "The omission or lack of action by the president on national security matters has created a climate of instability in the country. . . . I hope that in the next few days the president will make some decisions in this area or leave the space free so that Vice President Armando Aráuz can make them," said Interior Minister Carro (ICES 1987:77). On August 8 Security Minister Solano announced that "we have rumors of a coup d'état. We have been on maximum alert since receiving this news" (ICES 1987:62).

On August 11 President Monge finally capitulated to U.S. and right-wing forces, later asking for the resignation of his entire cabinet. He replaced pro-neutrality Security Minister Solano with ultrarightist Benjamin Piza, who years later was indicted by a Costa Rican judge for violations of national law in actions related to "Contragate." At the same time Monge named neoliberal economist Eduardo Lizano as Central Bank president. Lizano was later to serve as Washington's point man in the promotion of the policies described in this book.

Monge's next step in his surrender was to call the National Assembly, then in recess, into an extraordinary special session, which began on Friday, August 17. After a marathon debate on Sunday that lasted twenty-three hours straight, during which security forces prevented the deputies from leaving the building, the amendments to the currency law were passed (ICES 1987).

By November of the following year, 1 billion colones of fresh funds entered the Central Bank for distribution nationally as credit. Of these ¢900 million went to the private banks and only ¢100 million to the state banking system (ICES 1987:44). The private banking sector funds would be used primarily to provide credit for nontraditional production and export operations in the agricultural and industrial sectors (see, e.g., USAID 1982; "IMF Okays Contingency Loan" 1987). According to the 1988/89 USAID Action Plan,

> USAID programs have . . . responded to the lack of adequate credit available through the national banking system by channeling foreign exchange resources through private sector financial intermediaries and by establishing a special local currency credit line in the Central Bank. Through these mechanisms, approximately $150 million has been made available to private sector producers since 1982 [through early 1986] [USAID/Costa Rica 1986:6].

USAID had successfully weakened the state banks and redirected assistance funds to the private sector. This, however, was apparently not enough for one group of USAID project evaluators who concluded that "impacts from policy reform in exchange rates, import duties, banking and monetary regulations, and investment incentives can be substantial and warrant ongoing efforts." Furthermore, "AID should vigorously pursue its efforts at policy reform including greater emphasis on the 'carrot-stick' approach" (Lack et al. 1989:I-5, III-5).

▼ **A Parallel Ministry of
Agriculture and Export Promotion Office**

USAID created in Costa Rica a group of private institutions focused on the agricultural sector that were ultimately designed to do for producers of non-traditional exports what the Ministry of Agriculture and other government agencies had done historically for peasants and for producers of traditional exports. In 1983 a private sector business association was created with USAID funds, the Costa Rican Coalition for Development Initiatives (CINDE). During the first two years its activities included export promotion, investment promotion, lobbying of the Costa Rican government, and policy studies, all focused on the promotion of nontraditional exports, both agricultural and industrial. In 1985 a new division was created, the Private Agricultural and Agroindustrial Council (CAAP), which was charged with the specific promotion of NTAEs.

CAAP functioned partially as an export office, much as the government's export office, Centro de Promoción de las Exportaciones (CENPRO), had functioned in earlier years (though CENPRO also had regulatory responsibilities). Five foreign offices were created and their activities focused on deal making—putting potential overseas buyers of nontraditionals in contact with potential exporters (USAID 1990; Bolton and Manion 1989; Nathan Associates and Louis Berger International 1990). Other CAAP activities were directed toward pressuring the Costa Rican government, and, interestingly, the U.S. government, to relax constraints on nontraditionals. A USAID-commissioned evaluation explained that

> the first type of constraint . . . affects, in a very real manner, the comparative advantage or investment climate of producers, processors or exporters. . . . An example of this type of general constraint could be a tax on exports, a transport problem, cumbersome export documentation procedures that delay the export of products, importing country regulations, credit availability, etc. This type of constraint generally requires changes in public policies, laws, regulations or systems. These, in turn, require lobbying, changing public opinion, Congressional action, etc. [Bolton and Manion 1989:110].

The next constraint CAAP addressed was technological, and here it duplicated the Ministry of Agriculture's functions in agricultural research and extension.

The second type of problem that CAAP addresses in promoting exports are specific constraints. These usually affect the comparative advantage of a specific commodity in production terms. They might include a problem such as the lack of knowledge as to the best commercial variety of the crop, a disease problem or lack of packing facilities, or inadequate market information concerning the importing country. Normally the specific constraints are dealt with through adaptive research or through the advice gained by the use of outside consultants. . . . CAAP determines the type and importance of specific problems as a result of the studies that are carried out on each commodity that they consider supporting. These studies in turn identify the major constraints on the basis of market requirements needed to compete (e.g., quality of the product, form in terms of size, shape and color). . . . This is important in order to provide technical assistance [Bolton and Manion 1989:110, 113].

Between 1986 and 1990 USAID provided CAAP with $35 million (Sojo 1992). In 1988 alone CAAP received $10.3 million, while the budget of the entire Ministry of Agriculture totaled $7.7 million. The MAG had to attend to many times more producers and maintain a much larger infrastructure (Lindarte 1990; Sojo 1992). The operating funds available per professional at CAAP were close to $100,000 per year, while in the MAG in 1988 they were well under $10,000 (Lindarte 1990; Nathan Associates and Louis Berger International 1990).

In addition to CINDE and CAAP, USAID created a new, independent agricultural university to compete directly with Costa Rica's high-quality (but budget-constrained) public universities (Biehl 1988; "US AID Controversy" 1988). The Regional Agricultural School for the Humid Tropics (EARTH) draws students from all over Latin America to be trained as technical managers for agroexport farms. The regional nature of EARTH also puts it in competition for international funds with the Tropical Center for Agricultural Research and Education (CATIE), which had been developed by and is, to this day, owned directly by the governments of Central America. In addition to the agricultural institutions we have already mentioned, USAID also created an institution (Asociación de Carreteras y Caminos de Costa Rica—ACCCR) parallel to the Ministry of Transport.

In 1988 a scandal erupted in Costa Rica when John Biehl, the Chilean-born adviser to President Arias, made his now famous denunciation of USAID's parallel state (Shallat 1989). Biehl (1988:16A) charged that

the existence of a parallel structure of bureaucratic organizations to drive Costa Rican development is a fact. U.S. economic aid has been conditioned upon the creation of several institutions and upon the modification of the laws of Costa Rica, all to facilitate a particular model of development. . . . The bureaucracy created by this means is enormous. Many of the people that have been hired by these institutions have been recruited from the public sector itself, to do similar work, but doubling or tripling their salaries.

It is possible—and I make no judgment here—that these entities are good for the country. But I do contend that they are financed with public funds. I contend that their creation implies duplication, and that therefore they may be wasting national resources. I contend that they are not subject to control by the National Assembly, nor by the Executive Branch, nor by the Comptroller of the Republic, and that probably is not good. . . .

We must be alert against foreigners and their internal accomplices who wish to design Costa Rican development behind the back of its democracy.

In the resulting public furor, the Chamber of Commerce and the neofascist Movimiento Costa Rica Libre demanded that Biehl be deported. It was reportedly U.S. pressure that finally led to his dismissal from his United Nations Development Programme advisory post, when he returned to his native Chile (Shallat 1989).

Looking a bit more closely at Biehl's allegations, how was it that CINDE and the other institutions were funded with Costa Rican public funds, if 100 percent of their financing came from USAID? The answer to this question is very interesting. Between 1982 and 1987 USAID deposited an estimated U.S.$700 million in Economic Support Funds (ESF) in the Central Bank, awaiting disbursement to Costa Rican institutions ("US AID Controversy" 1988:559; Shallat 1988:25). According to the *Tico Times,*

> this standard AID arrangement came with an expensive and apparently unique twist in accords signed between 1983 and 1987. The Central Bank was to pay market interest rates—averaging 21 percent—on funds transferred into AID's account but not yet disbursed. As ESF transfers multiplied 36-fold over the five-year period, AID collected a total of $100 million in interest payments. This money was plowed back into the "special account" as supplementary funds controlled entirely by U.S. AID [Shallat 1988].

A USAID document prepared in 1982 foreshadowed this issue:

> These funds would be used primarily to finance credit needs of the private sector and cooperatives engaged in employment-generating, productive activities, especially export ventures, and to stimulate agricultural production activities. However, given the enormous amount of local currency expected to be generated during the period 1982–1986, the Mission will also be evaluating the need to "sterilize" a portion of the *colon* generations in an effort to control their potential inflationary impact [USAID 1982].

Even if we accept Biehl's more conservative estimate of the amount earned in interest on these funds, $48 million dollars, it still accounted for more than one-third of the Central Bank deficit—then the principal stumbling block to the signing of a stabilization accord with the IMF ("US AID

Controversy" 1988). As Biehl put it, "you demand cuts in government deficits and then institute a system that creates a deficit" (quoted in "US AID Controversy" 1988:559). According to both Biehl (1988:16A) and independent press reports ("US AID Controversy" 1988:559; Shallat 1988:25, 1989:221–222; Carvajal 1988d:1, 22), these were precisely the funds that were used to finance CINDE, CAAP, EARTH, and other institutions—the parallel state. So, in a sense, Costa Rican public funds, tax payers' colones, were used to create development institutions over which the Costa Rican government and people had no say.

▼ Evaluating the Parallel State: USAID's Own Criteria

John Biehl declined to make a value judgment on the parallel institutions themselves, though he didn't hesitate to criticize the manner in which they were created and financed. But we, with the advantage of the time that has passed, will in this section attempt an evaluation of CINDE/CAAP based on the same criteria by which USAID judged the public institutions of the reformist state: bureaucracy and efficiency, subsidies and deficits, favoritism and special interest groups, and corruption. We rely as much as possible on USAID's own internal and external evaluations.

Bureaucracy and Efficiency

Although the institutions were part of the private sector and thus, according to neoliberal ideology, bound to be more efficient than state institutions, history does not bear this out. According to the *Final Evaluation Report* of the cross-cutting evaluation of USAID's Agricultural Crop Diversification/ Export Promotion programs,

> CAAP has developed a substantial bureaucracy and from interviews with the AID project manager inside CAAP, the team had the impression that there are some project implementation bottlenecks owing to CAAP's lack of initiative and excessive attention to bureaucratic detail. These shortcomings have not been conducive to the establishment of an effective implementation strategy. The team also sensed that CAAP was "doing too little of too much" [Lack et al. 1989:III-9].

Another evaluation that USAID commissioned contained similar language. "In our review of the plan that has been developed to date, and in interviews with various CAAP Executives, we have come to the conclusion that the Export Promotion Program is highly theoretical." The authors went on to state that it "has not been adequately thought through" and "is the subject of a substantial amount of confusion" (Bolton and Manion 1989:117).

As far as the new private financial sector was concerned, it began to unravel as early as 1987. New financial companies took advantage of easily available money to overextend their credit portfolios, with the logical outcome. "As might be expected, the collapse of eight finance and loan houses (10 percent of the total operating currently in Costa Rica) was followed by a run on others, and even some of the most solid found themselves hard-pressed to meet payment demands" (Carvajal 1987). By early 1988 there was a full-fledged panic (Carvajal 1988a).

Subsidies and Deficits

Though USAID had repeatedly criticized the Costa Rican state for maintaining programs through subsidies and deficit spending, the parallel state was in reality financed by a large Central Bank deficit mandated by USAID itself. While USAID criticized price supports and credit subsidies for peasant producers of basic grains, it in fact provided an immense subsidy for an entire industry—from export offices abroad, to free technical and market information, to generous credit provided by USAID loans placed directly with private banks.

NTAE institutions were so heavily subsidized, in fact, that many of USAID's own evaluations expressed concern that they would cease to exist on the day USAID funding ran out. For example, Lack and coauthors (1989:III-10) finished a review of similar institutions in more than ten countries by saying that "most of the above institutions are not self-sustaining. In the team's view . . . it is imperative that they implement revenue-generating operations. . . . This will not only help to reduce 'make-work' bureaucracy, but it will also help to reduce dependence on AID." A 1990 USAID evaluation made the following assessment:

> Less clear is the issue of sustainability of promoter-type projects—or of any trade and investment project. The concept of sustainability means that projects should, within a reasonable amount of time, become financially self-sufficient, or at least be able to support themselves from a combination of revenue generation and contributions from non-AID government, private, and international sources. . . .
>
> Evidence clearly indicates that investment promotion activities *cannot* support an investment promotion agency without some form of public or private sector grant support. Limited experience also indicates that export-promotion activities are not financially sustainable [USAID 1990:41].

In the case of the private banking sector, one group of evaluators expressed their "concerns [for] the sustainability of most of the development banks which have been supported by AID. These banks—which are specifically mandated to do NTAE loans—face especially high risks." The reviewers went on to say that the viability of these banks depended on "below-market interest for their funding," and that "the Agency has been concerned . . . about the long-term effect of lending to these institutions at 'subsidized' rates" (Lack et al. 1989:III-38–39). Thus it became clear even to USAID that the parallel state institutions were no more able to survive without subsidies and deficit financing than were the state agencies they were designed to replace. Yet USAID has yet to publicly acknowledge what its own internal reports conclude.

Favoritism Toward Special Interest Groups

The reformist state was accused of favoring special interest groups, namely import substitution industrialists, producers of traditional export crops, peasant producers of basic foodstuffs, and public sector unions. We must ask, therefore, if institutions such as CINDE/CAAP responded to their own special interest groups.

When USAID first began to promote NTAEs, a common justification was the importance of raising the incomes of the rural poor. Lack and coauthors' evaluation (1989:II-1) noted that "various AID missions had envisaged the export of non-traditional crops as a means of helping farmers, especially small farmers, to diversify from crops that had been unprofitable. Farmers with small acreages were encouraged to grow higher value crops (e.g., snow peas, broccoli, cauliflowers) and to reduce acreage in traditional crops such as corn and beans."

Nevertheless this began to change, as did the mix of clients attended by USAID-sponsored institutions, following the recommendations of its own evaluators.

> Although shifting in approach, AID still exhibits a bias in favor of early involvement of small farmers in CD/NTAE initiatives. The nature of these initiatives and the high risks involved, however, call for larger farmers and agribusiness to lead the way.

> Recommendation: AID should spend more time identifying and working with these larger farmers and agribusinesses in NTAE projects [Lack et al. 1989:I-17–18].

This point was emphasized in various documents. Bolton and Manion (1989), for example, concluded that "a paternalistic approach will only tend to attract the weaker elements in the community, and cause an erosion of credibility [among] the more competent exporters."

Small farmers were less likely than ever to benefit from these institutions. Meanwhile, promotion and lobbying for a new agroexport sector clearly favored those entrepreneurs and producers who were well placed to invest in these new activities; and the repeal of laws, the shrinking of programs, and the reduction of productive activities of traditional farming and manufacturing sectors were clearly detrimental to the interests of those sectors.

The USAID interventions in Central America of the sort discussed here (structural adjustment and promotion of nontraditional exports) have created substantial political realignments, according to some observers (Crosby[1] 1987). These realignments are a function of who wins and who loses under the modified rules of the game. According to Crosby's analysis, the losers, and thus opponents of the new strategies, included conservative capitalists, import substitution industrialists, traditional conservative parties, leftist parties, traditional agroexport producers, the professional and urban middle class, trade unions, peasants, and farm workers. The winners clearly were a narrow sector: entrepreneurs with the verve and wealth to take advantage of new opportunities in a new industry, and foreign corporations and investors.

This focus on specific groups by export promotion institutions is thought to be a key factor in their success. The authors of one USAID document emphasized that "the promoter approach . . . weighs the project portfolio toward 'winners.' . . . It does not try to work with too many new target groups" (USAID 1990:37). The selection of a small number of targets is part of the strategy: "Two projects, CINDE and PROEXAG, had a strong promoter orientation," notes one evaluation. "Both were well targeted, proactive, and emphasized the selection of and assistance to a few firms, sectors, and products. Both are being used as models . . . for elsewhere in the region" (USAID 1990:36). However, this selection of a few firms came dangerously close to favoritism, and it was criticized in the USAID cross-cutting evaluation as "excessive, direct involvement in linkage of exporters with selected receivers and over-involvement in trade arrangements" (Lack et al. 1989:III-17).

The profile of the target group, and thus the clientele of these institutions, was defined in one USAID document by the characteristics thought to be necessary for success: "nontraditional exporting usually requires business acumen, good contacts and information, conformance to product standards, financial resources, and willingness to take risks." In the same document the authors express concern that "attempts to target winners and to register early successes can make a project vulnerable to the criticism that it is playing the role of the private sector rather than a developmental role" (USAID 1990:37–38). The principal difference between these institutions and the reformist government, it would seem, is in the selection of favored groups.

Corruption

A further criticism of the Costa Rican state institutions replaced by the parallel state was that they were corrupt. In October 1987 the Scripps Howard

News Service published a two-part series in various U.S. newspapers. A draft of a classified memo written by the inspector general of USAID, Herbert Beckington, had been leaked to the press. The memo charged that

> in 1982 AID and a small group of influential Costa Ricans had formed the Costa Rican Coalition of Development Initiatives (CINDE) to promote private sector economic development. CINDE allowed at least 23 of its former and current officials to evade Costa Rican taxes by diverting AID funds to companies they own through consulting contracts. CINDE created contracts with these companies for consulting services which were not actually provided [Dyer 1988a:1, 23].

USAID later released several internal audit memos in Washington. Among the charges contained therein was that "millions of dollars in foreign aid funds for Costa Rica were mismanaged and misspent, including providing college scholarships for the children of influential citizens and creating a development agency [CINDE] that largely benefited politicians." The reports went on to claim that $33.8 million of USAID money "was used to establish CINDE in 1982, without proper approval from the State Department. This organization has done little to promote development, but appears to have been utilized by a few prominent Costa Ricans to advance their own personal and political interests, and as a temporary resting place or springboard for aspiring politicians" (Dyer 1988a:3). Referring to Corporación Financiera del Desarrollo, S.A. (COFIDESA) a private financial house that received $10 million from USAID in 1982, it was stated in one memo that "at least 8 of the institution's 14 directors have taken personal or corporate loans from the money" (Dyer 1988a:3).

Ironically, one of the influential individuals implicated in the leaked reports was Guido Fernandez, then Costa Rica's ambassador to the United States. He had just been accused by Under Secretary of State Elliot Abrams of having meddled in U.S. internal affairs by lobbying Congress against approving contra aid. He was eventually recalled at the insistence of the U.S. government, and the Arias administration complained that the release of the USAID audit memos was timed to discredit him in punishment for having opposed U.S. policy toward Nicaragua ("'Vendetta' Charged in AID Affair" 1988).

Controversy ensued when the directors of CINDE were called to testify before the Costa Rican National Assembly. At first they refused, claiming that, as a private company, they had a right to keep their accounts private. Pressed by the legislature because they had received funds donated by USAID to Costa Rica, a CINDE representative stressed that when the Costa Rican government and USAID had agreed to provide the funds, "CINDE was never told that it was being given public funds or that it would have to account to the government for their use" (Carvajal 1988c:21).

The parallel state institutions USAID created in Costa Rica were not managed with the minimum degree of transparency that one expects from public institutions, nor did their directors feel they were accountable to the Costa Rican citizenry or their elected representatives.

▼ Other Criticisms of the Parallel State

The critiques presented above, mostly from USAID's own documents, fail to touch upon the central criticisms of these institutions that were leveled within Costa Rica. These were essentially that the creation of the parallel state represented an infringement of national sovereignty; reflected a lack of democratic control and a lack of political checks and balances; and involved a loss of control by the elected government over national planning and development.

These criticisms struck at the heart of Costa Rican national identity and provoked sufficient controversy to lead to the resignation or removal of a number of high-level officials. In chronological order, the first to go were the members of President Monge's cabinet who were sacked in the midst of the crisis surrounding the currency law and the contra war. Next was Eduardo Lizano, the Central Bank president who had backed USAID's strategy. He briefly resigned in early 1988 when the minister of agriculture refused to go along with massive cuts in price supports for basic grains. He returned to the fold a week later, however, when Agriculture Minister Alberto Esquivel was forced out, paving the way for the cutbacks (Carvajal 1988b). On his way out Esquivel denounced the "coffee and cakes economists who think they can fix all of the problems of the country without taking into account social and political reality" (quoted in Vermeer 1989:55). The next to go was Biehl, whose parting words were, "[When institutions] are created, one proposes them and one creates a political party. That is the Costa Rican democratic way. But I would like to know in what political campaign the Costa Rican people said that they agreed with the creation of institutions like EARTH, CINDE and CAAP, that capture public funds" (López and Ramírez 1988:20). The last to leave was Minister of Planning Otton Solís, saying that, "it would be deeply disturbing if, given the impossibility of doing things openly and thus democratically, subterfuges and economically inefficient Machiavellianisms were adopted. The principles of productivity would be grotesquely contradicted if attempts were made to wear down and bankrupt state institutions via the creation of parallel structures organized as private entities" (quoted in Shallat 1989:223).

If one evaluates USAID's new development institutions, then, using the criteria with which USAID judged the Central American states, they clearly fall short. New financial institutions, in addition to being unstable, wound up providing subsidized interest rates to select clientele; and parallel service institutions proved to run up further the Central Bank deficit, to be bureaucratic and inefficient, prone to corruption, and to favor special interest groups at the expense of the larger population. Many of these ills are symptoms of what John Biehl and others highlighted as the underlying malaise inherent in the way they were created. They were built by foreigners in alliance with narrow elites, they were financed through highly irregular means, and they were in no way accountable to any body, elected or otherwise, of the sovereign state of Costa Rica.

It comes as no surprise that in the 1990s, with dwindling U.S. resources available for Central America, these institutions are reaching the limits of their ability to exist. "Each of the AID-assisted NTAE organizations [in Latin America] faces a long-term problem of how to ensure sustainability beyond the life of the AID project funding currently supporting them," says the most recent USAID evaluation (Byrnes 1992:88). USAID is seeking to set up permanent endowments for these organizations, which would, in effect, permanently institutionalize their lack of accountability and continue their ability to selectively serve wealthier clientele.

The Ministry of Agriculture in Costa Rica has further reduced its attempts to support farmers in many crops. In 1987 it had programs to assist farmers planting eighty-eight crops; in 1992 that was reduced to twenty crops, and it is considering reducing that number even further. One group most clearly affected are the small-scale farmers producing foodstuffs for local consumption. USAID's evaluation summing up a decade of policy is brutal in its conclusions:

> There has been a shift away from a USAID Mission's portfolio reflecting a country's needs and toward reflecting the interests of the US as a donor country [and] an emerging shift away from public sector and researcher control over the research process and toward greater private sector and client control over agricultural research. . . . As scarce resources were being redirected to support the development of private sector research on the NTAE crops, there was a failure to realize the negative consequences for the basic food crops. The new private organizations focus their attention on technologies, that, by their very nature, allow for the private appropriation of profits. Their activities cannot thus be expected to cover the development of technological potential in the broadest sense, that is, including education, training, etc.; without these functions, however, the ability of the rest of the system to develop new technologies would quickly be exhausted. . . . The new private organizations are not interested in developing certain agronomic techniques (cropping practices, pasture management, etc.) because of the difficulty of privately appropriating their benefits. . . . Yet there is a continuing need for technology generation and transfer for basic food crops. *But the tens of thousands of commercial small farmers who grow food crops for the market have little, if any, say in ensuring that adequate resources are allocated for research on these crops or*

that they are effectively involved in the design, implementation, and evaluation of this research (Byrnes 1992:62–63, 91–93, emphasis added).[2]

▼ Parallel State Structures in Other Central American Countries

Despite the criticisms, both external and internal, of the parallel institution strategy, USAID continues to duplicate the Costa Rican experience in other countries of the region. In Table 3.4 we outline the new private sector structures in each country that have been created or strengthened by USAID in conjunction with the promotion of nontraditional exports. In each country local commentators have raised the same issues that were raised by John Biehl in Costa Rica: the infringement of sovereignty; the lack of accountability; and a loss of control by the elected government over the planning and development process (Perdomo and Noé Pino 1992; Saldomando 1992; Rosa 1993; Escoto and Marroquín 1992).

Table 3.4   Comparable Parallel State Institutions Across Central America

Purpose	Parallels	Costa Rica	Guatemala	El Salvador	Honduras	Nicaragua
Export promotion	Government export office	CINDE	CONACOEX GREXPNT	FUSADES PRIDEX	FEPROEX-AAH	APENN
Agricultural research and extension	Ministry of Agriculture	CAAP	FUNTEC	DIVAGRO	FHIA FPX	CPXNT
Training	Public universities	EARTH	URL	FEPADE	EAP	INCAE
Infrastructure development	Ministry of Public Works	ACCCR	PIPD	FUSADES	MEA	MDA
Holding and investment	State investment funds and holding companies	CIP	CLE	FIDEX	FIDE	CIP
Banking and finance	State banks	SFP	FODEX	FIDEX	FIDE	BANCENTRO BANMER

Sources: Biehl (1988); Perdomo and Noé Pino (1992); Saldomando (1992); Rosa (1993); Escoto and Marroquín (1992); Byrnes (1992).

The amounts invested by USAID have been large, as in the Costa Rican case. From 1984 through 1992 the largest of these institutions, Fundación Salvadoreña para el Desarrollo Económica y Social (FUSADES) in El Salvador, received a total of $107 million dollars, of which at least $46 million went for agricultural projects (Rosa 1993). Even in Nicaragua, where USAID got off to a late start, more than $1 million per year were committed to private sector agriculture from 1991 through 1996 (Saldomando 1992:45). At this point in history it appears unlikely, however, that in El Salvador, Guatemala, Honduras, and Nicaragua these new organizations will eclipse their agricultural public sector counterparts to the extent that occurred in Costa Rica. To the extent that they focus, nonetheless, on the promotion of USAID-sponsored NTAEs, the dismal prognosis with respect to Central America's rural poor from USAID's cross-cutting evaluation (Byrnes 1992) is likely to continue. We will now turn to the concerns of the rural poor majority.

▼ Notes

1. Benjamin Crosby is a professor at the conservative Central American Institute for Business Administration (INCAE), which is affiliated with Harvard Business School.

2. It is worth noting that the author of this scathing report, Kerry J. Byrnes, wrote a 1989 report extolling the success of a USAID project promoting melons across Central America. Byrnes is presently employed by Chemonics International, the consulting company that ran PROEXAG—the principal vehicle created by USAID to promote nontraditionals across the region.

▼▼▼▼▼▼▼▼▼▼▼▼▼▼▼▼▼▼▼▼▼▼▼▼▼▼▼▼▼

4

UNDERMINING SMALL FARMERS: THE STRUCTURE OF THE CENTRAL AMERICAN NONTRADITIONAL AGRICULTURAL EXPORT INDUSTRY

▼ Globalization of the Fruit and Vegetable Industry

Recent decades have seen the progressive globalization of many industries, ranging from electronics and automobiles to raw agricultural commodities. The fruit and vegetable industry has been no exception, as attested by the boom in production of nontraditional export crops in Central America. In his influential book *The Work of Nations* (1993), U.S. Secretary of Labor Robert Reich laid out a vision of how globalization will restructure the international division of labor by the twenty-first century. In his view, increased competition and diffusion of technology are leading to a declining rate of profit in those industries and other enterprises engaged in the production of physical goods, from cars to tomatoes. This, combined with the worldwide trend toward free trade policies, produces a progressive relocation of these activities toward low-wage countries. Reich predicts that the commodity with the highest value in the future will be information—and he presents the outline of a strategy to ensure the future competitiveness of the United States by focusing on investment in education geared toward the high-paying jobs in the information management industry. While it may seem unlikely at first, this and similar analyses are actually useful for understanding the NTAE industry in Central America.

In this new world order, driven by constantly falling costs of transportation and communication, it is increasingly likely that lower production costs in poorer countries will more than compensate for the costs of shipping goods back to wealthier (higher-wage) countries, particularly when poorer countries are played off against each other in a global competition to produce the same goods for less. Thus the Ford Motor Company can produce a "world car," where each component is produced in several countries. This is known as outsourcing; parts are manufactured outside the walls of the assembly plant, outside the firm itself (through contracts with independent parts suppliers), and often outside the boundaries of the country where final assembly takes place. If a trade union threatens to raise production costs in one country through, say, successful demands for higher wages, Ford can simply shift production to factories in other countries that are able to produce the same parts at lower prices. In the same way, then, a transnational fruit company may outsource melons from various Latin American countries, shifting production quotas from site to site as production and marketing conditions vary. This organization of industries is sometimes referred to as "flexible accumulation" (Sabel 1993).

If different melon-producing operations are analogous to the different autoparts factories in Reich's scheme, then the fruit and vegetable brokers in Miami, Houston, and other U.S. ports of entry, who dominate the NTAE industry, are surely the equivalent of the well-remunerated information managers he describes. The commodity they sell is the knowledge of both who is selling each nontraditional commodity on a given day and who is buying, as well as the sundry details of shipping, storage, and financial transactions. To the central role Reich assigns to information brokers under flexible accumulation in a global economy, we might add shippers, as both international and domestic transport make up an increasing part of the value-added of goods that, for example, while sold in Des Moines, may be produced anywhere from El Salvador to Malaysia. Indeed, the economic analysis of Central American melon production we present at the end of this chapter provides strong evidence that shipping companies, followed by brokers, are the big winners in the fruit and vegetable industry that has been spawned by the promotion of NTAEs. In this chapter we show how globalization, while providing substantial opportunities to firms in the advanced industrial countries, has a downside in the developing world—the increasingly powerful squeeze in which peasant farmers are caught between suppliers of inputs and the buyers of their produce.

▼ The Structure of Commodity Systems

Industries that produce and market a particular agricultural commodity can be characterized as commodity systems (Friedland 1984; Gereffi 1994), each composed of a vertical chain and a horizontal structure (see Figures 4.1 and 4.2). The vertical chain leads from suppliers of inputs (chemicals and machinery) through actual farming—a small part of the system—to packing, shipping, wholesaling, and retailing. The horizontal structure refers to the different actors or firms involved at each link of the chain. The particular structure and organization for a given commodity are determined by the interplay of different factors, including the crop's agronomic requirements,

Figure 4.1   A Typical Commodity Chain for NTAEs

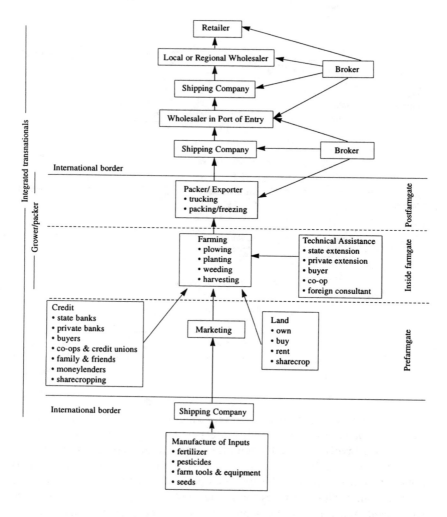

the amount of processing that takes place, the product's perishability, transportation difficulties, market variables, and the relative presence or absence of powerful national or transnational firms.

Though there is considerable variation among the commodity systems that comprise the Central American nontraditional export sector, certain common conditions within those systems foster and/or grow out of the domination by large national and international companies. These conditions include the fact that the most profitable nontraditionals are commodities

Figure 4.2   Horizontal Structure of Alternative NTAE Commodity Systems

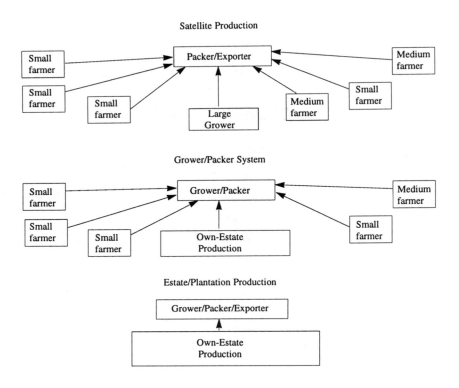

consumed or used in a fresh state (e.g., melons, snow peas, broccoli, cut flowers, strawberries). Although these perishable products bring the best prices, they involve unusually complex transportation problems and experience extreme volatility in prices. When they are processed by being cut, parboiled, and/or frozen, they become less perishable. But they are then also a simpler commodity that faces far greater global competition. In either case significant transport problems are inherent to these commodity systems, which implies the need for substantial access to information, infrastructure, and financing. In addition, the extreme price fluctuations that fresh produce systems worldwide tend to experience also lead to the need for significant capital resources to withstand these vagaries. Finally, while some nontraditionals are crops of local origin (e.g., passion fruit, cashews), most are Temperate Zone plants that have been transplanted to the Tropics (melons, broccoli, snow peas, cauliflower, strawberries), so that a Temperate Zone technical base is a valuable resource for any firm involved with such commodities, a condition that, again, favors transnational corporations.

In analyzing any commodity system we consider three basic segments (see Figure 4.1). *Prefarmgate* refers to the manufacture, procurement, and delivery of all goods and services the farmer needs to produce the crop. *Inside-farmgate* refers to all activities carried out by the farmer within the physical boundaries of his or her farm. Finally, *postfarmgate* operations include all actions between the farm and the final consumer. In modern agricultural systems, in contrast to more-traditional ones, the vast bulk of the value-added, and consequently the lion's share of the profits and the bulk of the power within the industry, tend to lie at the extremes: the pre- and postfarmgate segments. The farmer is the weakest link, inside the farmgate. When farmers move from traditional toward modern systems, as many peasants do in their switch to nontraditionals, they move toward a still weaker position in the commodity system. Below we outline a generic commodity system for an NTAE, adapted largely from How (1991), in order to show how the deck is stacked against the small, independent farmer.

▼ Prefarmgate Characteristics of NTAEs

Land is the most basic commodity needed for agricultural production. While peasant producers generally have some access to land before they attempt nontraditional farming (i.e., some landownership, some rental, and perhaps sharecropping), outside investors, entrepreneurs, and foreign corporations often do not. These individuals or companies, whether from local urban areas or from foreign countries, generally rent or buy land in the local market. As we saw in Chapter 2, this can have profound consequences for local land markets and thus for the availability of land for peasant farmers.

Technical information on how to grow a crop—including which variety of seed to use; how to prepare the soil and fertilize; how to manage weeds, diseases, and insect pests; how to thin, prune, and harvest; and how to pack—is increasingly a commodity bought and sold in modern agriculture. The same is true for marketing information. As we saw in the previous chapter, while small farmers must rely on national extension services of dubious quality, or on development projects, larger firms and transnationals obtain the best advice money can buy, generally in the form of foreign consultants from Temperate Zone countries. Giants such as some fruit companies usually have in-house experts on whom they rely.

As noted in Chapter 2, credit and other forms of capital to invest in production are key obstacles to entering the nontraditional business. State banks, and (increasingly) private ones, are key suppliers of credit to Central

America's farmers. Private investment houses, or *financieras,* are another important source. These function like investment funds, where urban professionals invest their money in shares. Increasingly, urban import-capital groups, such as those that own foreign automobile and computer dealerships, are entering nontraditional production. The impetus for these groups may sometimes be to guarantee an influx of foreign exchange for their import operations, making them less interested than other players in a profit in their agricultural operations per se. Finally, transnationals, such as the fruit giants, use their own capital for direct investments.

Key agricultural inputs in the Central American NTAE system include fertilizers, seeds, farm machinery, irrigation equipment, petroleum and electricity, pesticides, trucks, packing materials, and cooling or refrigeration equipment. All of these except electricity are manufactured abroad, though some, notably fertilizers and pesticides, are formulated or repackaged nationally, contributing some value-added within domestic boundaries. The production and international trade in all of these commodities are controlled by transnational corporations based in developed countries, though local importers and distributors may play significant roles.

▼   Inside-Farmgate Operations and the Firms Involved

An estimated 60 percent of nontraditional producers are small farmers (Kaimowitz 1991). Medium-scale and larger individual farmers, national commercial/corporate operations, and foreign companies make up the remainder of NTAE participants. The relative contribution of these groups to the total value exported, however, is skewed. Foreign companies account for 25 percent of the value exported, medium and large national companies about 40 percent, while the 60 percent of small farmers account for only 35 percent of the value (Kaimowitz 1991). The relative share of profits is even more skewed, as many of the larger producers are grower/packers, grower/shippers, and/or grower/exporters. As we saw in Chapter 2, small farmers often sell their production to these larger growers, who often pay below-market prices.

Farmers and farm managers are the actors who carry out the key operations inside the farmgate, including labor management, supervision of agronomic operations, harvesting, and sometimes packing. Labor sources include farmers themselves and their immediate families in the case of peasant production, and hired labor—both seasonal and permanent—in the case of larger producers. Some tasks in Central America are more usually performed by women, such as thinning, sorting, and classifying. Others, such as plowing, spraying, and mechanical cultivation, are usually done by men. Here we find the principal factor that favors small farmers over larger growers in a number of crops—the exploitation of family labor. As many NTAEs are heavily labor-intensive, labor contracting and management impose substantial costs on larger-scale producers. Family labor generally requires less supervision and is rarely considered a measurable cost by the family farmer (Barham et al. 1992; von Braun et al. 1989). This is particularly true when family labor has low opportunity costs, such as when social customs or local labor market conditions restrict women's ability to find work outside the home (de Janvry et al. 1992). A local manager of VERDIFREX (a frozen vegetable packer/processor that exports from Guatemala's Altiplano) told us that he "simply cannot find enough producers" from year to year. The profit margin for producers of broccoli and snow peas, for example, was so slim that he could find no farmers with even a single hectare of land willing to dedicate it to broccoli; no grower who had to pay prevailing wages for non-family workers could make a profit at the current prices. This went a long way, in his view, toward explaining the predominance of microfarmers in the production of that crop (Rosset 1992b).

The other dimension was the implicit cost of land. No farmer who needed to cover the implicit rental costs of land, that is, the income lost from not renting it to someone else, according to the VERDIFREX manager, would find broccoli or snow pea production economically sustainable. This explained why he was unable to contract with farmers who had more than one or two hectares of production, and it left him constantly seeking producers who were willing to use smaller parcels, one or two *cuerdas* (tenths of a hectare), for production.

The spatial and social organization of farming operations in the nontraditional sector can be categorized into three basic horizontal structures—satellite production, grower/packer production, and plantation production—with considerable variation within and between each.

Forms of Satellite Production

Many producers and exporters have relied on satellite production, where a packing shed buys from many individual farmers (see Figure 4.2). This is the principal direction in which transnational agribusinesses have moved in recent decades, as flexible accumulation schemes have been deployed to minimize the risks associated with fixed investment (Watts 1990). Fruit companies and other transnationals discovered that landownership and large investments in infrastructure put them at risk during the periodic crises that plague the Third World. Political crises could lead to expropriation, while ecological degradation could reduce land quality (see Chapter 5). Flexible accumulation, on the other hand, means minimal infrastructure and the purchasing of produce from local producers, thus avoiding the risky and relatively unprofitable business of actual farming. When a crisis arises, the company simply pulls up and moves, often leaving local economic devastation in its wake (see Box 4.1).

The satellite system has developed in two forms, one relying on independent producers (satellites) and open market or noncontractual purchasing; the other relying on a contractual satellite-core relationship (Williams and Karen 1985). In the classic satellite production system, producers of many different sizes plant one or more nontraditional crops on land they own, rent, or sharecrop. They obtain financing from a variety of sources, including family savings, other family members, local usurers, banks, or credit unions (if they have title to their land or other assets to use as collateral), and government credit programs. They grow their crops relying largely on their own experience and whatever information or technical assistance they might obtain, whether from a neighbor or friend, an occasional visit from a government technician, or information from an exporter,

---

Box 4.1   "Slash and Burn Capitalism": The Broader Industry Implications

Large-scale and transnational operators have employed a variety of strategies to cope with, and to benefit from, the crisis tendencies in nontraditional agriculture in Central America. The strategies are not entirely new. Earlier in this century banana companies negotiated their century-long concessions under the crisis conditions of the Great Depression. They then maintained idle plantations throughout the region, first to convince all potential competitors that they could expand production and undercut any competition, but more importantly to provide the opportunities to shift production from site to site in response to any problems that might arise. As ecological problems (plant diseases), social problems (labor unrest or the organization of contract producers), and economic problems (any attempts by local governments to tax them) arose, they simply abandoned whole areas, ripping out their irrigation systems and moving on.

These tactics, of course, invariably left in dire straits the local labor force, as well as the less mobile smaller-scale producers who were dependent upon the transnational's packing and shipping infrastructure. Today's large-scale operators in nontraditional agriculture, often the subsidiaries of the same banana companies, pursue similar strategies. Melon exporters in southern Mexico, for example, plan for a seven-year cycle of production in any given location, after which they expect to relocate as both ecological problems and the rising discontent of their contract producers make melon production untenable in the existing location (López 1990). Dominican exporters of Oriental vegetables moved to Guatemala "virtually overnight" when a pesticide-generated crisis hit their exports from the Dominican Republic (see Chapter 5). While these growers renewed their ecologically and socially destructive processes in other locations, they left in their wake several thousand small-scale Oriental vegetable producers in severe economic crisis. A spokesman for the Honduran melon exporters association candidly observed that they would have to move "like the Mexicans," if the pest crisis confronting Cholutecan farmers (in the South of Honduras) during the 1989/90 season did not subside (see Chapter 5). "If we have to, we can move these packing sheds and equipment in two days" (Murray 1991).

Ironically, these flexible accumulation strategies may not only allow larger-scale operations to escape the consequences of unsustainable farming, they may also benefit the largest, best-financed firms. A crisis, once brought under control by state policies or market forces, may lead to new investment opportunities.

With the economic collapse of a particular crop or agricultural system, land prices decline, unemployment rises, and wages become depressed, inviting new investment by those with financial resources. The rise of Honduran melon production in the 1970s, for example, was predicated in part on the previous crisis in Honduran cotton and on the decline of cattle and sugar production. With the collapse of cotton, many farmers went bankrupt and unemployment soared, pushing down land value and wages. These factors became part of Choluteca's "comparative advantage" of cheap land and labor, much touted by USAID (USAID/Honduras 1990) and industry developers alike (Zind 1990) as they promoted the nontraditional export process. The cotton crisis created investment opportunities for nontraditional investors, as the continuing crisis in nontraditional agriculture presently provides. This dynamic leaves the permanent residents of these regions more deeply impoverished, living amid ecologically deteriorated landscapes, while the large-scale local and transnational investors blithely move on.

processor, or packing company. At harvest time the producer relies on various options or combinations of options. He can sell his crop to a local intermediary, or coyote, who will in turn sell the produce either to an exporter or in the local domestic market. Or the producer can sell his harvest directly in the local market, or directly to the exporter, processor, or packing company.

This form of production has been referred to as involving a "low-intensity" relationship between producer and processors, packers, exporters, and others (Glover and Kusterer 1990). Noncontract satellite farming was employed in Guatemalan melon and snow pea production through the mid-1980s (Hoppin 1991), coexisting alongside more "management-intensive" contractual relationships (Glover and Kusterer 1990). Noncontract farming was also the predominant structure in the successful development of the Dominican Oriental vegetable sector, an important part of the Dominican Republic's regional ascendency in NTAEs during the same period (Murray and Hoppin 1992; Chapter 5 in this book). Even today, one can find local intermediaries in communities around Sacatapéquez, Guatemala, with signs posted in front of their houses or warehouses announcing "Snow peas Purchased Here," suggesting a continuation of this low-intensity relationship between producers and buyers.

This production structure appeals to risk-averse exporters for several reasons. By waiting until harvest to purchase a crop that producers or coyotes deliver directly to the packing or processing facility, they avoid assuming many of the risks associated with adverse agricultural production conditions, such as weather and pests. Problems with overproduction or a drop in demand can be passed back to the producers with limited risk to the exporter. On the other hand, the absence of contracts makes efficient, planned utilization of packing capacity difficult, and often results in failure to establish sufficient quality control during production, optimal timing of production with respect to market prices, or appropriate selection of products for the market, all affecting exporters' profits.

The alternative classic form of satellite production, the satellite-core form, is similar to the first in that it relies on small to medium-sized independent producers or producer cooperatives. But unlike the first, the second uses contracts, written or verbal, linking producers and exporters (Goldsmith 1985). This alternative form provides exporters with greater involvement in, and control over, the production process through increased management intensity (Glover and Kusterer 1990). This has been the case for broccoli packers in the Guatemalan highlands, where competition for growers apparently makes contracts necessary, as noted in Chapter 2 (see also Rosset 1992b). The exporters often provide credits or financing, some material inputs (particularly pesticides, fertilizers, and hybrid seeds—all offered on credit against the harvest), and technical assistance. Producers are given a preplanting contract that usually requires growers to sell all their harvest to the exporter at planting time.

A typical contract provides the packer with substantial control over the production process, including timing of planting, timing and dosage of fertilizers and pesticides, and frequent on-site inspections. In addition the packer may reject produce for a variety of reasons, ranging from insufficient size or cosmetic quality to the presence of insects or insecticide residues. The packer performs residue analyses, sometimes in the farmer's field, before giving permission to harvest; and often at the packing shed after harvest. The discovery of illegal products or excessive levels of legal ones leads to the rejection of an entire harvest. In the case of insects, a subsample of the produce is examined, and if the percentage contaminated is above a certain threshold, then, once again, the entire lot is rejected. In the case of other quality concerns, only the portion that is unacceptable is rejected. It is critical to note that there is no price guarantee whatsoever.

Rejection of harvests is a constant problem and one that creates great anxiety for producers. In interviews covering forty-seven small producers in the municipality of Santa Lucía de Utatlan, AVANCSO found that almost half reported having between 25 and 100 percent of their product rejected because of one of these factors (Rosset 1992b).

Contracts can benefit small farmers when harvest prices are stipulated beforehand, allowing the grower to make rational economic decisions throughout the growing season. Most of the contracts used in the NTAE situations we investigated in Central America, however, specify that the product is to be purchased at the going price the day of harvest, or worse yet, a percentage of the price received in the importing country, with payment to be made a considerable time later, once the product has been shipped, evaluated, and sold. In our Santa Lucía interviews, many farmers complained of late payments, often as long as three months after harvest and sometimes as much as one year later. Glover and Kusterer (1990) observed that to a significant degree the extent to which smaller farmers benefit from contracts depends on whether or not contract terms are determined through some form of collective bargaining (as through a co-op or farmers' union) or through individual negotiations with each farmer. In the latter case farmers usually lose out both on contract terms and on prices.

United Brands employed a satellite-core contract farming system in its melon export operation PATSA (Productos Acuáticos y Terrestres, S.A.) in Choluteca, Honduras. It was also the structure employed by United Brands' banana industry on the Caribbean coast of Honduras. One of PATSA's rivals, CREHSUL (Cooperativa Regional de Horticultures Sureños Limitada) employed a variation of the satellite-core contract system in Honduran melon production. The cooperative provided similar assistance to producers who were members of CREHSUL. But instead of a preplanting, fixed-price contract, CREHSUL paid a market-based price at the time of sale, after deduction of various cooperative fees and costs. In effect, the cooperative producers were upping the ante in a high-stakes gamble to obtain higher prices for their melons at harvest time instead of the lower, but guaranteed, prices set through preplanting contracts.

Generally, these satellite (or outgrower) production schemes that rely on small farmers provide exporters with potentially cheaper produce than if they produced it themselves with hired labor. That is because peasant farmers generally overexploit family labor and discount their land, as described above, such that labor and land costs are in effect lower than could be achieved with contract labor (Watts 1990).

Grower/Packer System

This system is found in Salvadoran production of melons, described in Chapter 2. Large growers have their own packing sheds, where they pack both their own produce and that of smaller farmers in the surrounding area (see Figure 4.2). The function of the smaller growers is basically to maintain the packing shed at capacity, and to provide flexibility in the event of market fluctuations. As we saw, they can be paid less, or let go altogether, when prices drop.

Estate/Plantation Farming

The second structure commonly found in nontraditional agriculture is estate farming, or the "new plantation" system (Raynolds 1994:230). This production structure relies on large tracts of exporter-owned or rented land (see Figure 4.2). Producers are generally salaried employees, or employees who receive payment based on a percentage of the harvest price of the crop, again after deduction for inputs and other costs. This was the system employed by companies like Standard Fruit (Dole) in Honduran pineapple production, and increasingly by various national and transnational producers in Guatemalan melons (Murray and Hoppin 1992).

In some instances large growers and/or transnational corporations maintain both a plantation structure and a satellite-core relationship with small independent producers, functioning as grower/packers or grower/exporters. This combination assures exporters a more stable supply for their processing and packing facilities, while still allowing them to benefit from the satellite production structures, which require less capital and less management intensity, to cover peak demand periods (Glover and Kusterer 1990).

In the latter part of the 1980s exporters were faced with an array of production problems, including grading and quality requirements imposed by

U.S. government agencies and various commodity producer associations, pest and pesticide restrictions imposed by the U.S. Department of Agriculture (USDA) and Food and Drug Administration (FDA), and other production, transportation, and distribution problems. These obstacles led many exporters to abandon the noncontractual forms of satellite production by the late 1980s (see Chapter 5). Even the appeal of the management-intensive style of contract farming with small producers faded for exporters in some NTAEs, such as melons. In Guatemala and Honduras exporters began shifting to the more directly controlled estate farming in the late 1980s and early 1990s. In the process, significant numbers of small producers were either transformed into employees of large-scale operations or driven from the NTAE sector (Murray 1992).

▼ Postfarmgate Operations

Smaller exporters are not part of integrated enterprises that include receivers in destination ports. Thus they must rely on brokers or sales agents to receive their product and arrange for its sale. Brokers arrange sales (selling brokers) or purchases (buying brokers) without taking title to the product. They are paid a percentage of the sale. Exporters sometimes retain agents to negotiate sales on their behalf. The international transport of Central American perishables is a tricky business, where timing and shipping conditions, such as refrigeration and speed, must be balanced against cost. Types of transport of these products from Central America include airfreight for high-priced speciality items (mainly cut flowers), overseas shipping (in refrigerated containers or holds), and overland transport through Mexico by refrigerated truck.

There are a variety of private commercial firms that transport fruits and vegetables from Central America to the United States and to other developed country markets. However, there are substantial problems related to the optimal use of shipping capacity and to timing. There is limited refrigerated space available, especially on short notice, and firms compete for it. Larger firms may occupy space by reserving entire containers, planes, or ships in advance, thus excluding smaller firms. It all adds up to a substantial problem for all but the largest companies, as noted by Soule (1990:33):

> Frequently, an exporting country may have one container ship calling each week, while others sometimes have two or three vessels within a week, with a period of 10 to 14 days ensuing before the next visit. It is often difficult to hold fruit and vegetables in the field or to stagger harvests or locations until the next ship is in port and still obtain maximum yields, maintain market-quality size, configuration, quality standards, etc., given the perishable nature of the product. The upshot is that the product may be har-

vested too early or too late, or it rots in the field, especially if cold storage facilities are not available so as to accumulate sufficient volume for the arrival of vessels later.

These complexities in shipping create a substantial advantage for the largest fruit and vegetable companies over their competitors. They have their own transportation network, including in some cases their own ships, established over more than a century in the banana business. They plan trips to suit their own production and marketing plans, sometimes selling excess space to other exporters at higher rates, and at other times exploiting their control of transportation to gain greater advantage over growers and competing exporters. In Figure 4.2 we show the relative control over the commodity chain that an integrated operation exerts, compared to a grower/exporter or an individual farmer.

A change of ownership often takes place again (except in the case of fully integrated operations like the fruit companies) at the port of entry in the United States or other importing countries. The exporter's representative or a broker arranges for the product to be sold to a wholesale shipper who takes responsibility for moving the product to destination markets, usually in or around major cities. In some cases the large supermarket chains take over at this point, while smaller retailers buy in destination wholesale markets. The destination markets often have wholesale produce markets where fruits and vegetables arrive from many places to be bought by retail purchasing agents. Retailers, both chains and independent operators, do a large percentage of the advertising associated with these products, though to the extent that integrated concerns are involved they may advertise themselves to achieve brand differentiation, as do Chiquita or Dole (How 1991).

▼ Minimizing the Farmer's Shares: The Melon Commodity Chain

At each step along the commodity chain some value is added to the product. The difference between the price at which it is sold to the next step, minus all the costs at the current step, approximates the net margin, profit, or value-added at that step. In Figure 4.3 we present the distribution of estimated value-added of Salvadoran melons in early 1991. The overwhelming bulk of the value is added postfarmgate (89%). Less than 4 percent of the value is added at the farm, and the remaining 7 percent is provided by the prefarmgate supplying of inputs and services.

The distribution of revenues from a pound of melon produced by a small farmer and retailed in the United States for 65 cents is even more illustrative (see Figure 4.4). These calculations, which are intentionally

**Figure 4.3   Distribution of Value-Added in the Melon Commodity Chain
(melons from El Salvador, 1991)**

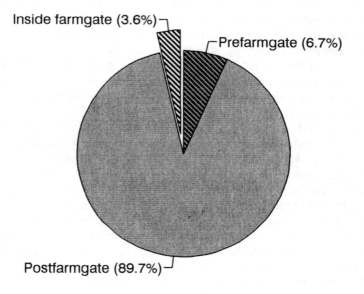

Source: Codas (1991).

**Figure 4.4   Distribution of Revenues in the Melon Commodity Chain (melons
from El Salvador, 1991)**

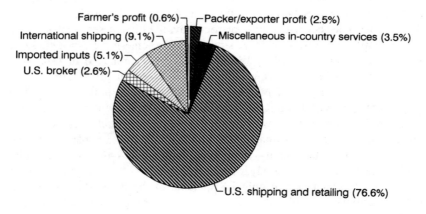

Source: Codas (1991).

conservative, indicate that, at best, 0.6 percent of the revenue, or about half a penny, accrues to the farmer as income. Some 5 percent goes for imported inputs such as fertilizer, pesticides, and seeds, and about 2.5 percent winds up as profit for the packer/exporter. A much larger proportion (9%) is spent on international shipping, while more than 75 percent of the final value is added through U.S. shipping, wholesaling, advertising, and retailing. Even assuming that the packer/exporter is local (e.g., in this case, a Salvadoran firm), more than 90 percent of the revenue accrues outside the country. In the case of integrated concerns like the big four fruit companies, that proportion is even higher.

It is probable that the 0.6 percent of the revenue that stays with the farmer is an underestimate, as these calculations assume that labor is contracted for. If, as is indeed likely, it is entirely family labor, then 2.3 percent of the total revenues accrue to the farm family. However, these revenues break down as 74 percent minimum wage for farm labor and only 26 percent profits from the farming operation. In fact, the return on the farmer's investment in this case (excluding wages) was a mere 7.2 percent, far below the prevailing rate of risk on capital at that time, closely reflected by interest rates on farm credit, which were 20 percent. In essence, the small farmer who grows melons for export to the United States is a farm worker paid to work on his own fields, who additionally must personally assume 100 percent of the risks of crop failure, lessened quality, or market vagaries.

The clear winners from the globalization of the melon commodity chain are international shippers and brokers, or the giant fruit companies in the case of integrated enterprises. By globalizing production outside U.S. borders, these firms account for the bulk of the new value-added. Those companies that carry out shipping and marketing operations within the United States would probably have similar profit opportunities even if production took place within U.S. borders, so the gains for this sector are less dramatic, though they may benefit from year-round availability of seasonal produce and perhaps from lower costs. A similar picture emerges from a study of Honduran melons reported by Weller (1992) and reproduced in Table 4.1. He gives a breakdown of revenue allocation based on the price (CIF, or cost, insurance, and freight) of melons in Miami, the U.S. port of entry. The largest proportion of that total, almost 29 percent, goes to international shipping (broker fees accrue within the United States, and thus were not included). Though he estimates the farmer's profit at 8.6 percent of the value-added up to that point—a relatively high figure—this is in fact misleading. In Table 4.1 we reanalyze his data based on U.S. retail prices, which produces a farmer profit of only 1.8 percent of the price of a melon in a U.S. supermarket, results that are in the same range as the Salvadoran figures.

Table 4.1   Allocation of Revenue for Honduran Melons Exported to the United States, 1988 (percentages)

	Based on CIF/Miami	Based on U.S. Retail
Farm labor	6.6	1.4
Other production costs	14.1	2.9
Farmer's profit	8.6	1.8
Packing	14.6	3.0
National shipping	2.6	0.5
Port fees	0.5	0.1
Exporter's profit	24.4	5.1
International shipping	28.6	5.9
CIF/Miami	100.0	20.7
U.S. broker, shipping, wholesaling, and retailing		79.3
U.S. retail		100.0

Sources: Weller (1992); review of 1988 U.S. supermarket advertisements giving retail prices.

▼ Concentration of Exporting in the Central American NTAEs

As we move up the in-country nontraditional commodity chain from farmer to exporter, we move toward greater relative concentration of the industry. Few good estimates exist of the total number of farmers who grow nontraditionals in Central America. While Kaimowitz (1991) estimates that there are between thirty-five and forty thousand growers, this seems low compared to another estimate of eighteen thousand producers of broccoli alone in Guatemala (Rosset 1992b). Whatever the true number, it is several orders of magnitude larger than the number of exporting firms, who are therefore able to play farmers off against each other in an attempt to obtain produce at lower prices. In Table 4.2 we present figures on concentration among exporters of fifteen crop types in Costa Rica and Honduras. In the least concentrated commodity, Costa Rican cassava, the three largest firms out of a total of thirty-three control fully one-third of the export business. At the other extreme is pineapple, where Del Monte exports 95 percent of the Costa Rican production and Dole 96 percent of the exports from Honduras. In many cases the three largest firms account for greater than 50 percent of the exports of each crop from each country.

Dole and Del Monte both use the grower/packer/exporter system, producing the bulk of their pineapples on two to three thousand hectares each, which they supplement with purchases from small farmers and cooperatives

Table 4.2   Concentration Among Exporters of NTAEs, Costa Rica and Honduras
(percentage of total exports of each product)

	Costa Rica			Honduras		
	No. of Enterprises	Largest Enterprise	Three Largest Enterprises	No. of Enterprises	Largest Enterprise	Three Largest Enterprises
Flowers	79	31.1	53.6	2	—	—
Foliage	41	23.9	45.3	4	48.5	—
Ornamentals	92	20.0	35.6	15	20.9	53.3
Chayote	28	51.3	69.7	—	—	—
Vegetables	—	—	—	17	39.7	77.8
Cassava	33	16.8	33.0	—	—	—
Roots and tubers	—	—	—	8	24.3	—
Pineapple	22	94.9[a]	97.3	10	96.3[b]	98.3
Strawberries	13	26.2	62.7	—	—	—
Citrus	—	—	—	25	52.7	72.3
Plantains	31	32.1	59.7	25	22.3	47.2
Papaya	7	94.0[a]	98.7	—	—	—
Tropical fruits	—	—	—	20	62.8	84.4
Cacao	6	63.2	95.6	8	34.9	79.1
Pepper	—	—	—	6	40.3	78.1

Source: Based on Weller (1992).
Notes: a. Largest firm is Del Monte.
b. Largest firm is Dole.

(Kaimowitz 1991). Of an estimated twelve thousand hectares of melons in the entire region, about four thousand hectares are either satellites or estates of the big four fruit companies, the bulk under various contract arrangements (Kaimowitz 1991; Byrnes 1991). Multinationals are also important in crops such as papaya, where Del Monte exports 94 percent of the Costa Rican production (Weller 1992; Kaimowitz 1991), as well as substantial quantities of mangoes and strawberries (Kaimowitz 1991). ALCOSA, a subsidiary of Hannover Brands, is the largest exporter of frozen vegetables from Guatemala (Rosset 1992b).

In addition to this heavy concentration at the level of exporters in those crops where transnationals dominate, there is substantial concentration at the level of growers in those crops where the grower/packer and grower/exporter models are common. In these cases it appears that the operative factor is the relatively strong position of these individuals and firms relative to the individual farmers who sell to them, as seen in Chapter 2. These grower/packers are particularly important for that portion of melons not controlled by the fruit companies. In Costa Rica six grower/packers dominate, in El Salvador four or five, and in Nicaragua's new melon sector a total of only three or four (Kaimowitz 1991). Essential oils, cut flowers, and certain vegetables in Guatemala are other examples of the same phenomenon

(Kaimowitz 1991). These types of operations tend often to be in the hands of foreigners, as is the case of cut flowers in Costa Rica, where twelve of the fourteen largest firms are owned by non–Costa Ricans; and foliage, where the figure is twenty-nine of thirty-two total producers (Thacher 1990).

Peasant producers remain important for crops such as broccoli, cauliflower, snow peas, miniature vegetables, plantain, cassava, taro, sesame, cacao, and chayote, though they always face a reduced number of buyers who, by virtue of the numerical imbalance, hold the bulk of power in the transactions (Kaimowitz 1991). Melon is a crop where small farmers were once common but where their numbers had dwindled to some seven hundred in the entire region by 1990 (Kaimowitz 1991), as a result of the processes described in this book.

▼ Conclusion

The structure and organization of the nontraditional commodity system in Central America favors brokers, shippers, transnationals, and larger national packing operations, while hurting small farmers. The logic of flexible accumulation in the global marketplace pits producers in one country against producers in many others, and means that transnational firms have no commitment to a given place, pulling up and moving out when crises appear, leaving devastation in their wake. Power in the country portion of the commodity system is concentrated in the hands of exporters, who often are foreigners, placing small farmers in a relatively weak bargaining position. The distribution of profits along the commodity chain clearly demonstrates this fact, as farmers receive a tiny portion of the final retail sale value.

5

ERODING THE PRODUCTIVE BASE: THE ECOLOGY OF NONTRADITIONAL AGRICULTURAL EXPORTS

Pesticides are a critical component of the high-technology production systems that characterize much of the nontraditional sector. The problems associated with agrochemical technology demonstrate some of the obstacles to, and consequences of, introducing new crops and new technologies into the socioeconomic and ecological setting commonly found in the developing world. The impact of nontraditional agriculture's heavy reliance on pesticides raises serious questions as to the appropriateness of the current agricultural diversification strategy for Central America's rural majority.

▼ Pesticides and the Cotton Culture

A pattern of heavy pesticide use was established in Central American agriculture several decades before the current wave of NTAEs.[1] Pesticides became an integral part of Central American farming largely through the expansion of cotton, one of the main nontraditional agricultural exports from the 1950s through the 1970s (Williams 1986). While pesticides were also increasingly important in coffee, bananas, and other crops, cotton accounted for as much as 80 percent of all pesticides imported into the region during the 1960s and 1970s (ICAITI 1977).

Cotton farming provides a classic example of the problems associated with monoculture production, as cotton was grown year after year over vast expanses of land in the same area. Seeking ever-higher yields from an increasingly degraded productive base, producers applied increasing amounts of chemical pesticides and fertilizers. In part at the frequent urging of chemical salesmen and agricultural technicians trained in chemical-intensive production systems, farmers came to adopt a strategy of total pest eradication.[2] The discovery of even small numbers of insect pests was sufficient cause to call in the pesticide spray planes.

Access to pesticides was virtually uncontrolled in Central America during the cotton era (Weir and Shapiro 1981). The region was a prime testing ground for new chemicals (Swezey et al. 1986). Pesticides that were banned or never registered in the United States because of various public health, environmental, or other problems continued to be used throughout the region. In addition, pesticide use was further promoted through government subsidies that made chemical use less expensive than running the risk of pest-related crop losses (Repetto 1985; Rosset 1987). Bank loans for cotton production included line-item categories requiring high rates of pesticide applications (Williams 1986).

In Nicaragua, the regional leader in cotton production throughout much of the postwar period, pesticide application rates soared from an average of five to ten applications per season in the mid-1950s to twenty-eight by the late 1960s, or an application every four days during the cotton-growing season (Swezey et al. 1986:9). In El Salvador pesticide application rates reportedly reached thirty-five to forty per season during the 1960s (Williams 1986:18).

Central American pesticide use escalated throughout the cotton era. During the mid-1960s the region consumed 40 percent of the total hemispheric exports of pesticides from the United States, the world leader in pesticide production and sales (Swezey et al. 1986:8). By the early 1980s Latin America as a whole led the developing world in the volume of pesticides applied per hectare (WHO 1989:25), with pesticide use increasing 32 percent from 1980 to 1984 (WHO 1989:14).

The heavy reliance on pesticides was obviously inefficient. One study of Central American cotton in the mid-1970s concluded that pesticide use could be reduced by 50 percent without decreasing yields (ICAITI 1977).[3] In the late 1960s and again in the late 1970s insecticides alone (roughly 80% of all pesticides used in cotton) accounted for nearly one-third of total cotton production costs in Nicaragua (Swezey et al. 1986).

But the inefficiency of pesticide use was a relatively minor part of the overall problem with technology during the cotton era. More importantly, heavy pesticide use was causing serious ecological disruption, which in turn was driving the need for greater pesticide use. Because of their broad-spectrum nature, many of the chemicals killed not only target pests but a range of beneficial insects as well. These beneficial insects normally prey upon other insects, keeping their populations in balance. Once the beneficial insect populations declined, pest populations were liberated from natural population controls and exploded into secondary pest outbreaks. An early example was the regionwide outbreak of the tobacco whitefly *(Bemisia tabaci)*, a cotton virus vector, in the mid-1960s, which wrought havoc on cotton harvests and drove many small and medium cotton producers bankrupt (Williams 1986:35). Other secondary pests appeared, including the bollworm *(Heliothis zea)*, and the armyworm *(Spodoptera* spp.), and became increasingly difficult to control (Vaughn and Leon 1977).

Growers responded in the only fashion they knew, by applying higher doses of insecticides at shorter intervals, as they found themselves on the pesticide treadmill (Swezey et al. 1986:29). Some pests evolved resistance to the pesticides, compounding secondary pest problems. A study of the bollworm in Nicaragua in the late 1960s found the cotton pest to be forty-five times more resistant to methyl parathion, the most heavily used insecticide, than any field population ever studied (Swezey et al. 1986:9).

Cotton production went through several boom and bust phases in Central America. But increasingly, traditional problems such as weather, international market prices, and rising chemical costs combined with pesticide-generated pest problems to erode the viability of cotton production. With the onset of the regional economic crisis near the end of the 1970s, cotton production began a relatively steady decline through the 1980s, from which it never recovered (see Figure 5.1). But the wholesale importation of

Figure 5.1   Central American Cotton Production (area harvested, 1940–1990)

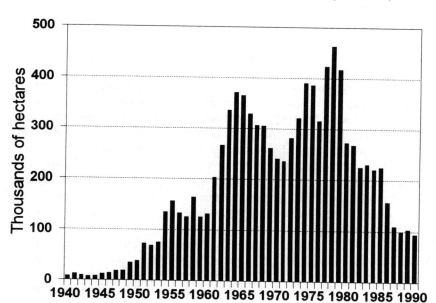

Source: FAO *Yearbooks* (various years).

Figure 5.2   Central American Pesticide Imports

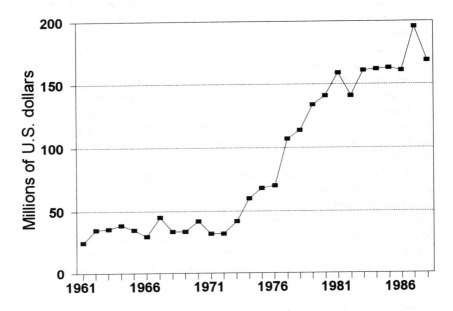

Source: USDA (1992).

pesticides and fertilizers continued (see Figure 5.2) as the profile of Central American exports began to change.

The heavy promotion and use of pesticides in cotton soon spread to other crops as the promise of "miracle" technology reached an ever-wider range of farmers. Relatively inexpensive pesticides, particularly the older organochlorines like aldrin/dieldrin, heptachlor, and chlordane, were being applied to a wide range of crops destined for both export and domestic markets. Pesticide use even increased in basic grains like corn and beans, crops traditionally grown with relatively little technological input, leading Humberto Tapia (1984), an international specialist in bean production, to bemoan what he described as the *"algodonización del frijol"* (the cottonization of beans).

One USAID study of pesticide problems in Central America observed that, with the decline of cotton, the most worrisome area of pesticide use was to be found in Central American vegetable production destined for domestic or Central American markets (Contreras 1990). Crops like cabbage and tomatoes were being sprayed at rates approaching those of the cotton era as farmers maintained the intensive chemical control strategy (Rosset and

Secaira 1989). To varying degrees, the heavy reliance on pesticides in the cotton sector began to spread throughout Central American farming.

▼ Pesticides and the New NTAEs

The rate of growth in pesticide imports to Central America tapered off somewhat during the mid- to late 1980s (as seen in Figure 5.2), as it did throughout much of the developing world (Knirsch 1991), but agricultural chemical imports remained very high even though cotton production collapsed. This was the result of a number of factors, including the decline of cotton, the continuing effect of the regional economic crisis on the ability to pay for pesticides, the soaring price of petrochemical-based inputs,[4] and the more general decline in agricultural development and production as a result of the crisis-generated economic stagnation. But even with the declining imports, pesticide use remained high in selected crops and selected agricultural zones.

In Costa Rica, where cotton was never a significant crop, pesticide use per capita was five to ten times higher from 1982 to 1984 than in a selection of other Latin American countries (see Table 5.1). While an estimated 35 percent of Costa Rica's pesticides were applied to bananas, a range of the newer nontraditional crops, such as ornamental plants, accounted for an increasing percentage of the country's pesticide consumption (Trivelato and Wesseling 1991:2).

Table 5.1 **Pesticide Use, Population, and Agricultural Land Area in Five Latin American Countries, 1982–1984**

	Population (millions)	Agricultural Area (km^2)	Pesticides Used		
			MT	kg/Capita	MT/km^2
Costa Rica	2.6	31,844	8,000	3.10	0.25
Guatemala	8.4	42,000	3,000	0.36	0.07
Colombia	29.0	310,000	21,000	0.72	0.07
Mexico	81.0	600,000	53,000	0.65	0.09
Brazil	136.0	1,200,000	42,000	0.31	0.04

Source: WHO (1989:28).
Note: MT = metric ton.

Predictably, with the spread of pesticide dependency from the cotton sector to the new nontraditionals, there came the spread of many of the problems associated with the earlier generation of nontraditionals. One telling factor has been the almost universal reporting of escalating pesticide use, an indicator of increasing pest problems, among producers of nontraditionals throughout Central America. A USAID-funded survey in the Guatemalan highlands in 1987 found that 82 percent of NTAE producers interviewed reported increasing pesticide use (CICP 1988:48). When asked if pests were becoming "stronger" each season, 85 percent answered yes. In our more recent regional survey, our Central American collaborators found this pattern to be consistent throughout Central America (see Table 5.2). This raises the fearful prospect of the re-creation, possibly at an accelerated rate, of the pesticide treadmill that plagued Central American cotton production.

Table 5.2   **Reported Increase in Pesticide Use Among Small-Scale NTAE Producers in Central America**

Question: Three years ago, did you spray more often or less often than you sprayed this year?

	More Often	Less Often	Same	N
Guatemala	2.2%	88.9%	8.9%	45
El Salvador	21.9%	56.3%	21.9%	64
Honduras	27.91%	55.8%	16.3%	43
Costa Rica	0.0%	91.3%	8.7%	23

Source: Texas Regional Project Pilot Surveys, 1990–1991.

The Problem with Residues

The heavy reliance on pesticides in the new nontraditional crops was not immediately apparent to development planners and policymakers, in part because nontraditionals were only a small portion of Central America's agricultural export sector until the latter part of the 1980s. But a growing consumer awareness in the United States of the presence of pesticide residues in food brought pesticide use among NTAEs to the forefront of the concerns of producers and development planners throughout the region. In 1987 consumer and environmental groups demanded that the FDA more stringently monitor pesticides in domestic and imported produce. The following year Congress passed legislation mandating closer surveillance of pesticide residues (PL 100-418 102 Stat. August 23, 1988).

Even before the passage of the new law, the FDA had begun increasing surveillance of imported produce (FDA 1988). NTAEs from Central America and the Caribbean drew particular attention as early FDA sampling found relatively greater numbers of shipments in violation of pesticide residue standards than had previously been found in comparable sampling of U.S. produce.[5] In 1989 the FDA detained nearly four thousand shipments of fresh and processed foods from Central America and the Caribbean, the majority of which were found to have illegal pesticide residues (see Table 5.3). The Central American and Caribbean shipments found in violation of residue standards accounted for 11.2 percent of the global food imports detained that year.

Table 5.3   FDA Detentions of Food Imports from Central America, Mexico, and the Caribbean, Fiscal Year 1989

	Number of Detentions
Mexico	1,919
Dominican Republic	1,429
Bahamas	25
Turks and Caicos Islands	6
Haiti	38
British Virgin Islands	6
Barbados	5
Grenada	5
Aruba	24
Guatemala	87
Honduras	50
El Salvador	160
Costa Rica	85
Panama	37
Jamaica	39
United States (U.S. goods returned)	195
Global detentions	26,013

Source: FDA (1989).
Note: Countries are those with five or more detentions.

The most striking example of the impact of the residue problem in non-traditional agriculture did not occur in Central America, but in the nearby Caribbean nation of the Dominican Republic. The Dominican Republic was the early leader in nontraditional growth in the Caribbean Basin. Dominican NTAEs grew at a 13 percent annual rate from the early 1980s, reaching $44.9 million in 1986 (CEDOPEX 1987). The Dominican Republic was also the regional leader in attracting foreign investment in nontraditional development (Mathieson 1988). In 1986 one writer for a British magazine, the *Economist,* predicted a bright future for the Dominican economy based on the investment prospects in the nontraditional sector. He described the Dominican Republic as "the Caribbean country which offers by far the most important agricultural and agro-industry (investment) opportunities" in the period from 1986 to 1991 (cited in Raynolds 1994:227).

The Dominican Republic, while not directly part of the Central American focus of this book, is important to understanding the development of nontraditional export agriculture because it was initially the most successful of the countries participating in the new development strategy. It was frequently pointed to by USAID and others during the early to mid-1980s as the showcase of the new development policies. Its subsequent experiences with the implementation of these policies is suggestive of the kinds of problems that may yet await those Central American countries that followed the Dominican lead.[6]

Dominican nontraditionals included a range of fruits and vegetables, from Oriental vegetables such as eggplant, bitter melon, and fuzzy squash, to melons (cantaloupe and honeydew), tomatoes, snow peas, string beans, okra, and others. Oriental vegetables, along with melons and pineapples, were among the most dynamic components of the nontraditional sector. By 1987 Oriental vegetables brought in an estimated 11 percent of Dominican NTAE earnings (Raynolds 1994:229).[7]

Production was carried out largely through satellite farming, with twelve exporters shipping produce to the United States that they bought from two to three thousand small farmers (Raynolds 1994:228). Satellite production appealed to risk-averse exporters. They merely waited until the harvest and paid the going rate for the crop upon its delivery to the packing or processing plant. If there was overproduction or a drop in demand, the exporters passed on adverse market conditions to the producers. Likewise, farmers bore the financial impact of common agricultural problems such as weather, pests, and transportation. Investment requirements were also relatively low for the Oriental vegetable exporters, with some setting up little more than cement block sheds with refrigeration units, sorting and packing tables, and a loading dock for truck-drawn containers headed to the local port.

Exporter control of producer pesticide use and other farming practices was negligible. Similar to their Central American counterparts, Dominican producers had relatively easy access to a wide range of pesticides. New pesticides were being registered by the Secretaría del Estado de Agricultura (SEA) at a rapid rate, growing from an estimated twelve to fifteen products available in the mid-1970s to over nine hundred products by 1989 (Murray et al. 1989:9). Small farmers routinely applied highly toxic pesticides, often mixing several at a time, which they applied on a calendar, or prophylactic, basis to control existing or anticipated pest problems.

Dominican exports of key nontraditionals, including Oriental vegetables, peaked by the mid-1980s, as illustrated in Figure 5.3. They subsequently fell into a gradual and then accelerating decline as a combination of increasing FDA surveillance and worsening pest problems (discussed below) significantly undermined the promise of continued economic growth throughout much of the nontraditional export sector. From 1987 through 1989 the Dominican Republic achieved the dubious distinction of being the regional leader in the percentage of samples of exported produce found to

Figure 5.3   The NTAE Gamble in the Dominican Republic

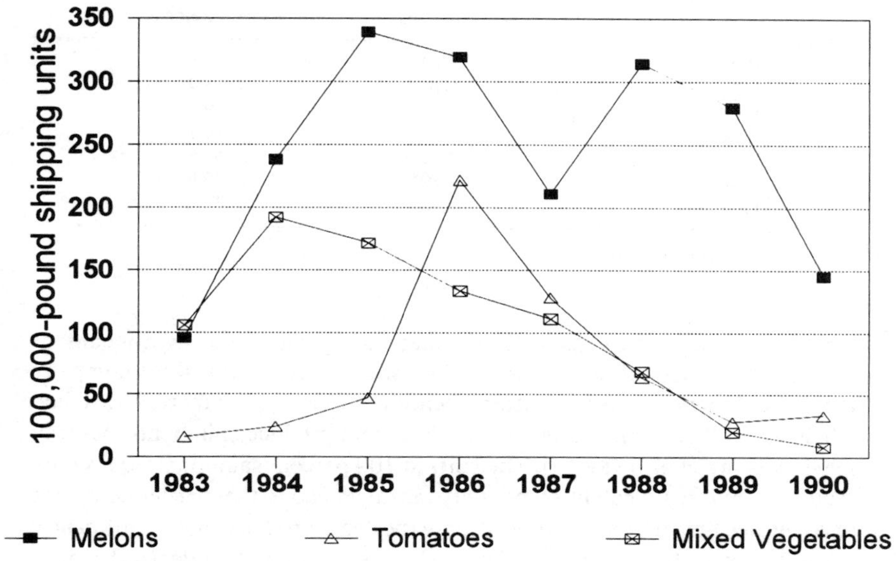

Source: USDA Market Research Service (1991).

have illegal pesticide residues (as seen in Table 5.4),[8] and was second only to Mexico in the total number of detentions (see Table 5.3).

Oriental vegetables were among the main culprits identified by FDA surveillance. By 1988 Oriental vegetable exporters were reporting significant losses from residue detentions, with some losing hundreds of thousands of dollars in a single month (Murray 1989). The FDA soon followed with a cropwide, automatic detention on five Oriental vegetables, requiring that every Dominican shipment be sampled before acceptance into the United States.[9] This was a major change from the traditional FDA sampling rate for imported food of 3.4 percent (Mott and Snyder 1988).

The low-cost, low-risk structure of satellite farming had allowed exporters to avoid assuming the greater costs associated with more-direct control of producer pesticide use and other farming practices. With the relatively infrequent FDA sampling of the early Reagan years, risk of detentions had been a minor problem. Some exporters even developed strategies to evade FDA sanctions. For example, one exporter reportedly chose to use several brand names for his exports by registering different brand name

Table 5.4   FDA Rejections of Nontraditional Produce Shipments from the
Dominican Republic for Pesticide Residues

	Samples	Percent Rejected
1985	103	4.8
1986	165	5.4
1987	481	9.3
1988	1,216	14.1
1989	2,531	53.5
1990	701	35.9
1991	427	32.3

Source: FDA (various years).

labels in the names of his wife or other family members, as a means of avoiding FDA detentions. When residues were discovered and his company faced the threat of FDA's exporter detention provisions, he merely switched labels to another brand name on his subsequent produce shipments (Murray 1994; Murray et al. 1989:11). The shift to 100 percent sampling required by cropwide automatic detention not only meant an end to that particular means of avoiding the FDA's scrutiny of an exporter's produce, but significantly raised the probability that many more shipments would be rejected because of more-complete sampling.

The Problem with Pests

Oriental vegetable producers complained that the primary reason for heavy pesticide application was a tiny insect pest, *Thrips palmi.* The pest had become increasingly difficult to contain, and by 1988 it was completely out of control. Producers reported applying nine different insecticides recommended by agricultural technicians, chemical salesmen, or others, with little effect (Murray et al. 1989:4). Some producers lost their entire crop to thrips. One producer observed that the pest had not been a problem until a tiny spider that had preyed on thrips disappeared from the Oriental vegetable fields, presumably a victim of heavy pesticide application rates.

The inability to control thrips led to a second problem that, when combined with FDA residue detentions, brought the Oriental vegetable export sector to a halt. On May 8, 1989, the USDA placed an emergency quarantine on five Oriental vegetables because they were found to be infested with thrips that might threaten U.S. agriculture. The virtual elimination of the primary export market was devastating.[10] Seven Oriental vegetable growers reported a 57 percent decrease in the area under cultivation for the 1989/90 season (Murray 1994; Murray et al. 1989), leading to an estimated $16 million loss for the year as packing sheds and processing facilities stood idle.

Pesticide-induced pest problems also plagued Dominican melon producers as an explosive outbreak of another secondary pest, the tobacco whitefly, in 1988, undermined further growth in melon production in the Azua Valley (see Figure 5.3). In early 1989 one melon exporter reported the loss of forty containers;[11] USDA inspectors had found the fruit infested with whiteflies, and had quarantined it, as they had several shipments of Oriental vegetables infested with thrips (Murray 1994; Murray et al. 1989:2). Whitefly problems seriously reduced melon yields as well, and melon farming had virtually disappeared from the Azua Valley by the 1990/91 production cycle (personal interview, Lorena Lastres, June 27, 1991).

Tomato production also declined in Azua as the whitefly outbreak reduced per-acre yields in 1988/89 by 20 to 25 percent from 1987 levels, accompanied by a 50 percent decrease in land under tomato cultivation, and a resulting $5.9 million loss in export- and domestic-processed tomato production. Meanwhile Azua producers were reporting increasing problems with six other pests by early 1989, including leafminers, leafrollers, fruit worms, mites, loopers, and tomato hornworms.

The ecological and economic disaster continued through the first half of the 1990s. By the summer of 1995 there was still no sign of melon production in Azua (personal interview, Laura Raynolds, July 19, 1995). The 1994/95 cycle of tomato production saw the first indication of recovery from the crisis as tomato yields reportedly returned to 1988/89 levels. It remains unclear whether a recovery to precrisis levels in tomato production is possible.

The Dominican experience is a graphic example of the crisis-generating potential inherent in heavy dependence on pesticides in nontraditionals. The question still remains whether this case is indicative of conditions throughout Caribbean Basin nontraditional agriculture, or merely an isolated example, peculiar to this island nation.

▼ The Crisis in Cholutecan Melon Production

Much of Central America's NTAE development has followed, lamentably, the pattern set in the Dominican Republic. In the last several years various crops in different Central American countries have become increasingly important to the local and national economies. As these countries have caught up with or surpassed the Dominican nontraditional export sector, they have begun to reproduce some of the pesticide-related crisis tendencies seen in the Dominican Republic.

The case of Honduras's export melon industry provides ample evidence that the Dominican experience with pests and pesticides is not an isolated incident. Choluteca, on the southern Pacific coast of Honduras, was Central

America's leading melon-growing region by the end of the 1980s. Melon production in Choluteca was initially developed in 1975 by United Brands, under the name Productos Acuáticos y Terrestres, S.A. (PATSA). The venture into nontraditionals was part of the company's efforts to diversify beyond its $100 million banana industry on the Caribbean side of Honduras.

PATSA produced melons through a relatively more sophisticated form of satellite farming than the one employed by Dominican Oriental vegetable exporters. PATSA contracted with small and medium-sized melon producers before the season began, providing a pre-determined, fixed price in exchange for exclusive rights to the producer's harvest. PATSA provided technical assistance, credits, and inputs.

In 1983 a number of small and medium producers split off from PATSA, in part because of the encouragement of USAID, to form a producer cooperative, the Cooperativa Regional de Horticultores Sureños Limitada (CREHSUL). CREHSUL, in contrast to PATSA's fixed price arrangement, marketed the cooperative's melons at harvest time through brokers in the United States, seeking potentially higher prices on the international market than PATSA offered.

But the gamble taken by the small producer cooperative almost ruined USAID's nontraditional export promotion in southern Honduras. The Standard Fruit Company flooded the international market with melons after a bumper harvest in the Dominican Republic in the 1983/84 season, driving melon prices down and causing major losses to the Honduran producers.[12] PATSA survived the bad market relatively better than CREHSUL because PATSA had fewer liabilities under its fixed-price contracting system, and since many producers had been convinced to shift to the higher-risk producer cooperative.

In spite of the economic losses, CREHSUL continued to pursue export melon farming, with significant financial assistance from both Honduran banks and USAID. Melon production began to expand rapidly after 1985 when the Israeli company Hondex brought more than 1,200 manzanas under direct production, followed in 1986 by another transnational, Seaboard Marine's Chestnut Hill Farms, which planted an area of similar size. Several other Honduran companies and cooperatives followed as melon production rose rapidly throughout the latter half of the 1980s (illustrated in Figure 5.4).

Pesticide use in the Honduran melon sector was somewhat better than in the Dominican Republic. Small producers also had easy access to a wide range of pesticides, including products not approved by the U.S. Environmental Protection Agency (EPA) for application on melons. But exporters were alerted relatively early in the development of the Honduran melon industry to the potential risks involved in melon pest control. The disastrous experience in the Dominican Republic served as one lesson. Several detentions of melon shipments from Choluteca gave further warning of the

Figure 5.4   Melon Exports from Honduras (thousands of 35–40 pound boxes)

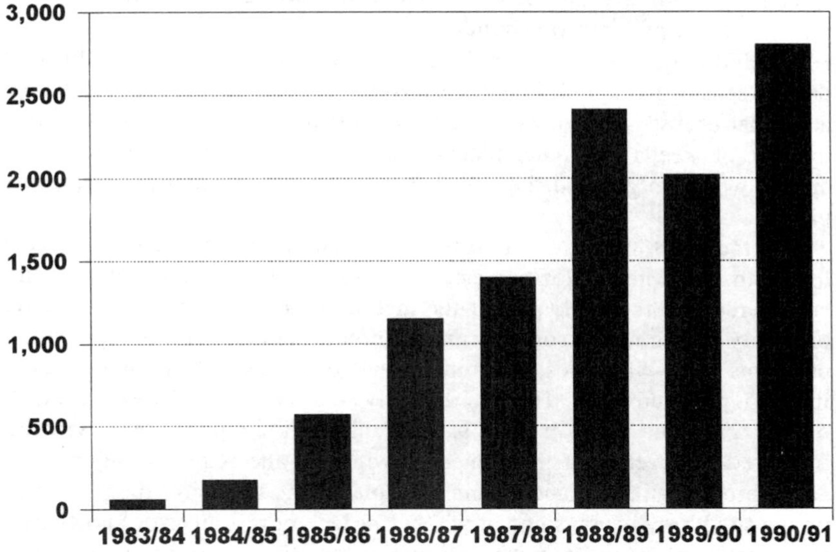

Sources: 1983/84, 1984/85 from Byrnes (1989); 1985/86–1989/90 from FPX (1990); 1990/91 estimated by G. Garcelon.

potential for major problems. Exporters, large growers, and USAID all took measures to gain greater control of pesticide use (discussed in greater detail below).

Control of pest-related pesticide problems proved harder to achieve. Producers had always experienced a certain amount of pest problems, particularly with plant viruses and several insect pests, which they considered part of the costs of participating in the melon gamble. Consistent with the standard pest control paradigm of the period, farmers sprayed a range of chemicals on a calendar basis to control existing or anticipated problems. Yet given the experience of the cotton era, some technicians and researchers were already warning that continued reliance on the techniques associated with the cotton culture would soon re-create the very same problems that plagued cotton.

The chief research entomologist for United Brands during the 1970s, Dr. Eugene Ostmark, was one of those expressing concern. Describing the pest control practices in the early years of Choluteca's melon industry, Ostmark (interview, May 25, 1990) observed, "PATSA had a brilliant field manager. But he really pushed calendar spraying to control aphids, which transmitted a virus to the melon plants. We knew by then that it would cause problems, and science has since shown that virus can't be controlled with insecticides. But he didn't believe it. He would say, 'See, we don't have any virus.' But the problem was building."

Aphid populations grew with the increasing area planted in melons. In the off-season the aphid colonies survived in surrounding areas of weeds and other crops. The viruses that attacked the melons survived as well in a number of weeds and other plants. Once the melon fields appeared, the aphids would migrate to the vast expanses of melon plants, carrying the virus.

In the 1988/89 season producers experienced an estimated 10 percent loss of the projected melon harvest. The losses were significant but were still considered an acceptable part of the melon production game. Losses were primarily due to aphid-borne virus, but producers also reported increasing problems with whiteflies, leafminers, and other secondary, or pesticide-induced, pest outbreaks. Then, in the early stages of the 1989/90 season, all of the previous pest problems, particularly the aphid-borne viruses, increased to levels that threatened to wipe out the region's melon crop. Large producers, and some technicians, placed the blame for the pest crisis on the small producers, some of whom, for lack of resources or knowledge, had failed to plow under their remaining melon plants after the previous harvest, creating an ideal environment in which the pests could multiply during the off-season (Murray 1994, 1991). Others pointed to late rains that delayed planting, or to the overall increase in the area under melon cultivation, which generated increasing pest problems. But most readily agreed that the history of frequent pesticide applications had fostered both chemically resistant pests and secondary pest problems.

As evidence of the pesticide-induced nature of the pest problem, one survey of whitefly populations found less than 1 percent of the whitefly eggs in Choluteca had been parasitized by beneficial predatory insects (Marenco 1990). These beneficials, which normally kept whitefly populations in check, were presumably early victims of the heavy pesticide spraying in the melon fields. In contrast, whitefly surveys taken in other regions, where melons were not grown, including San Pedro Sula (20% parasitized) and Zamorano (15% parasitized) found significantly higher rates of whitefly control by beneficial insects.[13] Researchers also found a 200 percent increase in leafminer eggs in the Cholutecan melon fields, suggesting a decline in the predator populations that kept this pest in control as well.

Pesticide use, according to the pest control schedule that CREHSUL provided to its members, had reached fourteen applications for the two-and-a-half-month season in 1989. One survey of Cholutecan melon farmers reported application rates of nineteen per season and extreme cases of applications every two days (Marenco 1990), leading one melon pest control specialist to complain that the frequency of pesticide use was approaching, once again, that of the cotton era (personal interview, Alfredo Rueda, May 3, 1990).

Estimates of the overall losses to pests in the 1989/90 season ranged from 45 to 56 percent of preharvest projections, with some producers losing most of their crop (personal interview, Rolando Pretto, May 13, 1990; FPX 1990). The pest problem had reached critical proportions. One of the leading international pest control specialists in the region described the situation as "a crisis approaching disaster" that raised the very real question "of whether Choluteca will still be producing melons in four to five years" (personal interview, Keith Andrews, May 3, 1990).

The crop losses hit particularly hard among the small producers. Most had gone deep into debt to finance their entry into the melon sector. Many producers in CREHSUL found themselves unable to meet their debt payments for the second consecutive year. Yet most also found themselves unable to escape from the melon gamble. As one producer complained, "They can't pay back their debts with corn" (Perdomo and Noé Pino 1991:41).

But continuing in melon production became ever more difficult. A period of serious drought prior to the 1990/91 planting season provided Cholutecan melon producers with unexpected pest control assistance. The drought meant that the surrounding areas of weeds and other crops, which normally sustained the aphids and plant viruses in the off-season, were almost completely absent. When the rains finally came, melon planting immediately followed. Without a major threat from aphids, yields increased dramatically.[14] Some producers still experienced significant losses to whiteflies, leafminers, and a newly emerging nematode problem. But many producers harvested unusually high volumes of melons. Unfortunately for the Cholutecan farmers, other countries experienced similar bumper harvests during the same crop cycle, and the international market price for melons plummeted at the time much of the harvest was sold (Murray 1991). Financially strapped small producers found themselves again unable to meet their debts. The previous year's losses to pests still plagued them in spite of a bountiful harvest.

CREHSUL producers and others went to the Honduran national development bank, BANDESA, requesting the refinancing of their loans. Instead, BANDESA officials chose to cut off further loans to small producers because the burden of unpaid loans was undermining the bank's lending viability. USAID stepped in to purchase a portion of the small producers' debt from BANDESA, but many farmers still found themselves facing the 1991/92 season without secured financing for the upcoming melon planting.

Time appears to be running out for many small producers in Choluteca. If weather patterns return to normal, pest problems are likely to escalate again. Producers may find better pest control, such as the biological and nonchemical methods being promoted by technicians from the Panamerican Agriculture School in Zamorano. But even if they overcome their pest problems, they must count on unusually high international market prices, corresponding with even higher crop yields, if they are to have any hope of overcoming their debt burden. The pest and pesticide problems, when combined with international market forces, appear to have left the poor, small-scale melon producers in Honduras holding a losing hand in the high-stakes game of export melon production.

▼   Signs of Impending Crisis in Guatemalan NTAEs

Full-blown crises such as we have seen in the Dominican Republic and Honduras have not occurred in all the nontraditional crops and growing zones. But the buildup of problems that make crises more likely has been occurring throughout the region. The Guatemalan highlands offer an example of the incipient conditions that likely exist across a wide range of crops and growing areas in nontraditional agriculture.

Guatemalan nontraditional producers experienced many of the same pesticide-related problems seen in the preceding cases, but on a relatively less significant scale. For example, from 1985 through 1987 only fifteen instances of FDA pesticide residue detentions of Guatemalan exports were reported (see Figure 5.5). But an alarming increase in detentions began near the end of the decade with the increase in FDA surveillance. Twenty-seven percent (67 out of 247) of all Guatemalan shipments sampled in 1990 were found to have illegal pesticide residues. Rejections of Guatemalan nontraditional exports continued to climb through 1993, when the total economic losses from FDA detentions were estimated at $10.4 million (Thrupp et al. 1995).

Guatemalan NTAE producers also reported increasing pest problems in recent years, similar to the previous examples. Seventy-three percent of the farmers interviewed in one survey reported greater use of pesticides from 1986 through 1988 (Hoppin 1991:178). A second survey found that 82 percent of the producers reported increasing pesticide use, and 85 percent reported pests were becoming "stronger" (CICP 1988:48). The more recent regional survey (see Table 5.2) found 88.9 percent of the Guatemalan small farmers interviewed were using increasing amounts of pesticides on their nontraditional crops.

Pesticides have clearly become a major part of Guatemalan nontraditional production. Pesticide costs in melons were the highest among the tropical, or hot-climate, crops in Guatemala, with costs ranging from $735 to $2,206 per hectare (CICP 1988). Snow peas led temperate, or cold-

Figure 5.5   FDA Rejections of Guatemalan NTAEs (value of exports rejected for residues in thousands of U.S.$)

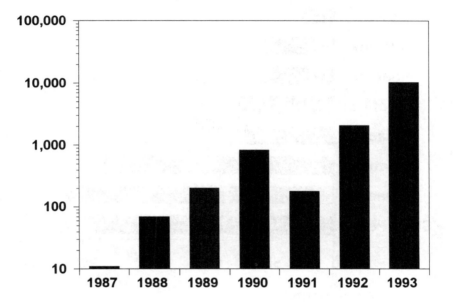

Source: Thrupp (1995).

climate, crops, with pesticide costs in excess of $2,206 per hectare. Pesticide costs per manzana in snow peas even surpassed those of bananas and cotton, historically the heaviest users of pesticides (see Figure 5.6).

AVANCSO conducted, in late 1992, what may be the first detailed analysis of the ecological impact of NTAEs in the Guatemalan highlands. They sought to determine the extent of the buildup of pesticide-generated and other ecological problems in the nontraditional sector. In addition, they wanted to compare insect populations, disease incidence, and soil conditions under both organic and chemical-intensive production technology. Conducted by a research team at the Instituto de Investigaciones of the Universidad del Valle de Guatemala, the survey was designed to compare ecological conditions in the six principal nontraditional agriculture zones of the Guatemalan highlands (Morales et al. 1993; MacVean et al. 1993). Although it was an extremely low-budget study, depending largely on the dedication and enthusiasm of the research team, its results are striking.

The survey compared various indicators of ecological problems on nontraditional farms, where chemical-intensive practices were used, with

Figure 5.6   Pesticide Costs in Guatemala (U.S.$ per manzana [0.7 ha], 1987)

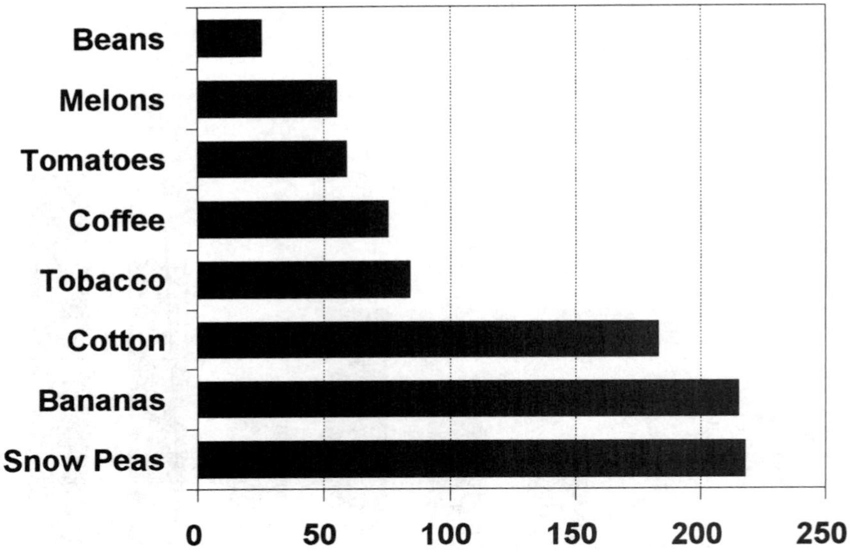

Source: de Campos (1987).

nontraditional farms where organic methods were employed. The study also compared ecological conditions in nontraditional crops (broccoli and snow peas) with traditional domestic crops (corn and beans). The researchers further compared soil, disease, and insect conditions in basic grain crops "close to" chemically intensive nontraditional production with conditions found farther away from the chemically contaminated environment.

Several pest problems were actually lower in plots of organically grown nontraditional crops than in nontraditional crops produced under the more common chemical-intensive approach. For example, pests such as the white grub and thrips (the most important insect pest in snow peas) were completely absent from plots of snow peas cultivated organically, while chemical-intensive plots showed relatively high levels of these pests. In the case of nematodes, plots of organically grown snow peas and broccoli had (statistically) significantly lower levels of these pests than chemically treated plots (Morales et al. 1993).

Even more striking was the comparison of damage due to plant diseases in organic and chemical-intensive nontraditional crops. Damage due to various diseases was considerably lower in organically grown broccoli and snow peas than in fields where they were grown chemically with the assistance of herbicides, pesticides, and chemical fertilizers. In the case of *Aseochyta,* the main plant disease in snow peas, the difference was statistically even more pronounced; the measured damage under the chemical regime was more than 10-times greater than under organic production. Organic plots of nontraditionals had, not surprisingly, more beneficial insects, the natural enemies of insect pests, than chemically treated plots, with both the total population and the number of species of predatory spiders significantly higher in organic plots than in chemically treated plots.

Also striking was the impact of nontraditional crops on the ecology of traditional subsistence crops grown adjacent to or near the chemically intensive nontraditional plots. There were significantly more pests found in corn plots close to nontraditional crops than in plots isolated from nontraditional crops. In the case of specific pests, such as leafhoppers and aphids, these effects were statistically significant. Corn and beans planted adjacent to chemically grown nontraditionals also were found to have significantly higher levels of plant diseases, similar to those found in the chemically treated nontraditional fields.

The rate of beneficial parasitism (the incidence of pests found to have been preyed upon by beneficial insects) was highest in corn, where pesticide use was much lower than in nontraditionals, with lower rates in broccoli and virtually no signs of parasitism among snow peas, where chemical spraying is greatest. The less ecologically disruptive bacterial pesticide, *Bacillus thuringiensis,* was the primary chemical used in the broccoli plots surveyed, while more highly destructive, broad-spectrum chemicals were commonly used in snow peas. This probably explains the relatively higher level of parasitism in broccoli over snow peas. Corn was also found to have lower rates of parasitism when it was grown close to nontraditionals than when grown farther away.

Soil quality and soil erosion may be the most powerful indicators of the ecological well-being of nontraditional agriculture. Survey results from Guatemala suggest that nontraditional crops have seriously undermined the long-term ecological sustainability of agriculture in the highlands through the degradation of soil. One indicator of soil quality is the amount of leaf litter or mulch on the ground surface. This material is important in controlling erosion and holds humidity in the soil. It also provides habitat for natural enemies of pests, and contributes to the organic content of the soil. The quantity of leaf litter in traditional crops (corn and beans) was found to be much greater than in nontraditionals. The quantity of earthworms in a plot of soil is also an indicator of soil quality, as well as an indicator of the impact of pesticides. The survey found far fewer earthworms in broccoli fields than in corn, and no earthworms in the soils sampled from snow pea fields, those with the heaviest uses of pesticides (Morales et al. 1993).

Relative levels of erosion are another indicator of the ecological impact of nontraditionals. The rate of erosion in fields of broccoli grown in San José Pinula was found to be twice that in traditional corn plots in this community during the same period. Finally, the level of aluminum residues in soil, an indicator of possible toxic buildup of microelements from fertilizer use, was also measured. Aluminum residues were significantly higher in broccoli (although still not at the phytotoxic levels that would hinder growth) than in corn. This illustrates that heavy fertilizer use in nontraditionals may create future problems with declining soil productivity due to toxic buildup.

The results of this survey suggest, first, that heavy pesticide use in Guatemalan highland nontraditionals may be creating the ecological imbalance seen so often in other parts of the world: heavy and inappropriate uses of chemicals worsen the conditions they were designed to remedy, creating an ecological imbalance for continued production of the same crop. Second, the promotion of pesticide-dependent nontraditionals is probably having an adverse impact on the ecology of other crops that traditionally have not been chemical-dependent. The findings also suggest that it is the chemical-intensive nature of nontraditional farming, not the nontraditional crops per se, that have generated this array of ecological problems.

▼   **Transnational Operators**
    Respond to Pesticide Problems

The problems generated by the continued heavy reliance on pesticides in nontraditional agriculture have not fallen equally on all players in the non-traditional gamble. Those firms with sufficient resources to ride out periods of economic and ecological problems have fared relatively better.[15] Large national and, more frequently, transnational operations have been able to cope with, adapt to, and overcome at least some of the obstacles posed by agrochemical technology.

One indicator of the differing success in dealing with pesticides is preliminary evidence of decreasing pesticide use among larger producers. Figure 5.7 shows a decline in the rate of pesticide application among larger melon producers in Guatemala, compared to a continuing increase in the rate of applications among smaller producers. As Byrnes (1989) suggested, such factors as the ability to survive the school of hard knocks (or, essentially, to gain experience without going bankrupt), combined with the greater technical assistance for which larger operators can contract, may explain why these larger producers have shown modest indications of bringing at least pesticide application rates under control.

Transnationals and operations capitalized by foreign investors have been particularly effective in coping with both crisis-generating factors and with the consequences of crises. Where production has been organized

Figure 5.7   Pesticide Use Tendencies of Small and Large Melon Growers, Guatemala

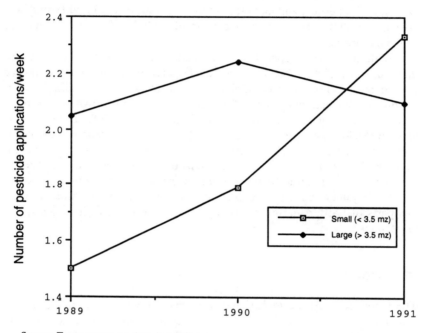

Source: From our survey (see Appendix).

through satellite farming, exporters have maintained considerable flexibility through relatively low fixed-capital investments. When problems reach critical proportions, these operations have little incentive to remain in existing communities or countries, particularly when faced with the prospects of an ecological crisis and the potential collapse of the productive base of the nontraditional sector.

The example of the Dominican Republic is again instructive of potential trends in transnational corporations' responses to pesticide problems in nontraditional agriculture throughout the developing world. When the Dominican Oriental vegetable sector collapsed in the face of the combined problems of pesticide residues and pesticide-resistant pests, Oriental vegetable exporters took quick steps to overcome at least their own misfortune. Of the dozen major exporters, most were Asian investors who ventured relatively small investments ranging from less than $150,000 to $3 million. With few local ties and limited capital at risk, these investors closed down their operations and abandoned the Dominican Republic "virtually overnight" (Raynolds 1994:230). Many moved to nearby countries such as

Jamaica, where they set up new Oriental vegetable export operations, no longer under FDA detention and (for the moment) free of the pesticide-generated ecological problems. Left in their wake were two to three thousand satellite farmers and an untold number of family and hired farm laborers whose options and prospects were considerably less favorable than those of the exporters.

With the increasing problems in the Azua Valley melon and tomato production, some of the largest transnational operations in the country chose a similar option. For example, Chiquita Brands, one of the leading melon-exporting transnationals in the Caribbean Basin, shut down an incipient melon project in the Azua Valley before the start of the 1990/91 season (personal interview, Dwight Steen, October 16, 1990). In addition to the pesticide-generated pest problems, the move was in part influenced by frustrations with the Dominican government over obstacles to the further development of nontraditional projects in pineapple production and other crops. Chiquita continued to expand and/or shift melon operations in various parts of Latin America, including Mexico, Honduras, Costa Rica, and Guatemala.

▼ Conclusion

The evidence available to date indicates that an array of pesticide-related problems are generating increased obstacles to small-producer viability in nontraditional export agriculture in Central America. In contrast, transnational corporations are responding to these technology-induced problems in ways that allow them to continue profitable production, export, and expansion throughout the region. Far from reducing inequity in the region, it appears that pesticide-dependent nontraditional farming is further contributing to the already wide gap between rich and poor in Central America.

Yet socioeconomic and ecological inequity are not the only negative effects of current chemical-intensive development. There are other realms in which nontraditional agriculture's dependence on pesticide technology threatens the productive base of the rural sectors of Central America: the very health of the producers themselves, their families, and their workers. It is to those problems we turn in the next chapter.

▼ Notes

1. See Murray (1994) for a more complete account of the role and impact of pesticides in Latin American development.
2. See Perkins (1982) for an account of the evolution of pest control paradigms.

3. A more recent study, focused on U.S. agriculture, concluded that similar reductions would have a limited impact on productivity in U.S. crops, and a beneficial effect throughout other areas of the economy and environment (Pimentel 1991).

4. UN CEPAL (1990:1) noted that rising fertilizer and shipping costs were two primary factors in the rapid increase in regional production costs that fueled the economic crisis after the second oil price hike in 1979.

5. Most residue rejections involve chemicals that are not registered by the Environmental Protection Agency (EPA) for use on the crop being tested. Rejections also occur when a level of pesticide residue is found that is registered for use on a particular crop, but is in excess of the "tolerance" (the level of residue of that particular chemical the EPA considers safe for human consumption). This latter type of violation is far less common than the former. For example, of the fifty-two samples of Dominican produce found in violation of FDA standards in 1987, only two involved pesticide residue levels in excess of EPA tolerance (Murray and Hoppin 1992).

6. This discussion of the Dominican case is drawn largely from a previously published article (Murray and Hoppin 1992).

7. Santo Domingo's leading daily newspaper placed the estimate at 25 percent (Raynolds 1994), which Raynolds believes to be an overestimate.

8. See FDA World Wide Import Detention Summaries, 1987 through 1989. The FDA did not publish this report before 1987 and discontinued its publication after 1989.

9. Automatic detention (also known as certification status) can be placed on individual exporters or on all exports of a given crop from a given country. A laboratory certificate verifying that no illegal residues are present must accompany any shipment under automatic detention.

10. Exporters found partial relief by shipping their produce to Canada, where they reportedly did not encounter significant residue or quarantine restrictions (Murray et al. 1989). But the Canadian market could not absorb the volume necessary to sustain the Oriental vegetable industry at the level it had reached by the late 1980s.

11. There are roughly a thousand boxes of melons, each containing from twelve to thirty melons, in a trailer-sized container drawn by truck, loaded directly on to ships, and delivered, still in container, to warehouses at the U.S. port of entry.

12. Personal interview, Eugene Ostmark, former chief entomologist for United Brands, May 25, 1990.

13. These contrasting rates are also relatively low, which may be explained by the fact that both comparative surveys were conducted in zones where pesticide use is also common.

14. Aphid problems were probably reduced as well by the increased adoption of integrated pest management (IPM) techniques by some producers in the region (personal interview, Lorena Lastres, June 27, 1991). The relative weight of the drought, IPM, and other factors in reducing the overall incidence of plant virus or other pest problems cannot be determined at this time.

15. See Byrnes (1989), for a discussion of the need for a resource base sufficient enough to allow participants in the melon sector to learn from the school of hard knocks. Byrnes estimates a minimum of five years is necessary to improve the probability that a producer will develop into a successful melon farmer.

6

RAISING THE HUMAN COSTS: PESTICIDES AND HEALTH IN CENTRAL AMERICAN NONTRADITIONAL AGRICULTURAL EXPORTS

One morning in the spring of 1989 a crew of fifteen field-workers, mostly women ranging in age from thirteen to eighteen years, began applying pesticides to a melon field in Choluteca, Honduras.[1] They moved through the field sprinkling the pesticide powder by hand from a small bag slung from each woman's hip, onto the ground surrounding the plants. They wore no protective clothing and applied the chemical bare-handed. Some worked barefoot. Late in the morning they stopped work. Since they had only about twenty minutes for lunch, they moved to a nearby shaded area and quickly ate their modest meal of tortillas, rice, plantain, or beans, then commenced working again. Soon after returning to the field, several of the young women began feeling dizzy and nauseated. Within the hour, the majority of the crew became seriously ill with vomiting and chills. Several collapsed. They were rushed to a hospital where they received treatment for pesticide poisoning. All the victims survived, although some continued to feel the effects of the poisoning for weeks after the incident.

This case was not an isolated one. In the Nicaraguan department of León, immediately south of Choluteca, there were an estimated two thousand cases of pesticide poisoning in 1986 and 1987 that occurred in precisely the same manner as the incident in Choluteca: workers applying a chemical bare-handed and either absorbing the poison through their unprotected skin or ingesting it from their unwashed hands (McConnell et al. 1990). While the precise numbers are unknown, some estimates suggest that pesticide poisonings in Central American agricultural zones are among the most frequently occurring, and among the most serious, causes of illness in the region (de Campos 1987; Cole et al. 1988; Keifer and Pacheco 1991). As we shall see, the evidence suggests that the human health problems associated with pesticides have not changed appreciably since chemical-intensive agriculture became a cornerstone of Central American development after World War II.

▼ Pesticide Poisoning: The Cost of Cotton

Pesticide-related health problems in the current nontraditional development process, similar to the pesticide-related socioeconomic and ecological problems discussed in the previous chapter, are rooted in the rise of Central America's cotton economy. Without pesticides, cotton production would not have been possible on the scale achieved in the region during the 1960s and 1970s (Murray 1994). With increasingly heavy doses of ever more toxic chemicals, cotton farmers were able to gain at least short-term control over cotton pests and reap the quick fortunes for which the Central American cotton boom was famous.

The cost of chemical-intensive cotton farming in human lives was high. An early indication of the problems ahead came with the introduction of one of the new products developed during and just after World War II. In February 1951 the German pesticide manufacturer Bayer tested its first commercial run of the organophosphate methyl parathion against the boll weevil in Nicaragua (Swezey et al. 1986). The tests were successful, and over 1.2 million pounds of methyl parathion dust were applied to forty-three thousand manzanas of Nicaraguan cotton the following year.

While the pest control efforts were impressive, the impact on farm workers was tragic. Workers accustomed to handling organochlorine pesticides like DDT were used to getting the pesticide powder on their skin and clothes, with little or no noticable effects to their health. DDT in particular has a very low acute toxicity. But the new organophosphate was hundreds of times more toxic than DDT. A very small amount of methyl parathion, if left on the skin for a few hours, is sufficient to cause serious pesticide poisoning. As a result of the introduction of the new chemical, hundreds of field-workers were poisoned and several dozen died during the 1952/53 season. The new chemical was banned by the Nicaraguan Ministry of Agriculture in 1953, but powerful cotton growers forced the lifting of the ban before the following season. Millions of pounds of methyl parathion, and a number of other chemicals of comparable toxicity, have been applied annually ever since, not only in Nicaragua but throughout Central America.

The full health impact of pesticide use during the cotton era throughout Central America has never been precisely documented. But increasingly reliable estimates have shown that the human health costs of pesticide use in the cotton era were severe.[2] One early report documented 19,330 poisonings in Guatemala, Costa Rica, Honduras, and Nicaragua from 1971 to 1976 (Mendes 1977). The vast majority of these cases were among cotton farmers and farm workers, although researchers acknowledged that these cases were likely only a fraction of the total pesticide-related illnesses in the region. More-recent studies have shown that pesticide poisoning was the leading cause of work-related illness in the Central American cotton sector, and in some agricultural regions rivalled the incidence of malaria (Cole et al. 1988; Keifer and Pacheco 1991; McConnell 1988).

The most reliable contemporary estimate of pesticide-related illness rates in Central America was conducted in León, Nicaragua, in 1989. Medical researchers, relying on a self-reporting survey technique,[3] cross-referenced with a well-maintained public health service illness registry, estimated that between 4,777 and 10,343 pesticide poisonings occurred annually in the department, among a rural population of about 300,000 (Keifer and Pacheco 1991). Government health records documented only 23 percent of the total estimated cases, even though the pesticide illness registry in the department was considered one of the best in the developing world (Cole et al. 1988; McConnell 1988). Based on the revised estimates, researchers calculated that one in eight people working with pesticides in León was poisoned annually, or 13.2 percent of all farmers and farm laborers who used or were exposed to pesticides (Keifer and Pacheco 1991).

As noted in Chapter 5, cotton production declined throughout the 1980s. With the decline of cotton, and the effects of the regional economic crisis, pesticide use declined as well in all countries of the region but Costa Rica. But as the cottonization of other sectors of Central American agriculture took place, pesticide-related illness problems reemerged among farmers increasingly relying on agrochemical technology.

The illness data from the León study were generated even though there had been a major shift away from cotton occurring throughout the region. The pattern of pesticide poisoning continued. Nicaraguan cotton production had declined to only forty thousand hectares by 1989, almost all of it in the department of León (FAO 1990). Corn production in León, meanwhile, expanded during the same period, with 125,160 hectares planted by 1988 (Appel et al. 1991). The shift in crops was reflected in the survey of pesticide poisonings, with 51 percent occurring in corn, and only 12 percent occurring in cotton (see Figure 6.1).

Farmers generally use a far smaller amount of pesticides on corn than cotton. The overall illness rates from León in 1989 were, for that reason, probably much lower than during the era when cotton was the predominant crop. Nevertheless, the rates seen in León indicated that health problems associated with pesticides were not limited to the historical pattern of chemical-intensive farming in cotton. Dependence on the technology, and the health problems it generated, had shifted to other crops as Central America sought to diversify its agricultural sector.

Figure 6.1   Pesticide Poisonings by Crop, León, Nicaragua, 1989

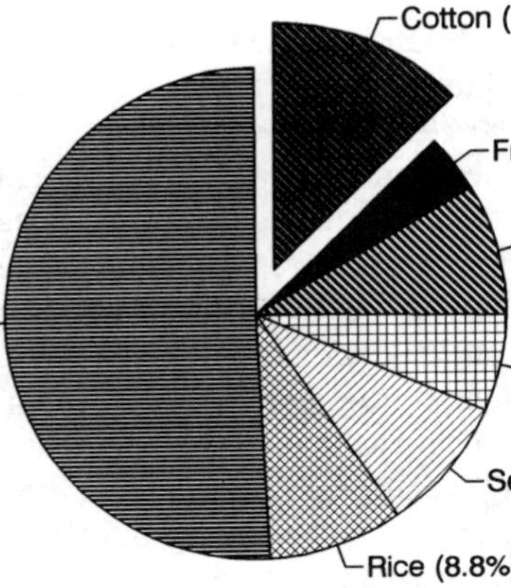

Source: Keifer and Pacheco (1991).

▼   **Acute Pesticide Illness Problems with NTAEs**

In the Nicaraguan data there was a nearly total absence of pesticide poisonings attributed to nontraditional crops. This was largely due to the economic embargo imposed by the United States against the Sandinista government during the 1980s, which meant that the U.S. market was not accessible for Nicaraguan NTAEs. In addition, no U.S. development assistance for nontraditional agriculture was provided to Nicaragua during the 1980s, as it was to neighboring countries. Consequently Nicaragua's agricultural development tended to concentrate in more-traditional export crops.

But in those Central American countries where nontraditional agriculture was heavily promoted by U.S. development agencies, pesticide-related illnesses soon became a serious problem. One of the first investigations into the pesticide problems in nontraditional agriculture was conducted for USAID in the Guatemalan highlands where the production of snow peas and broccoli had become particularly intense. Researchers found that 29 percent of the small farmers interviewed reported at least one instance of acute pesticide poisoning (CICP 1988:50). A second study found even higher rates among nontraditional export farmers in four different Guatemalan crops (melon, broccoli, snow peas, and strawberries), with 50 percent of the producers reporting an acute pesticide-poisoning episode (Hoppin 1989).

The most recent study, part of the survey of small-scale melon farmers throughout the region undertaken as part of the University of Texas Regional Project on NTAEs, suggests the problem has become even more serious than the previous investigations had indicated. Nontraditional farmers were asked if they had been poisoned while using pesticides in the previous two years. The data in Table 6.1 show that farmers in El Salvador reported a low of (only!) 28.4 percent having been poisoned. The highest proportion was encountered in Guatemala, where fully 57.8 percent volunteered that they had been poisoned by pesticides.

Table 6.1   NTAE Farmers Reporting Pesticide Poisoning During the Last Two Years Before 1991 Survey

	Percentage Reporting Poisoning	N
Guatemala	57.8	45
El Salvador	28.4	74
Honduras	28.9	45
Costa Rica	56.0	25

Source: University of Texas Regional Project on NTAEs.

These data suggest a disturbing comparison. Nicaragua had long been considered the worst-case scenario for pesticide-related health problems because of the historical predominance of cotton, discussed above.[4] But if one takes the estimated annual rate of poisoning of 13.2 percent of León's pesticide users, noted above, and if one doubles it to compare with the two-year poisoning rates reported in the regional survey (see Table 6.1), one would find that the poisoning rates reported by nontraditional farmers in Honduras and El Salvador are at roughly the same high level as in Nicaragua. But the pesticide poisoning rates in Costa Rica and Guatemala, where the development of nontraditional agriculture is considerably more advanced, are significantly higher than reported rates in Nicaragua. The pesticide-poisoning rates found among farmers producing nontraditional crops are at least comparable to those historically reported for the areas most afflicted with pesticide-related health problems.

▼ Chronic Health Problems Related to Pesticides

The long-term effects of pesticide exposure are not well understood. Research into potential chronic or permanent health effects of pesticides in human populations has demonstrated a number of serious problems, but to date such research has not led to a comprehensive understanding of the long-term hazards posed by the technology.

During the cotton era most of the concern over long-term problems focused on the potential cancer-causing capacity of organochlorine pesticides like DDT. By the late 1970s nineteen of the twenty-five most commonly used organochlorines had been found to cause cancer or other chronic effects in laboratory tests on animals, contributing to the eventual prohibition or severe restriction of the use of a number of organochlorine pesticides. Organochlorines were of particular concern because they were persistent in the environment and tended to accumulate at the higher levels of the food chain, most notably in humans. The pesticides were fat-soluble and thus concentrated in human adipose tissue, or fat cells.

Studies done in the 1970s on Central Americans living in and around cotton-growing zones found some of the highest levels of DDT and toxaphene (another organochlorine compound) ever measured in humans. A 1971 study of Guatemalan women found levels of DDT and its metabolites in human milk samples (high in fat content) of 12.2 parts per million (ppm), 250 times above the World Health Organization's (WHO's) maximum tolerance level (FAO 1990: annex 1:14). Similar levels of DDT were found in samples taken in El Salvador, and comparable levels of toxaphene were found in samples taken in Nicaragua. Samples taken from human body fat in 1980 found Nicaraguans had some of the highest DDT burdens in the world: 97 ppm, or eleven times the levels found in a cross-cultural and cross-socioeconomic strata survey done in south Florida (ICAITI 1977:129), and sixteen times the global average (Swezey et al. 1986). Yet in spite of laboratory research on test animals, there remained little conclusive evidence of the long-term health effects of organochlorines on exposed populations in Central America. So organochlorines continued to be applied heavily in cotton and elsewhere. El Salvador reportedly still used 3.5 million pounds of DDT in 1979 (FAO 1990: annex 1:14).

But the scientific uncertainty over DDT may have finally, although belatedly, begun to put an end to the use of this pesticide. A newly completed study of women in New York City found a fourfold increase in the risk of breast cancer among women with relatively high levels of DDE in their blood serum than among women with lower levels (Wolff et al. 1993). DDE is the metabolite produced by the breakdown of DDT in the human body. Breast cancer is one of the most frequent killers of women in the United States and an affliction that appears to have been on the rise in recent years. The authors of the study were led to conclude that "the implications are far reaching for public health intervention worldwide" (Wolfe 1993:648).

Indeed, the implications for Central American women may be of even greater significance. The fourfold increase in U.S. women occurred at 19.1 parts per billion (ppb) of DDE in blood serum, compared with "low levels" measured as less than 2.0 ppb. One study of DDE levels in the blood serum of Salvadoran women found average levels of 101 ppb, more than five times higher than the trigger level found in the U.S. study. Central American women are thus likely to be facing risks far greater than those causing great concern in the U.S. medical community.

The organochlorines were not commonly used in the newer nontraditional crops. Application of these persistent chemicals decreased considerably during the 1980s because they had become ineffective against chemically resistant pests, and because they remained as residues on harvested produce and could cause the FDA to reject nontraditional exports upon arrival in the United States. Yet even with the disappearance of the organochlorines from the nontraditional export sector, the chronic health hazards remained. A number of the new chemicals that were heavily used in nontraditional crops have been found to be the source of similar long-term hazards. Sixteen pesticides identified in a study of Guatemalan nontraditional farming were associated with cancer, birth defects, organ malfunctions, and other chronic disorders (Hoppin 1991:179–183). But again, there remained little or no conclusive evidence of actual long-term or permanent health effects among nontraditional farmers or farm workers.

Table 6.2, however, presents new findings from our regional survey of farmers producing nontraditional crops. When analyzed with the results of recently reported medical research showing permanent neurological damage among Central Americans poisoned by pesticides (McConnell et al. 1994; Rosenstock et al. 1991), our data suggest that long-term health problems may indeed be developing among nontraditional export producers in the region. The most commonly reported sources of acute pesticide poisoning among nontraditional farmers were the organophosphate methamidophos and the carbamates methomyl and carbofuran. This survey corroborated an earlier USAID-funded survey that found methamidophos and methomyl to be the two most frequently reported sources of pesticide poisoning among small farmers in the Guatemalan highlands (CICP 1988:49).

Researchers from the University of Washington and Mount Sinai

Table 6.2   Most Frequently Reported Sources of Pesticide-Related Illness Among Central American NTAE Producers, 1991

	Percentage Methomyl	Percentage Methamidophos	Percentage Carbofuran	N
El Salvador	37.1	37.1	2.9	45
Honduras	23.8	28.6	43.0	42
Costa Rica	50.0	23.1	0.0	26

Source: University of Texas Regional Project on NTAEs.

Medical Center in New York, in collaboration with Nicaraguan researchers, conducted a series of tests on Nicaraguan farm workers who had experienced a single episode of organophosphate poisoning, and found the poisoning victims had a significant and apparently permanent decrease in neuropsychological performance in comparison with farm workers who had not been poisoned (Rosenstock et al. 1991). Thirty-six workers who had been treated for pesticide poisoning from nine months to three years prior to the study were matched by age and sex with a community control group that had not been poisoned, and given a battery of tests to measure neuropyschological functions. The poisoned workers had statistically significant lower scores on five out of six tests developed by WHO, and on three out of six additional tests. The poisoning victims scored significantly lower on tests for verbal and visual attention, visual memory, visuomotor speed, sequencing and problem solving, and motor steadiness and dexterity. These data imply that the many nontraditional export farmers and farm workers who have been poisoned with organophosphate pesticides may be suffering permanent brain damage as a result of a single poisoning incident.

A second study by the same researchers produced further cause for concern. Workers previously poisoned with the pesticide methamidophos were found to have higher vibrotactile sensory thresholds, meaning their ability to detect sensations in their hands and feet was significantly weaker than the control group's (McConnell et al. 1994). The researchers concluded that the methamidophos poisoning victims had sustained damage to their peripheral nervous systems independent of the previously discovered effects of organophosphates on the brain.

The high incidence of acute pesticide poisoning discussed earlier, and particularly the role of methamidophos as a leading cause of acute pesticide poisoning among nontraditional farmers and farm workers, becomes even more alarming in this context. Indeed, the combination of the acute and permanent health problems documented by recent investigations suggests that pesticide poisoning may be one of the most serious public health problems confronting the rural agricultural labor force.

▼ **Responses to Pesticide-Related Health Hazards**

The reemergence of pesticide-related health problems in the nontraditional sector has not gone unnoticed by development planners and practitioners. USAID and the pesticide industry have recently initiated a series of independent and collaborative efforts to address at least some dimensions of the pesticide problems. USAID has initiated a multifaceted three-year, $4 million project called the Pesticide Management Activity (PMA) (DANIDA

1992). The project involves five components, focusing largely on training and education in the safe use and hazards of pesticides.

Most of the PMA involves the training and education of technicians, farmers, farm workers, rural community members, and physicians (through a correspondence course) in the proper use of pesticides and the recognition and treatment of pesticide illnesses. USAID has chosen the nontraditional export sector as the primary focus of these training efforts because, according to a USAID representative, this sector is the most viable avenue for diffusion of the pesticide safety message to small farmers and the rural populace.

In June 1991 the Central American pesticide industry organization, FECCOPIA, initiated a three-year project in Guatemala designed to raise user and public awareness of the safe and proper use of pesticides (DANIDA 1992). The international chemical industry organization, the Groupement International des Associations Nationales de Fabricants de Produits Agrochemiques (GIFAP), provided more than $1 million to FECCOPIA to finance the project as one of three industry pilot projects in the Third World. The other two pilot project countries are Kenya and Thailand.

The pesticide industry project also focuses on training and education measures, combined with the distribution of personal protective equipment and the creation of a toxic waste management facility. Educational materials and courses are being developed for use in primary schools, rural secondary, vocational, and agricultural schools, as well as in the agricultural departments of Guatemalan universities. Agricultural technicians and officials will also be trained under the pesticide industry project.

FECCOPIA has also developed educational materials such as posters and teaching materials for the USAID PMA project. Once the chemical industry pilot project has been tested in Guatemala, GIFAP plans to expand its efforts into eight Central and South American and Caribbean nations. GIFAP will provide an additional $400,000, and hopes to obtain additional funding for the project from USAID.

In spite of the impressive amount of activity and new funding going into the resolution of pesticide problems in the region, there remain serious problems and limitations in the overall response. We will now explore the inadequacies of each of the basic responses to the pesticide problems in Central American nontraditional agriculture.

The Increased Control of Access

As the discussion of the transformation of Guatemala's nontraditional export sector in the previous chapters demonstrates, exporters have begun to take much more direct control over nontraditional export production, in part to gain greater control of producers' selection and use of pesticides. Nontraditional producers appear to be increasingly relying on exporters or cooperatives to provide pesticides, often as stipulated in preplanting contracts. This is a marked shift from the earlier era when pesticides were generally obtained from pesticide salesmen and local pesticide distributors (de Campos 1987; Contreras 1990; ICAITI 1977).

But the reports on pesticide-related illness coming from recent surveys in the region suggest that the problems with pesticide residues and the problems with pesticide poisonings are running in opposite directions as high rates of pesticide poisoning continue to plague the nontraditional sector. One possible explanation for the lack of impact on health problems is that export controls have focused on the potential economic costs of pesticide use, which are internalized by the companies as a result of produce rejections, increased pesticide input costs, increasing losses to pesticide-resistant pests, and so on. Health hazards and illnesses are largely externalities to the company's business ledger, insofar as the victims bear the burden of the cost and suffering from the illnesses and as long as there are sufficient workers and producers to replace the poisoning victims. Thus health hazards may receive less careful attention in both the selection of pesticides and in the training and technical assistance dedicated to their use.

For example, the concern over residue problems in Mexican nontraditionals was considered the driving force in a drastic increase in pesticide poisonings as exporters shifted away from more-residual but less-toxic organochlorines like DDT and chlordane in the late 1970s and early 1980s, and began using less-residual but far more toxic organophosphates like methamidophos and parathion (Wright 1986). Notably absent from the Mexican export industry's concern over pesticide residues was a commensurate increase in attention to the health problems afflicting farmers and farm workers as they shifted to more-toxic pesticides. The apparent improvements in residue-based problems[5] and the failure to curb pesticide poisonings in Central American nontraditionals suggest a similar pattern may be developing.

Increased Technical Assistance and Supervision

The provision of technical assistance and training appears to be following a similar pattern. Increased technical assistance to Guatemalan nontraditional farmers (measured in number of visits by a technician) resulted in a decrease in the number of illegal or unregistered pesticides producers reportedly used (Hoppin 1989:30–31). Yet, in striking contrast, a higher percentage (66%) of producers who received no technical assistance reported using personal hygiene measures to protect themselves from pesticide exposure, than growers who received technical assistance (58%). In addition, snow pea producers in the Guatemalan highlands who received more-frequent technical assistance were more likely to store pesticides in their homes (85%), thereby exposing themselves and their families to greater risks than snow pea producers with less technical assistance (51%), leading one investigator to conclude that "agronomists that provide frequent technical assistance are not effectively addressing health problems associated with pesticides" (Hoppin 1989:50). Again, it appears that the needs of exporters and producers to maximize production have taken priority over, and at times have conflicted with, protecting the health of pesticide users and the rural populace.

Training and Education

The safe-use projects of USAID and the pesticide industry will undoubtedly have some positive impact on regional pesticide problems. The historical absence of pesticide user training and public education has contributed to the continued lack of awareness of pesticide hazards. But the heavy emphasis on training and education in the multimillion dollar efforts now under way are likely to have a relatively limited impact on the rate of pesticide poisoning and the more general unsafe conditions related to pesticide use in Central America. Consider the case of the poisoning of the young women working in Choluteca's melon fields, described at the beginning of this chapter. The most basic pesticide safety training instructions would have addressed the main causes of this poisoning incident. Ignoring for the moment the obviously inappropriate application technique employed throughout the region, the workers would have been instructed to use personal protective equipment, in this case rubber gloves and boots, which would have avoided the primary source of dermal contact. Instructions would necessarily have also included the need to wash one's hands before eating lunch, further reducing the likelihood of ingestion of pesticide residues.

But the reality of agricultural labor in Central America, and much of the rest of the Third World, belies the simplicity of these solutions. According to the government investigator of the Choluteca incident, the workers were not provided rubber gloves or other safety equipment, let alone required by their supervisor to use such equipment (Murray 1991). Furthermore, there is rarely enough water in the fields for hand washing, and the likelihood of finding soap in these settings is remote indeed.[6] Finally, according to local agricultural technicians, these workers were normally provided only twenty minutes for their lunch break before they returned to applying pesticides, hardly enough time to find a place to wash one's hands, eat, and then return to work.

The effects of training on pesticide hazards are mediated by the social relations in the workplace and the general lack of commitment by employers to improving worker protection. In the developing world, and certainly in the Central American nontraditional sector, worker health and safety have not been a central component of industry or government pesticide reforms.[7]

Use of Personal Protective Measures

Much of the training of pesticide users focuses on the proper procedures for selecting, mixing, and applying pesticides, along with the appropriate personal protective measures, hygiene practices, and so forth, The assumption is that, once trained, workers will take greater precautions, such as relying on personal protective equipment and hygiene practices to reduce pesticide hazards.

There is ample evidence that, for a variety of reasons, pesticide users frequently ignore safe-use practices. In one USAID-funded study participants in a Guatemalan workshop were surveyed about their use of personal protective equipment (CICP 1988:53). Only one out of twenty-six farmers reported using more than boots and a hat as protective equipment when applying pesticides. Another survey of Guatemalan nontraditional export farmers found that 89 percent of the respondents did not use gloves when applying pesticides, 87 percent did not use glasses, and 42 percent relied on a handkerchief over their face for respiratory protection when spraying chemicals (Hoppin 1989:39). Our regional survey found the use of personal protective equipment varied across the countries in the region but was consistently low for virtually all safety measures (see Table 6.3).

Table 6.3   Reported Use of Personal Protective Equipment by 192 NTAE Producers in Central America, 1991

	No	Yes	No Response
Gloves	64.1%	19.8%	16.2%
Boots	62.0%	22.4%	15.6%
Overalls	72.4%	7.3%	20.3%
Longsleeved shirt	64.1%	20.8%	15.1%
Hat	60.4%	19.8%	19.8%
Respirator	55.2%	18.8%	18.8%

Source: Regional farmer survey conducted for this study.

Where training in the use of safety measures has been carried out, it appears that personal protection has improved, although the degree of change leaves serious questions as to the ultimate impact such training will have on the actual reduction of pesticide hazards and pesticide problems. The following excerpt from one study in the Guatemalan highlands is enlightening (CICP 1988).

Those who stated that they had received a full and careful explanation from the pesticide vendors consistently reported taking more precautions in applying pesticide. In some cases, the difference between those who had received a good explanation and those who had not is significant. The following percentages of respondents reporting on use of various equipment items came from the good-explanation group: overalls when spraying, 55.1 percent, masks, 59.5 percent, gloves, 63.2 percent and 66.7 percent always used eyeglasses [p. 59].

Of those who stated that they always took a bath after pesticide use, 51.3 percent came from the well-informed group. Of those who said they changed their clothes after spraying, 50.0 percent came from this group, while 46.8 percent of those who stated they washed their faces after pesticide application also came from the group that had received the more complete explanation of the dangers of incorrect pesticide use. . . . Careful instructions . . . may play an important role in improving the safety precautions used by farmers [p. 60].

While indeed there may have been improvements in personal protection, with only 46 to 66 percent adopting safety precautions after careful instructions one must question what it will take to assure the safety of the large minority, and in some instances the majority, of trained workers who continue to use pesticides in hazardous ways.

Integrated Pest Management

Ultimately, the most effective means of significantly reducing pesticide illnesses in nontraditional agriculture, as well as many of the other pesticide-related problems we have documented, is to drastically reduce the use of pesticide technology, particularly the many pesticides that pose serious acute or long-term risks. Integrated pest management (IPM) is an alternative pest control strategy that seeks to reduce or eliminate pesticide use through reliance on changes in farming practices, combined with biological control agents and other alternative technologies. The shift to IPM strategies appears to be the only viable avenue for a major improvement in the course of this problem. For example, where IPM has been introduced in Nicaraguan corn cooperatives, the consequent decrease in pesticide use has been shown to significantly reduce indicators of pesticide poisoning (Keifer 1991). But in spite of the claims to the contrary, IPM has not yet become a major part of the response to pesticide problems in nontraditional agriculture. USAID's resource commitment to IPM continues to lag far behind the agency's commitment to promoting high-technology farming systems that by default, if not intent, depend on pesticides.

As noted in the previous chapter, USAID was instrumental in the development of a new IPM project in Choluteca's melon sector, although only after the disastrous explosion of pesticide-driven pest problems in the 1989 harvest. USAID has also helped expand the IPM activities at the

Panamerican Agriculture School in Zamorano, Honduras. But the scope of these efforts remains limited. The number of qualified IPM technicians in the region does not begin to approach the regional needs in either the non-traditional sector or the more traditional crops. As the director of the Zamorano school recently observed, "there are probably not more than a hundred qualified IPM technicians in the region, which falls far short of the regional needs" (personal communication, Keith Andrews, May 30, 1991).

The new USAID PMA project claims to include IPM activities along with the array of activities focused on the safe use of pesticides. Yet IPM is the focus of only one and a half days of the five-day agricultural techni-cian–training component of the PMA, which one international pest control specialist, after attending the course, deemed to be "woefully inadequate for the task at hand" (personal communication, anonymous). In addition, USAID intends to use Peace Corps volunteers to promote both IPM and safe-use strategies among nontraditional farmers in Central America. While this component of the PMA was not yet under way and could not be evalu-ated, it remains doubtful it will significantly fill the void of broad-scale IPM efforts that exists in the region. It appears, however, to be a step in the right direction (if somewhat overdue).

Further complicating the development of IPM is USAID's recent deci-sion to cut the funding for CATIE's IPM extension program. CATIE has been the leading source of IPM research and development in the region, but reportedly fell into disfavor with USAID, in part because CATIE personnel resisted USAID's demands that the IPM program shift its limited resources, away from working with small farmers producing basic grains and local market crops, to IPM development for nontraditional export farming (per-sonal communication, anonymous).

▼ Conclusion

The scope of the pesticide-related health problems in the nontraditional export sector of Central America is cause for serious concern. The incidence of acute pesticide illness remains high. The scope of the long-term problems associated with pesticide exposure is less well documented. But the increas-ing evidence of long-term hazards linked to many of the most frequently used chemicals in the nontraditional sector is sufficient to further heighten concern over pesticide-related health hazards faced by producers, laborers, and the rural population.

Responses to health problems have not been equal to the efforts to resolve problems that pose more-direct economic threats to dominant inter-ests in the nontraditional sector. While residue problems decrease,[8] illness rates and the use of chemicals posing potential long-term health risks continue unabated. Training and protective measures, while offering some degree of improved protection, have not shown the capacity to achieve a major reduction of health hazards posed by the technology.

The focus on the safe use of pesticides in the current USAID and chemical industry projects, while a laudable improvement over past neglect, really achieves only minor adjustments in the use of the technology without significantly altering the overall role of pesticides in the development strategy. It appears that the resolution of the pesticide problem has been subordinated to the continued promotion of nontraditional agriculture. If the needs of Central Americans were placed at the forefront of regional development strategies, it is likely these two priorities would be reversed.

▼ **Notes**

1. This account is a reconstruction of the description given in an interview with the government inspector who investigated the incident (see Murray 1991).

2. Estimates of pesticide-related acute illnesses have notoriously understated the scope of the problem in the Third World (Levine 1985). In 1973 the World Health Organization estimated an annual rate of 500,000 poisonings worldwide (WHO 1973). By 1989 WHO had revised this estimate to 2 to 3 million per year, with the vast majority occurring in the developing world (WHO 1989). While increasing pesticide use was believed to account for part of the difference between the two estimates, WHO acknowledged that both estimates remained very conservative and suffered from a lack of adequate data. A more sophisticated recent attempt to estimate illness rates set the annual global rate at 25 million (Jeyaratnam 1990).

3. Keifer and Pacheco (1991) evaluated the reliability of the self-reporting technique by checking such reports against illness registries. Self-reporting was determined to be over 85 percent reliable.

4. This was continued in anti-Sandinista rhetoric and sentiment in recent years. A USAID consultant, for example, objected to the inclusion of pesticide-related illness rates from Nicaragua in a Central American comparison, during a conference in Guatemala City in July 1991 focused on current pesticide problems in nontraditional agriculture. The consultant argued that Nicaraguan farmers and farm workers had not benefited from the training, education, and technological advances that had occurred in the rest of the region because Nicaragua had been isolated during the 1980s. That was the reason Nicaragua's pesticide problems might be expected to be worse than those of its neighbors. Similarly, a representative of the North American Chemical Association suggested to one of the authors that Nicaragua's pesticide problems were more indicative of the problems one would expect to find in a Communist country, where the regime cared less for the health and safety of the population.

5. See Thrupp et al. (1995: appendix 3) for the most recent data on FDA residue rejections, which show a decline in the number of rejections in most of Latin America, with the exception of Guatemala.

6. Of course, washing and sanitary facilities are still not available in many agricultural settings in the United States, in spite of decades of organizing and protest on the part of farm labor organizations.

7. It is again useful to note that worker health and safety in the United States

encountered similar problems. Training was of little use where workers had no power to act on or implement the measures they learned through training. The key to improving worker safety in the United States was the development of union representation and government regulation, combined with training in measures that could be implemented through the exercising of workers' rights (Berman 1978).

8. It is unclear which factors best explain the decline in residue-related FDA detentions in the last several years. In the case of the Dominican Republic, it appears to be a result of the disappearance of various nontraditional exports. In other countries where the nontraditional export profile has not changed significantly, the decline may be the result of better control of pesticide use, in-country residue sampling, or other measures. In the case of Guatemala, where USAID and pesticide industry efforts have been greatest, residue-based problems continued to soar through the first half of 1994.

7

SEEKING NEW DIRECTIONS:
THE SEARCH FOR ALTERNATIVES

> But gentlemen, if the prices of most of Central America's traditional
> exports are unstable and declining, if there is unlikely to be any interna-
> tional assistance for redevelopment of basic grains production, and nontra-
> ditional agricultural exports are impoverishing our small farmers . . . what
> alternatives does Central America have?
> —*Question asked at an August 1991*
> *Guatemala workshop on nontraditionals*

Simple criticism of a strategy that has had some apparent success in some
countries, for some producers, under some conditions, and at some times
is not a sufficient response to the problems that face Central Americans
today. In this concluding chapter we explore two classes of alternatives to
the region's contemporary NTAE strategy: (1) alternative ways in which
present production could be improved in order to lessen the negative consequences demonstrated by the research on this project; and (2) alternatives to
NTAEs as a basis for responding to the needs of Central America's poor
rural majority. This exploration of alternatives leads directly to recommendations for policies that could be implemented in the region by local governments as well as local and international nongovernmental organizations
to respond more effectively to the region's quest for an alternative, more
sustainable development future that is ecologically more appropriate,
socially more equitable, politically more feasible, and economically more
efficient.

The research project that led to this book did not pretend to provide
detailed exploration of a full range of alternatives to NTAEs. It was, rather,
an attempt to gather information from across Central America to draw attention to the crisis-generating potential of NTAEs as a new development strategy, particularly in the way in which it was being implemented by USAID.
The suggestions for alternative policies in this chapter should be taken as
recommendations for areas to explore, not as fully developed policies that
are ready for adoption or implementation.

There are many potential improvements in the ways NTAE products could be produced in Central America. If one seeks to respond to the inequities and inefficiencies discussed in the chapters above, one needs to find ways to lessen both the cost and the danger of producing these products, one needs to counter the biases against small producers, and one needs to find ways of increasing the proportion of the final value-added that reaches the farmer. The alternatives discussed here range from fully organic production of present crops to a wide range of alternative agricultural production techniques that could permit greater profitability for small farmers. These approaches, however, must also be viewed in terms that extend well beyond the profitability of individual farms; they touch on areas of greater long-term sustainability for Central American agriculture in general.

▼ Organic Production Techniques

The naysayers have been more common than the advocates when it comes to Central American production of organic products for export. USAID's regionwide PROEXAG program led the critics and provided great support for continued production based on imported chemicals. When Polly Hoppin suggested in 1989 that movement toward organic production might help improve Guatemalan NTAE production, John Lamb, PROEXAG team leader, wrote to her that "it remains the consensus of our team that organically-grown produce is now and will remain for the foreseeable future a niche market, not one that Central American growers should focus all or even most of their efforts toward" (Hoppin 1989; letter of August 28, 1989). This was an opinion that he later repeated in public at meetings organized by our project.

The debate over organic production in Central America covers several distinct issues. Are the markets for organic produce, in the United States and elsewhere, large enough to absorb a significant increase in Central American production? Is the state of organic production technology such that organic producers can, in fact, enjoy profits? And is it conceivable that Central American production, especially among small-scale farmers, could be organized to meet international organic standards?

Organic agricultural production and processing is generally defined to mean production that involves no use of man-made chemicals at any stage. Use of organic techniques could imply both significant theoretical advantages for Central American producers and potential theoretical disadvantages. The potential advantages include the following:

• Organic production is more labor-intensive than conventional production, for it requires much more labor in mulching and weeding (as an alternative to herbicides), in the application of manure instead of chemical fertilizers, and in the use of botanical pesticides and beneficial insects. This gives a potential advantage to poorer farmers, who have family available to them but little capital.

• Organic production economizes on the use of imported agricultural chemicals and chemical application equipment, reducing the component of production costs that has risen most rapidly in the region in recent years.

• There is strong evidence that the niche markets to which Lamb referred are, in fact, the fastest growing components of fresh food markets in most of the industrialized countries.

• There are large, and apparently sustainable, price premia available in principal markets for organically produced fresh foods. Wholesale prices of organic produce in the Los Angeles market area averaged more than 50 percent higher than conventional produce, in one USDA survey; they varied from less than 10 percent higher for easily grown red-leaf lettuce and radishes to more than 100 percent higher for carrots, cauliflower, and some squashes, and nearly 200 percent for eggplant and zucchini (Morgan et al. 1990).

• Other aspects of organic production may favor small-scale farmers, for it requires the kinds of detailed crop management (frequent rotation, diversified on-farm production, close attention) that are difficult to provide on a commercial plantation scale.

The Boom in Organic Production and Sales

The growth in the number of strictly organic farms in the United States has been very rapid. The total number of certified organic producers in the United States grew from an estimated 273 growers in 1982 to nine hundred in 1987, an estimated four to five thousand growers in 1990/91 and twelve thousand in 1995 (Cook 1990; PANUPS 1995). The demand for organic products still outpaces production. "We simply can't get enough organic produce," notes Margaret Wittenberg of Whole Foods Markets, Inc., the largest U.S. organic foods retailer (see Box 7.1). Estimated retail sales of organically produced foods in the United States increased five-fold between 1980 and 1988, from $174 million to $812 million; by 1992 they had nearly doubled again (see Table 7.1 and Figure 7.1). Current estimates put sales at about $2 billion in 1994, an increase of 22 percent over the previous year (PANUPS 1995). EarthTrade reports that growth rates in the United States from 1980 to 1990 totaled 600 percent, growing over 20 percent per year over the past five years (Clarke 1995), which must be seen in the context of overall stagnation and crisis in agriculture. The Organic Farming Research Foundation estimates that organics will surge from 1 percent of the total agricultural economy to 5 percent by the year 2000 (PANUPS 1995).

Box 7.1   Whole Foods Market, Inc.: Riding the Organic Foods Wave

When the *New York Times* focused on "Health-Food Super-markets" in a January 1992 feature article, it noted that the national leaders in the concept included the Whole Foods Market chain based in Texas, Mrs. Gooch's Natural Foods in California, and Bread and Circus Wholefoods Supermarkets in the Northeast. "These gleaming new supermarkets," it noted, "bear as much resemblance to the grungy, 1960's fern-bedecked natural food co-op, with its shriveled produce and flour stored in trash bins, as McDonald's does to Lutéce." They represent, it suggested, "an important milestone in the maturing of an industry" (*NYT,* January 8, 1992: C-1).

By the end of 1992, Whole Foods Market, Inc. had acquired both Bread and Circus and Mrs. Gooch's, converting the parent firm into the largest chain of natural foods supermarkets in the United States, with thirty stores and an estimated 1993 total sales of $300 million. When the firm issued its first public offering of stock, shortly after the *Times* article appeared, the price of shares jumped 60 percent in the first hour, and finished the first day of trading at more than 50 percent above the initial price.

This firm has developed a consistent in-store philosophy for the sale of organic produce. All produce is labeled by state or country of origin and production technology. Wherever possible, organic produce is offered. "But we can't get enough," according to Margaret Wittenberg, a Whole Foods spokesperson, in an August 1993 interview. "We constantly look for additional suppliers. Consumers are asking for organics, and we are doing everything we can to work with organic farmers across the country to increase our offering of organically grown foods." According to Wittenberg, during peak seasons as much as 80 percent of the fresh fruits and vegetables sold in some Whole Foods stores is organically grown. The stores require adherence to a strict code of organic production. As a condition for receiving their organically grown label, food must be certified by credible third parties (generally state agencies or known organic producer associations) to come from land totally free of synthetic compounds for at least three years and to be free of inorganic compounds from seed through postharvest processing.

Whole Foods has also been a significant national voice in major campaigns and coalitions supporting environmental responsibility, protection of endangered species, and the promotion of organic foods consumption. Its wholly owned subsidiary, Texas Healthfood Distributors, is now one of the largest wholesalers of organic produce in the nation, distributing to a wide range of smaller natural foods stores as well as the rapidly increasing demand for organic produce at conventional supermarkets.

Table 7.1   U.S. Retail Sales of Organic Food and Beverage Products (millions of dollars)

	Fresh Produce	Processed Foods and Beverages	Other (Bulk and Deli)	Total Sales
1988	200	431	180	812
1989	250	500	188	938
1990	280	585	200	1,065
1991	308	691	219	1,218
1992	330	842	228	1,400

Source: Organic Times (1993).

The expanding demand is based not simply on the demand for organic fresh produce in stores that are willing to stock it, but rather upon the proliferation of a rapidly expanding line of processed organic products. The number of new products introduced by organic food processors increased from ninety-eight in 1988 to 510 in 1992 *(New Product News)*. In 1991 and 1992 new organic products averaged 20 percent of all new food products introduced in the United States (MIS, Inc. 1993). The leading U.S. food-processing newspaper has reported expectations that organic practices will be "mainstream" by the year 2000 (Burnett 1990). And one major consultant reported that as much as 50 percent of agriculture could be using "some aspect of organic growing" by that date.

National attention to the importance of organic foods was greatly heightened in June 1993 with the publication of a report by the U.S. National Academy of Sciences on the potential risks of pesticides in the diets of infants and children (National Research Council 1993). The report, commissioned by Congress in 1988, suggests that children may be uniquely sensitive to pesticide residues. It called for changes in chemical regulations to protect infants and children and a change in the EPA's decisionmaking

Figure 7.1   U.S. Sales of Organic Foods (millions of dollars)

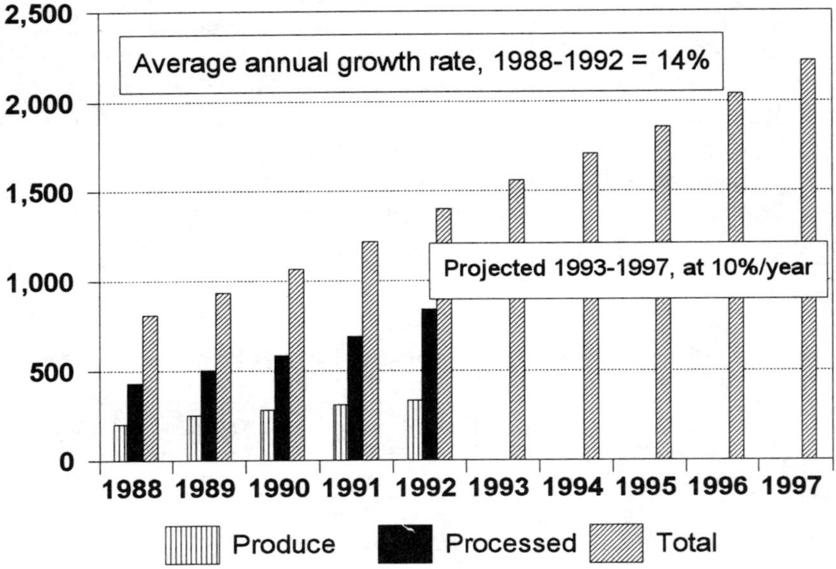

Average annual growth rate, 1988-1992 = 14%

Projected 1993-1997, at 10%/year

1988 1989 1990 1991 1992 1993 1994 1995 1996 1997

Produce   Processed   Total

Source: Organic Times (1993).

processes so that health considerations, rather than agricultural production, are foremost (*New York Times,* June 27, 1993).

The Clinton administration responded to the report by announcing "a major landmark in the history of food safety," creating a joint effort of the EPA, and USDA to reduce the use of chemicals in the production of the nation's food (*New York Times,* June 27, 1993). New U.S. federal legislation governing processed organic foods went into effect in October 1993 with the creation of the National Organic Standards Board.

Production Advantages of Organic Farming

Organic production has characteristically been associated with lower levels of productivity per hectare because of the simple comparison of production with fertilizers and production without. This issue is obviously linked to specific production technologies and to the costs of conventional agricultural chemicals. But farmers are increasingly focusing on the long-term costs of production with and without chemicals and the economic value of maintaining or sustaining the viability of land by avoiding the use of chemicals.

There have been few controlled studies of the full costs of production and profitability of organic production in Central America. But one study of coffee growing under completely alternative technologies, which compared organic with conventional chemical-intensive production, found that even though yields were often substantially lower in organic production, profits were usually higher when price premia for fully organic products were factored in (van Gillst 1994).

The attitude of organic farmers in the United States goes beyond healthier and higher-profit products. "Many growers new to organics try it to capture increasingly elusive market share," according to the Committee for Sustainable Agriculture (Burnett 1990). "But within six months those same growers are talking about the health of their soil, sold on the healthy land aspect of the system because it makes economic as well as ecological sense." For Central America this approach also illustrates the fact that the appeal of organics is not just the short-term direct return on investment. There is increasing recognition within the development community that we must maintain the resource base, or natural capital, if we are to sustain development. As we saw in Chapter 5, organic production of NTAEs offers tangibly improved prospects for ecological sustainability. Soil erosion declines and soil quality improves where chemical-intensive farming practices are abandoned in favor of organic production. In addition, we saw how chemical-intensive NTAEs have generated increasing pest problems in surrounding subsistence crops. These heightened pest problems have an economic as well as ecological cost. Small farmers respond to these problems with increasing pesticide use in corn and beans where such crops traditionally required little or no pest control. Increasing pest problems in surrounding crops make decreasing yields likely, which in turn is likely to further drive the shift to NTAEs because farmers are less able to meet the rising costs of land rent and debt payments.

The costs of the chemical-intensive paradigm are hidden in the ecological transformation it engenders. Not only does it generate higher input costs and potentially declining yields, but it also erodes the productive base upon which the rural poor depend. Organic agriculture offers not only direct economic alternatives for Central American farmers, but also offers an ecologically sustainable alternative that is essential to the region's long-term recovery and stability.

Is Organic Production and Certification Possible in Central America?

The disadvantages of organic production in Central America are not, however, insignificant. It has been difficult to create a credible certification program for organically produced fresh foods in the United States, and without credible certification the price premium rapidly disappears (Brumback 1990). There is little reason to believe that this will be any simpler in Central America, although significant areas have already been certified by foreign organizations at significant cost to local producers. Table 7.2 presents data on Central American acreage certified as organic by one such organization. In order to bring down certification costs, however, it will be necessary for national or regional certification to be set up.

Table 7.2   Estimated Acreage, 1994, of Organic Production in Central America Certified by the OCIA

	Costa Rica	Guatemala	Honduras	El Salvador
Coffee	1,488	3,072	n.a.	3,856
Cocoa bean	1,890	0	193	0
Blackberries	2,273	0	0	0
Cardamom	197	n.a.	0	0
Sesame	0	2,538	0	1,313
Cashews	86	0	0	886
Vanilla	42	0	0	0
Cinnamon	5	0	0	0
Pepper	5	0	22	0
Curcuma	0	0	0	12
Squash	0	0	0	1
Bananas	0	556	0	0
Papaya	0	0	3,487	0
Pineapple	0	0	248	0
Eggplant	0	0	1	0
Lemons	0	0	56	0
Oranges	0	0	32	0
Limes	0	0	56	0
Onions	0	0	1	0
Spinach	0	7	0	0
Lettuce	0	12	0	0
Carrots	0	5	0	0
Sugarcane	0	0	24	0
Ginger	0	0	3	0
Miscellaneous vegetables	0	15	0	0

Source: OCIA unpublished data.
Note: Nicaraguan data are not available.

The marketing of organically produced products is potentially more difficult than that of conventionally grown produce. Organic products are even more of a specialty item than conventionally grown fresh produce; organic markets remain less well organized; organic products are somewhat more perishable than conventional produce since fungicides cannot be used during shipping; and the risks of marketing failure may be greater. Discussion of these problems is left for the section below, where we consider alternative marketing arrangements.

What would it take, under Central American conditions, for production to expand rapidly using organic technology? Given the close links noted in earlier chapters between the technology used by small-scale producers and the technology packages provided by packers and exporters, is it conceivable that Central American farmers could introduce wholly new technology under the tightly controlled conditions needed for organic certification? In some cases this has begun to happen. The market for organic coffee from Central America and Mexico (which is, in fact, a nontraditional export) is booming, providing premium prices despite the glut of conventionally grown coffee in recent years. EarthTrade, a U.S.-based alternative trade company, has worked with the Organic Crop Improvement Association (OCIA), to certify organic soy beans, sesame, cashew nuts, and other nontraditional export items, with significant quantities now coming from Nicaragua and El Salvador (Clarke 1995). In 1995 they expect sales of over $3 million of organic products from Central America and Mexico (EarthTrade, personal communication).

The full range of opportunities for Central America remains to be explored. A shift toward other nonperishable organic NTAEs, such as spices, dried fruits, and herbs, would lessen the problems of perishability. And transportation technology for organics is improving continuously. Once again, the criterion cannot be simplified: organic production promises not only access to markets with price premia but also reduction in the risks of chemical poisoning for the farmers, their families, and their workers.

USAID has begun to take note. PROEXAG, in spite of its public rejection of Polly Hoppin's suggestion that Guatemalan farmers pursue greater organic production, has begun the development of a regionwide initiative on organics. Within four months of writing to Hoppin, PROEXAG proposed "Preliminary Steps Toward the Establishment of an Organic Certification Program and Organic Agriculture Research Program in Central America" (PROEXAG 1989).

▼ Other Alternative Production Technologies

Alternative agricultural practices are becoming a touchstone of modern agriculture worldwide. As awareness rises of the contamination of groundwater, the poisoning of workers, and the effects of residues from agricultural chemicals of all sorts, the development of alternatives becomes essential (Curtis et al. 1991). For Central America the rapid movement toward these alternatives promises to increase, rather than decrease, the region's comparative advantage for NTAEs. And the beneficial effects in terms of biasing production toward greater labor intensity, smaller-scale production, and safer farm worker environments give even greater urgency to these strategies. In fact, the increasing awareness of the problems of pesticide residues in fresh and processed foods, noted above, means that Central American produce will encounter greater disadvantages in export markets unless the use (and abuse) of agricultural chemicals is reduced dramatically.

IPM has been demonstrated to be a viable alternative to chemical-intensive agriculture (Andow and Rosset 1990). New techniques, procedures, tests, and studies of IPM efficacy are now abundant (Curtis et al. 1991). Yet IPM has not been widely adopted by producers of Central America's NTAEs. For the small farmers surveyed in our research, the explanation is simple: those who received any technical support received it solely from the packers and exporters who provided both the agricultural chemicals and the detailed schedules for applying them. Nonetheless, there is evidence that the historical bias toward chemical-intensive agriculture is beginning to weaken. As demonstrated in previous chapters, the change is often coming in desperate response to the crisis-generating effects of pesticides in NTAEs (see also Murray 1994).

Rosset (1992a) warned that, in order for IPM to have a chance with small producers of nontraditionals, certain criteria would have to be met. The crops selected for peasant production would have to be of local origin and nonperishable, have adequate marketing channels, and ideally provide the possibility of local artesan value-added processing or transformation (e.g., drying of fruit). He cautioned that IPM technology would have to be generated with farmer participation (see below), and should not emphasize the use of expensive substitute biological pesticides because of their prohibitive cost. Finally, he predicted that any efforts would fail if certain national and macroeconomic policies were not changed, including the reorientation of NTAE incentives and technical assistance toward small farmers, and the assurance of adequate prices for basic grains as a necessary buffer against the risks inherent in nontraditionals.

▼   "Farmer-First" Strategies

Farmers commonly fail to adopt new technologies because these practices are often inappropriate to their social, economic, and environmental milieu. This is a product of the top-down nature of conventional agricultural research, which excludes producers from most stages of generating new technology (Chambers 1990). Both conventional technologies and alternative ones like many IPM programs have fallen victim to this problem.

There is, however, an emerging new paradigm for the development of agricultural technology, called "Farmer-First," that is starting to catch on in Central America and that appears to hold great promise (Nelson 1994). Farmer-First approaches differ from conventional agricultural development strategies in that the latter are based upon top-down development of agricultural technology, primarily in the advanced industrial countries (and to a lesser extent in the laboratories they dominate in the Third World). Agricultural research priorities are established by research scientists, funded by national and international agencies, and then transferred by being taught to farmers wherever it is thought they might usefully be applied (Chambers 1990). When transfer fails to generate significant success, it is often assumed that the farmers are incapable of adopting it, for reasons of ignorance or culture or because their fundamental resources are insufficient.

Farmer-First approaches look for reasons farmers do not adopt technology, "not in the ignorance of the farmer but in deficiencies in the technology and the process that developed it" (Chambers 1990). Built from the farm back to the laboratory, Farmer-First development processes begin with farmers' group discussions and visits and proceed to a search for effective, locally adapted innovation with which others might experiment. This often leads to farmer-to-farmer innovator workshops, rather than lectures by extensionists trained by outsiders in techniques never before seen in a specific context. Traditional research can be grafted onto this process in the search for information and material to respond to farmer-generated questions. This then leads to an array of choices from which farmers can select, experiment, and adapt, rather than a laboratory-designed "ideal" response to categories of problems, with little or no adaptation to local conditions far from the lab (Altieri and Hecht 1990).

For Central America the Farmer-First approach calls for fundamentally new and different modes of research and extension. It offers the prospect of rediscovering successful historical practices, of distancing local production from technology heavily dependent upon imported seed and chemicals. In Honduras, for example, melon farmers have found that IPM techniques offer an escape from the escalating pest problems and consequent increasing pesticide costs and harvest losses that reached crisis proportions in 1989/90 (Murray 1991). USAID increased funding to the Panamerican Agriculture School in Zamorano, Honduras, in 1990 in order to provide greater assistance in IPM extension to the nontraditional export sector. Working with small farmers in Choluteca's largest cooperative, a Zamorano-based IPM specialist developed a series of demonstration plots to identify pest problems and test responses. The strategy employed in Choluteca moved away from the traditional, top-down technology transfer approach to IPM promotion, and instead drew heavily on small farmers' experience and participation. As the Zamorano specialist, Lorena Lastres, observed, "in this model of work we do not use the conventional experiment stations. Everything is carried out at the farm level"(quoted in Barletta and Rueda 1991).

If organic NTAEs are to be a viable option, then IPM must become a more widely researched, promoted, and adopted strategy in the region. In addition, IPM that draws heavily on traditional and cultural management techniques could counter the increasing economies of scale that have expelled growing numbers of small farmers from the NTAE sector. To the degree that these techniques are knowledge-based, and noncommodifiable, they provide greater insulation from the volatile and crisis-generating effects of imported technologies.

Two alternative successful examples of developing new production technology can be found in recent Guatemalan experience with NTAEs (see Boxes 7.2 and 7.3). In these cases sheer economic pressures, based on the low prices being paid by packers and the rising prices of imported chemicals, have encouraged indigenous communities to develop new strategies that are actually a return to ancient production techniques. In fact, there are an increasing number of examples of rediscovered (or newly appreciated) ancient agricultural practices that warrant reevaluation (Altieri and Hecht 1990). University of California scientists have recommended that farmers in the Andean mountains return to techniques used in pre-Columbian times. Archeologists found fields on the Bolivian side of Lake Titicaca that displayed tilling on raised beds with deep channels of water between them. Reconstruction of the practices demonstrated that this technique preserved vital nutrients and produced greater yields (*Rocky Mountain News,* July 12, 1993).

▼ Other Changes in NTAE Production

There are a variety of other policies that could improve the ability of NTAEs to raise the incomes of the rural poor. These policies should be directed at other principal characteristics of this industry that have led to impoverishment of those who seek to participate.

Government supervision of the contracting process could require that the final risks of price fluctuation and variation in harvest quantity and quality be carried more equally by producer and packer/exporter. It would not be difficult to develop model contracts for producers that do more than protect the investment of the packer/exporter with respect to seed, technical assistance, and agricultural chemicals provided to the producer. Protection for the producer should include: guaranteed minimum payments on the basis of areas sown, mid-season field conditions, or total quantity harvested; formal, government-supervised grievance procedures for recourse at the time of harvest if the packer/exporter alleges excess pesticide residues or inferior cosmetic quality; and procedures that free the producer to sell his or her product to alternative buyers after settling debts to the contracting firm if there is price competition at the moment of harvest.

The producers who have historically been most successful in the region are those who have negotiated collectively with packers and exporters,

Box 7.2   Rediscovering the Wisdom of the Old Ways

The community called Hacienda Vieja, near Santa Apolonia in Chimaltenango, Guatemala, has developed (or rediscovered) labor-intensive soil conservation practices that combine with non-traditional agriculture to give them an advantage in marketing from rain-fed production areas. The origin of the technique seems to be from ancient practices, recently re-introduced.

Twenty years ago they produced only corn, beans, and potatoes. Now local farmers also produce vegetables, including vegetable crops destined for the international market such as broccoli and snow peas. Each farmer must generate a considerable output from each plot, because the average size of plots is less than half an acre. They produce in a series of overlapping cycles during the seven or eight months of rain each year, yielding six or seven crops of different products at different times.

Their techniques begin with mild terracing, wherever possible to lessen the runoff of moisture and the loss to erosion. Once terraced, they disturb the soil as little as possible. Brush, leaves, and stalks are laid down to mulch the paths between planting rows, preserving moisture and lessening weed growth.

At the end of the rainy season, as each of the last crops of the year are harvested, a mixture of compost and mulch is spread and only lightly chopped into the top two or three inches of soil, using the foot-wide local hoe. As the dry season progresses, this mixture turns into a relatively rigid crust that retains much moisture.

Several weeks before the onset of the next rainy season, the farmers break through the crust and plant in the moist soil beneath. By the time the rains come, their new plants are well established. They grow well ahead of the competition and can be harvested two to three weeks before other producers, just in time for the season's best market prices.

Source: AVANCSO/PACCA (1992).

**Box 7.3   COCADI: Indigenous Community Action
in the Search for Agricultural Alternatives**

Chimaltenango is part of Guatemala's historical bread, fruit, and vegetable basket. A predominantly indigenous area with many tiny plots of intensively cultivated volcanic soil, it has reached into community roots to develop new sets of survival strategies. Buffeted by the decline in seasonal work for local laborers after the collapse of cotton production in the early 1980s and focal point for often brutal counterinsurgency activities throughout the 1980s, the community has developed a Cakchiquel-controlled development organization called COCADI (Cakchiquel Coordinating Group for Integrated Development). The initial goal of COCADI was to provide bases for the simple survival of small-scale farmers. According to Roberto Muj, the local agronomist responsible for the program, "We are not just getting higher yields and lower costs of production, we are also making a long term investment in forming healthier and more fertile soils."

COCADI has promoted local alternatives to high technology agriculture, including the development (and patenting) of insecticides based on native plants, development of sequences of crop rotation specifically designed to undercut local insect infestations, and the promotion of integrated farming at the community level, including the use of additional farm animals as a source of compostable material and as a store of community wealth for times of economic difficulty. The only external resources that they have used has been a small amount of financial assistance to purchase cattle, pigs, and chickens.

The "campesino researchers" of COCADI make and distribute an extract of cypress bark that works as an insecticide. They have found a local weed which, when boiled produces an effective fungicide. And they have spread the use of fermented urine as a foliar fertilizer and insect repellent. The combined effect of these alternative technologies has been a doubling of the yields of traditional corn farming.

Source: AVANCSO/PACCA (1992).

whether through a local cooperative or a regional marketing organization. Once again, the principal basis for expanding the income of the producers is to create bargaining power with which they can share in the total profitability of the industry more than they traditionally have. The difficulty of this form of collective bargaining is most apparent in the cases of those packer/exporter firms, especially the transnationals, who invest little more than the cost of a temporary sorting shed and a few mobile chilling units (which may be no more than a fleet of refrigerated tractor-trailers). The history of these operations indicates that the packer disappears when local bargaining becomes too demanding. This form of improvement in NTAE strategy is most likely to be successful in those cases where local and international capital invests in fixed, permanent processing plants.

Although farmers have long been encouraged to specialize, in order to reap economies of scale, the fundamental nature of NTAEs suggests that diversified production of these products and of traditional crops for local markets is the wisest choice. Although the production of basic grains has fallen dramatically in Central America since the mid-1980s, largely in response to structural adjustment requirements of the multilateral lending agencies and to liberalization of local markets, subsistence remains the crucial variable for small-scale producers. AVANCSO found in Guatemala that indigenous producers of NTAEs were most likely to continue to produce, from year to year, if they were using only small proportions of their land for these export cash crops. But the encouragement of this diversification at the farm level will require improved incentives for local production of food crops, discussed below.

The effective linking of technology packages to production contracts in NTAE strategy severely limits the ability of local producers to improve their productivity and decreases the ability of producers to move toward alternative agricultural processes. The presupposition that the packer/exporter or the distributor of agricultural chemicals knows best how to produce the product in each region, every microclimate, and under all variations in soil types, rainfall averages, and seasonal patterns applies far less in the enormously variable agricultural setting of Central America than it might apply in the homogeneous regions of the United States. If the governments of Central America wish to encourage the modernization of this production and, especially, movement toward alternative techniques and organic production, independent technical assistance needs to be developed and extended to farmers. The Farmer-First approach being explored by the Panamerican Agriculture School in Honduras and CATIE's Nicaraguan IPM project provide potentially successful examples (Nelson 1994).

The development of new, more varied markets for Central America's NTAEs would also increase the economic stability of the industry and might raise producer incomes. Diversification of markets doesn't necessarily have to mean different countries. Production of NTAEs for which there is a larger local market, in tourism or among local "yuppie" consumers, is one strategy. Movement toward nonperishables, which permit storage until final market prices are best, is another. Or the processing and freezing of perishables, to focus on the much more stable global market in frozen foods, provides effective diversification away from the high risks of solely perishable shipments.

If, as we attempted to indicate in the chapters above, NTAE suffers acutely as a strategy for improving the lives of small-scale farmers in Central America precisely because of the structure of production and marketing, it is worth considering the possibilities for alternative marketing strategies that might be attempted. USAID's PROEXAG strategy provided a top-down model in which foreign aid funds were dedicated, effectively, to increasing the access that U.S. fruit and vegetable brokers (and their Central American representatives) had to expanded Central American production of NTAEs. This may have been the most practical method for increasing the aggregate exports of NTAEs most rapidly, without regard for the local consequences. And it appears to have succeeded in generating significant increases in the gross exports related to nontraditional products. But it has, in effect, created a centralized, subsidized packing and exporting structure for much of the region, which effectively squeezes the individual producers, inhibits the creation of alternative marketing networks, and lessens the beneficial impact of these exports for the majority of small-scale producers.

Alternatives to this model of expanded production and exports do exist. One kind of alternative consists of producer-based marketing efforts that capture a much larger proportion of the final value-added for the producers and their communities. The other model consists of international marketing by nonprofit organizations that seek deliberately to share more equally with producers the value that is added in marketing and distribution. There are concrete examples of successful implementation of both approaches, including some presently under way in Central America, that offer potentially viable alternatives.

There has been a significant increase in the availability of external marketing channels for Central American products, especially goods produced by cooperatives or by groups of small farmers. The history and scope of these organizations vary considerably, but their potential impact is large, especially because they are dealing with relatively small numbers of producers (Central Americans) who are shipping into a very large U.S. and European market. Among the most interesting of them are Equal Exchange, which markets coffee in the United States, Europe, and Japan from a number of Central American countries; Pueblo-to-People, which has marketed handicrafts, cashew nuts, and other products to the United States and Canada from Central America; and EarthTrade, a start-up company that focuses on trade that revolves around sustainable development. Equal Exchange and Pueblo-to-People are formally organized as nonprofit organizations, but EarthTrade is a profit-making organization with a rather unique orientation (see Boxes 7.4 and 7.5).

It will clearly be some years before organizations of this sort are capable of marketing a significant proportion of Central America's NTAEs. But the success of their experiences is encouraging. It gives hope beyond the negatives more commonly heard about the inevitability of exploitative marketing when producers are poorly educated, distant from market information sources, and competing against government-subsidized large-scale and foreign-owned packers and exporters.

▼ Alternatives to NTAEs

Central America will remain a primarily agricultural region for the foreseeable future. Its greatest natural resources are its rich volcanic and alluvial soils combined with a creative, hardworking agricultural labor force. The scourge of Central America's agricultural past has been the concentration of production in the hands of transnational export-oriented plantations and in locally owned, large-scale, inefficient production units. The most important hope for future agricultural progress rests in the hands of the hundreds of thousands of small-scale farmers who have shown themselves, time and again, to be rapidly responsive to modifications in the incentives and opportunities for production.

The constraints placed on USAID programs in the region by the Bumpers Amendment and other congressional pressures, and the convoluted internal logic of development alternatives to which these constraints have led, should not be permitted to leave us with the conclusion that the full range of alternative agricultural development strategies has been attempted. There remain many alternatives to an excessive focus on subsidized exports of nontraditional agricultural products.

Capitalizing on the Assets That Small Farmers Already Possess

A key notion is that supposedly resource-poor farmers do possess significant assets that could, at least in theory, be mobilized under an alternative development strategy. In Central America these assets often include land, albeit a small parcel of dubious fertility that nevertheless could be made productive with alternative agronomic practices; a family network extended over long, often international distances; and a flow of potential investment capital in the form of remittances from family members living in the city or abroad (Elisabeth Wood, personal communication). Two things are needed to

Box 7.4   EarthTrade, Inc.: Sustainable Marketing for Central America

Imagine the possibilities for a trading company that announces in its earliest prospectus that it is setting out to connect environmentally conscious consumers in the United States and elsewhere with cooperatives and small producer associations associated with progressive and environmental currents in the developing world. Founded in 1992 by a group of businesspersons experienced in socially responsible investing, EarthTrade, Inc. is a for-profit socially responsible enterprise that provides:

- Marketing of environmentally sensitive products in the United States and other countries
- Purchasing of products and services needed by cooperatives and community businesses engaged in environmentally sensitive agricultural production
- Consulting on the development of environmentally responsible new products, production processes, and sources of investment capital
- Networking among environmental, religious, cooperative, and other nongovernmental organizations and socially responsible businesses worldwide

In particular, EarthTrade has begun to export organically produced sesame seed from El Salvador and Nicaragua (which commands a nearly 70 percent price premium over commercial grade sesame), and to provide training in organic production, certification, and marketing to local peasant farmers.

EarthTrade has found that the business niche for supplying cooperatives and marketing their products under more-responsible pricing arrangements can generate significant profits. It has attracted investment capital in preferred stock, low-interest commercial loans, and strong support from Central American nongovernmental organizations seeking new modes of insertion into the ever-more open global economy.

According to EarthTrade, it makes sense for Central American farmers to enter the international organic foods market (Clarke 1995). Central American farmers with limited resources cannot consistently compete with large transnational agribusinesses in conventional commodity markets. Small farmers run the highest risks in the chain of production because of climate variations, world price fluctuations, and local political or currency instability. EarthTrade's model of involving producers directly in marketing and processing offers long-term economic stabilization for disadvantaged and small-scale farmers.

The organic market is a relatively small but fast-growing niche market that offers a price premium and is not yet dominated by large agribusiness. This allows a relatively easier entry for small producers. Organic production methods are less cash-intensive and more labor-intensive, factors favoring peasant and cooperative producer associations.

Organic methods are more knowledge-intensive and require greater attention to human development. Likewise, organic production models generate a higher return on investment for training and technical assistance, as compared to conventional monocrop agriculture where human capital is not as important in generating value. Investment in skills development, information systems, and training programs also have wider social benefits in the farming community.

Environmental degradation caused by overuse of agrochemicals and soil erosion in many regions has reduced yields per acre to half of previous levels. Organic production techniques such as intercropping, rotations systems, and other soil improvements raise yields within two to five years, resulting in higher farm income while also reversing environmental damage.

The biggest barriers for Central American farmers seeking entry to the international organic market are: fair marketing mechanisms, including training to meet certification standards and information about product quality and pricing structures; efficient processing and distribution systems that allow farmers to provide the reliable, high-quality supply needed to retain buyers; access to investment capital and credit at fair interest rates. The EarthTrade model of partnership with producers (who actually co-own local processing and export facilities), nongovernmental organizations, peasant organizations, and financial institutions seeks to give Central American producers a foothold in each of these areas. Together they create a more level playing field for small farmers from the developing world to compete with those who benefit disproportionately from expensive agricultural research programs, extension services, state subsidies, and biased product and capital markets.

Further information is available from EarthTrade, Inc., 1814 Franklin Street, Suite 710E, Oakland CA 94612.

Box 7.5   Pueblo-to-People and Equal Exchange: Nonprofit Marketing from Central America

"Businesses with a social purpose" is the name sometimes given to nonprofit alternative trade organizations (ATOs) that have proliferated in recent years in the United States and Europe. The North American Alternative Trade Organization, founded in 1992, started with fifty organizations that had some $15 million in sales that year. Their European counterpart organization reported more than $100 million in sales, largely in Germany and the Netherlands.

ATOs tend to select their trading partners on the basis of criteria established by the Fair Trade Foundation. The criteria include fair distribution of income among workers, often meaning a cooperative organizational basis; healthy working conditions; concern for the environmental impact of their products; worker participation in decisionmaking; support of community life and cultural traditions; commitment to product quality; and reasonable cost to the consumer (*Co-op News* 1992).

Pueblo-to-People is a Houston-based ATO that has worked since 1979 to market the products of cooperatives in Latin America. By 1992 it had developed marketing ties to eighty-five production groups in nine Latin American countries, including four Central American countries, Mexico, Peru, Bolivia, and Brazil. Its products include cashews and dried cashew fruit from Honduras, a variety of organic coffees, Brazil nuts from the Amazon rain forest, and handloomed clothing from Guatemala, Peru, and Bolivia. It produces a catalog three times a year, which is distributed nationwide; it has a retail store in Houston, and it sells extensively at fairs, festivals, and conferences throughout the United States.

Equal Exchange, Inc. is the largest U.S.-based ATO focused on the coffee trade. It pays growers a guaranteed minimum price, which in 1992 was more than twice the international price. Growers using organic methods received even more. Standard coffee profit margins were so high, according to Equal Exchange's president, that it could pay producers large premiums, sell the coffee on gourmet markets, and still make money (*NYT,* June 26, 1992).

Although still far too small to account for any significant pro-

portion of Central America's nontraditional export capacity, the existence of these trading organizations illustrates the possibilities for shifting more of the value-added in distribution back to the original producer without requiring subsidies or other artificial and nonsustainable processes.

Further information is available from Pueblo-to-People, 2105 Silber Road, #101, Houston TX 77055 (713/956-1172) and Equal Exchange, Inc., 101 Losca Drive, Stoughton MA 02072 (617/344-7227).

mobilize these resources in a productive manner conducive to improved circumstances for rural families: a new type of marketing system that takes advantage of family members living in the city and/or abroad; and a price/cost structure that makes investing in agricultural production, artesanry, or small-scale local industry a reasonable way to spend one's money. This last item is of course the hardest to achieve, as recent trends toward free trade and tariff lowering have flooded Central America with cheap imports that make local production unprofitable. Thus it is no surprise that most family remittances are currently spent on consumption rather than production, since investment would mean almost certainly losing money and thus having still less for consumption. Yet, should macroeconomic change prove to be possible, there is an enormous amount of progressively distributed remittance income available to finance peasant production.

Food Security and Basic Grains

USAID argued that Central America could not compete with U.S. production of corn, beans, and rice and that, therefore, any local attempts to encourage continued production of these crops meant inefficient and otherwise inappropriate policy. As a result, virtually every Central American country has dismantled programs that had been relatively successful prior to 1980 in maintaining some significant local basic-grain production. In Costa Rica this meant dismantling the whole Consejo Nacional de Producción (CNP) structure for restraint on corn prices and the implicit subsidy to local corn production. In Guatemala this meant eliminating all protection for wheat production that had previously provided the basis for diversified highland agriculture for tens of thousands of farmers. With the importation of wheat, local prices fell, the balance of payments worsened, and local production virtually disappeared. Of course the argument as to the superior competitive ability of U.S. farmers is dubious at best, given the extraordinary level of U.S. subsidies, which dwarf Latin American support programs (see, e.g., Calva et al. 1992).

There remains a significant argument that is being heard, once again, for basic grain production as a component of food security (ICCARD 1989). The pursuit of comparative advantage through tariff reductions presupposes that producers of previously protected products can move, relatively easily, into production of alternative commodities for which there is local comparative advantage and from which the nation can gain the foreign exchange needed to purchase imported commodities.

In Central America the continuing debt crisis, the worsening balance-of-payments picture, and falling income levels throughout the region raise serious questions about the ability of many previous producers of basic grains to convert to production that allows them to purchase now-imported foodstuffs. Research by AVANCSO/PACCA (1992) in Guatemala indicates that small farmers have been forced into further-impoverishing NTEAs in the wake of dramatic plunges in the prices of traditionally produced basic grains. The greater the likelihood of balance-of-payments problems and resulting foreign exchange shortages, the greater the incentive to continue to provide support for some share of the nation's fundamental foodstuffs, albeit with improved technology. It is time to seriously reconsider the dismantling of the tariff barriers that once protected Central American food production (Rosset et al. 1994). Though it would certainly mean confrontation with the United States, the General Agreement on Tariffs and Trade (GATT), and other powers that be, it is a critical issue, of national defense–like importance, for Central American well-being, both in terms of guaranteeing the nutrition of the entire population and the possibility of improved incomes for peasant farmers.

Maquila Operations and Other NTAEs

Much of our argument in this book hinges on the specific characteristics of the NTAE industry, the markets it serves, and the conditions created for small-scale rural producers in Central America. The risks borne by producers at the bottom of the production chain because of the local nature of the industry, the chronic price volatility in international markets (which makes those risks enormous), and the environmentally unwise and personally dangerous technological basis of the industry all suggest that Central America's small-scale farmers are gambling recklessly when they attempt to improve their lot through NTAEs.

The same is not necessarily true of nonagricultural nontraditional exports. For most of the region this consists of a wide variety of labor-intensive processing industries, *maquilas* in the Mexican experience, that have expanded rapidly in recent years. The dramatic expansion of the apparel and electronics industry in Costa Rica provides an example of nonagricultural exports that have generated employment without forcing the majority of the burden of risk on individual small-scale producers. This is not, in general, an ideal industry on which to base one's long-term development strategy. It is rapidly becoming, in fact, the most competitive kind of employment generation in the world. Success depends upon providing wage and productivity combinations that can be shown to be the least expensive in the world. For a relatively well-educated labor force, such as that of Costa Rica, this may provide growth in higher-skill jobs. For the majority of Central America it promises little but low-wage jobs for low-productivity workers, under constant pressure to reduce wages further.

▼ **The Continuing Need
for More Fundamental Reforms**

One thing has become apparent in our review of the NTAE experience. If development planners are really committed to overcoming the decade-long crisis in the region, are committed to significantly altering the historical pattern of poverty and inequity, and if they have any hope of sustaining these important changes in the future, then profound and sweeping reforms must be made. The historical pattern of superimposed development, adopted by the Kissinger Commission to explain the impoverishing and inequitable pattern so characteristic of the region, has been further deepened by a decade of USAID support for NTAEs.

As we have argued elsewhere, NTAE as a development strategy (Murray 1994) and the broader development vision of the past decade (Rosset and Vandermeer 1986b) were promoted largely on assumptions that more-fundamental changes could be avoided. The record now demonstrates that such assumptions were foolish, indeed.

If a stable, peaceful, just, and, one hopes, someday prosperous process of development is to be established in Central America, it will require major policy reforms, including sweeping agrarian reform, greater local control over transnational corporations, a genuine commitment to democratic, grassroots reform, and the generation of indigenously developed strategies.

Agrarian Reform

As has been argued for years, agrarian reform is key to sustainable and balanced economic growth in the region (de Janvry 1981). Land reform will help create the necessary internal markets that, while possibly not producing spectacular annual increases in growth, will provide a more stable and sustainable foundation for growth, and will also produce far more equitable distribution of the benefits of that growth than has been seen to date. In addition, agrarian reform is likely to provide more ecologically sustainable growth. During the 1980s, for example, the rate of deforestation in Nicaragua was Central America's lowest, in part because of the agrarian reform that provided effective access to land for more than a hundred thousand families (Vandermeer and Perfecto 1995). When farmers own the land, they are more likely to have a long-term commitment to its sustainability and are less inclined to pursue ecologically destructive practices in the interest of short-term gain.

While some feel that land reform is a dead issue (de Janvry et al. 1989), others have recently made powerful arguments for reopening that chapter of Central American history (Rosset et al. 1994; Sobhan 1993). Clearly it cannot be the same kind of land reform that predominated in the past, when farmers were given useless land in remote places unconnected to markets. Rather, it must be a true reform that redistributes quality land (Rosset et al. 1994), and must be accompanied by credit, price, marketing, and technical assistance policies designed to remove the biases against small farmers (de Janvry et al. 1989).

In fact, a significant redistribution of land has occurred in two countries, providing the basis for guarded optimism vis-à-vis the future (Rosset 1994). In Nicaragua a significant number of state farms, which the Sandinistas had expropriated from Somoza and his associates a decade earlier, have recently passed into the hands of their employees. Violetta Chamorro's government had planned to privatize the entire state sector, either returning the lands to the former owners or selling them to private interests, but was thwarted when the workers armed themselves and refused to yield the properties.

After a few tense moments, which even saw the Sandinista police and army ordered to throw them off, a compromise was negotiated. Twenty-five percent of the farms were turned over directly to their employees, and another 25 percent were given as cooperatives to ex-combatants of both the Sandinista army and the contras (who seem to be getting along pretty well, based on their shared origin as peasants). The remaining half are being privatized as originally planned, but the 50 percent now belonging to the workers and ex-combatants include some of the country's best cotton and coffee lands.

Orlando Núñez, director of the Center for Research and Promotion of Rural and Social Development (CIPRES) in Managua, has estimated the impressive importance of alternative land tenure and organization in postrevolutionary Nicaragua (Rosset 1994). Adding together all of the beneficiaries of the Sandinista agrarian reform, plus other members of the Sandinista peasants' union, other cooperatives, and the half of the former state farms referred to above, one comes up with fully 50 percent of the national agricultural production of Nicaragua and a hefty chunk of the best lands under alternative forms of tenure and/or organization. This is both a truly progressive structural reform and a historic opportunity to build a more sustainable development model.

That of course will depend upon whether these dispersed and diverse new landowners can come together in a cohesive way. If they did, they could exercise the power in the marketplace that would be conferred by control over half of an entire country's farm output. It is much too early to say whether they will in fact be able to do it—though that is precisely CIPRES's goal. The former state farms are now organized as shareholder enterprises, where each former employee, whether farm worker, agronomist, secretary, or accountant, owns one share, which confers one vote in electing management teams. This is analogous to the United Airlines union buy-out applied to Third World agriculture. Several of these enterprises have embarked upon ambitious plans to convert their lands to organic farming, with substantial quantities of organic coffee, sesame, and soybeans already exported through alternative trading companies like EarthTrade and Equal Exchange.

El Salvador presents a similar situation, though at an earlier stage of development. Adding together the farmland transferred to peasants in the 1980s by the agrarian reforms implemented in response to the Farabundo Martí National Liberation Front (FMLN), plus that turned over to ex-combatants under the peace accords, gives a figure of almost 25 percent of all agricultural land in new hands. That percentage is scheduled to rise to more than 30 percent if the peace accords continue to be implemented (Rosset 1994).

In the San Vicente area about five thousand hectares of prime cotton and sugarcane lands have been turned over to ex-combatants of the FMLN and their families. These lands were abandoned by their owners twelve years ago, because of the war, and thus are excellent candidates for organic certification and other agroecological alternatives. The new landowners are already starting to produce small quantities of organic sesame and cashew, and have impressive plans for sustainable development.

Thus, although a cursory view of each country is depressing—60 percent unemployment in Nicaragua and the right-wing National Republican Alliance (ARENA) government dragging its feet on the peace accords in El Salvador, with major divisions within both the Sandinista Front for National Liberation (FSLN) and the FMLN—the changes in land holdings give real hope for the future. It may take five or ten years to see if the new owners of these lands will make it economically, but if they do they may create new models for more-sustainable rural development in the process. This may prove to be one, if not the only, true legacy of both the Sandinista revolution and the FMLN's long struggle.

Harnessing Transnational Capital

Transnational corporations continue to be the dominant economic forces in the region, the principal vehicles for new foreign investment, and the principal instruments of trade liberalization. In some cases the biggest and most successful players in the high-stakes game of nontraditional agriculture are the same fruit companies that have dominated the small economies of the region throughout the past century. These companies have taken advantage of development policies to mine the region's natural resources and extract large profits. They have been particularly adept at shifting production sites and investments to exploit intraregional conditions and avoid regulation. They have left little behind in the way of local benefits and sustainable development.

Devising strategies to more effectively regulate these interests and to make transnational participation in national economies more beneficial to national and local interests is one of the basic and fundamental changes that must occur in the region if long-term, sustainable, and equitable development is to be achieved. Demands for such changes are being heard throughout the developing world. Even in the United States proposals for more-profound policy reforms to address poverty and the decline of the inner cities are challenging the relatively free hand that transnational corporations have had in exploiting and then abandoning one locality after another around the world.

Expanding Economic Democracy

While democratic reforms are under way in the region, they must go much deeper into the political culture of Central American, and international, society if they are to be the foundation of sustainable and equitable development. This means much greater empowerment of poor and rural people, not just occasional participation in elections (itself a significant advance over previous decades). It means not just formal participation in the development process (as has often been the case with USAID, World Bank, and other development agency programs), but genuine participation in the development of project goals, strategies, technologies, and outcome assessments. This has been shown to be the key to successful IPM (Nelson 1994), as well as the key to sustainable development more generally (Altieri and Hecht 1990; Korten 1983). In Box 7.6 we present the voices of Central American farmers themselves.

Indigenously Developed Strategies

Finally, regional development strategies must grow out of indigenous visions of Central America's future, locally developed and locally implemented. The recent formation of the Central American Commission on Development and the Environment (CCAD) is an example of the emergent opportunities to chart a new course. If regional strategies are to become effective, U.S. and other international interests must make a commitment to support local goals. USAID and U.S.-controlled lending institutions in particular must avoid the divisive role they played in previous decades, which undermined efforts at regional coordination through bilateral agreements benefiting relatively narrow interests in the region.

Clearly, Central America needs the reincorporation of its poor majority into any development strategy that is to have any hope of success. Not only should improving the livelihood of the poor be the principal goal of development, but only by broadening the social base of the region's economies can economic recovery be achieved. "Magic bullet" policies like NTAE strategy that seem to repeat the worst mistakes of earlier cycles of export agriculture-led development are most definitely not the answer.

Box 7.6   The Voice of the Central American Small Farmer

Central American small farmers received their first formal voice in regional negotiations in December 1992 when a delegation of farmers was invited to participate in the annual regional economic summit of Central American presidents. The organization invited to select and send representatives was ASOCODE, the Central American Association of Small Farmer Organizations, which claims to represent 80 percent of Central America's organized small farmers. Wilson Campos, ASOCODE coordinator, was interviewed in July 1993 on the attitudes of small farmers in the region toward structural adjustment, free trade, and nontraditional agricultural exports (Korten 1993).

Why are so many farmers shifting from basic grains to non-traditional export crops?

"The new dependency on export crops is a product of policies that our governments have imposed on small farmers. If I go to the bank for credit, but the bank says it will only give me credit if I plant macadamia nuts for export, then that is what I will plant. The government has used mechanisms such as credit to force small farmers to abandon the goal of food sovereignty."

What is fueling the new unity apparent among Central American small farmers?

"Several factors have changed within Central America. First, new political opportunities are opening up within the region as Guatemala and El Salvador end their civil wars. . . . Second, free trade policies and structural adjustment have given small farmers a common concern. We are all struggling to find our place within an increasingly globalized economy. . . . We cannot forever use up our energy saying no, no, no to structural adjustment. Now we are looking for ways to join the dialogue to ensure that structural adjustment does not wipe us out.

"If we are to survive, structural adjustment has to happen much more slowly. Producing non-traditional export crops requires an entirely new form of production for us. We need time to organize exporting cooperatives. These cooperatives need to make contacts with foreign markets and gain access to international transportation systems. . . . To successfully make such a transition takes many, many years.

"Third, since farmers themselves have begun to lead the small farmers' movement, we have gained a new credibility. . . . That small farmers will disappear as countries develop is a central belief of both the capitalist and Marxist ideologies. But now we are able to see ourselves as a potentially powerful and positive economic force."

Do you believe that Central American small farmers are sufficiently organized to manage their own processing facilities?

"Gaining control over processing and marketing facilities is fundamental if we are to become a powerful and dynamic regional force. . . . Small farmers in every Central American country already have experience managing companies. In Costa Rica we have a long tradition of cooperatives. . . . Through the Sandinista Revolution, small farmers in Nicaragua have even more experience in managing agricultural firms."

What is the most important idea you would like to convey to a U.S. audience?

"At the most fundamental level, we are all threatened, North as well as South, by economic policies that are destroying the little this planet still holds. The development strategy currently advocated by the U.S. is simply suicidal. . . . What structural adjustment, and the economics behind it, advocate is violence against both the environment and the poor."

Appendix

▼▼▼▼▼▼▼▼▼▼▼▼▼▼▼▼▼▼▼▼▼▼▼▼▼▼▼▼▼▼▼▼

Statistical Profiles of Central American Producers of Nontraditional Agricultural Exports

▲▲▲▲▲▲▲▲▲▲▲▲▲▲▲▲▲▲▲▲▲▲▲▲▲▲▲▲▲▲

Table A.1   Average Melon Producers in Central America by Size Class, 1991
(surveyed in Guatemala, El Salvador, Honduras, and Costa Rica)

	All	Micro[a]	Small[a]	Medium[a]	Large[a]
General characteristics					
Number of observations	192	94	64	21	13
Age[b]	39.7	40.3	39.2	39.9	33
Years of education[c]	4.8	4.3	5.4	7.8	7.3
Member of a cooperative					
(% of all producers)	47	55	39	48	31
At least one child of producer					
participates in production (%)	28	32	31	14	0
Mean experience in melon					
production (years)	6.7	6.3	7.7	6.3	5.3
Yield (boxes per mz)[d]	356.4	354.4	320.4	278.9	656.1
Percentage of land in melon					
production[e]	76	81	80	57	58
Percentage of land rented[e]	36	24	48	38	50
Percentage of land irrigated[e]	45	47	43	49	31
Access to technical assistance (% of all producers)					
Received technical assistance	84	94	80	62	77
From a state extension agent	25	27	23	19	31
From a cooperative	16	3	30	33	8
From a distributor of					
agricultural inputs	13	15	9	10	15
From a buyer of harvest	64	85	50	29	38
Access to credit (% of all producers)[f]					
Received formal credit	70	63	81	67	77
From a private bank	16	21	6	10	38
From a public bank or program	27	20	39	29	15
From a cooperative	20	11	34	24	8
From other sources	10	12	8	10	15
Received input credit	63	70	56	43	77
From a public program	10	13	6	5	15
From a distributor of agricultural					
inputs	8	3	5	5	46
From a cooperative	26	28	30	24	0
From the buyer of harvest	20	15	31	14	8
From other sources	8	13	1	5	15

(continues)

Table A.1   (continued)

	All	Micro[a]	Small[a]	Medium[a]	Large[a]
Main buyer of product (% of all producers)					
Private national company	22	27	19	14	23
Private foreign company	57	68	42	38	77
Cooperative	18	3	34	48	0
Other marketing characteristics (% of all producers)					
Sold part of output in a local market	46	33	64	48	46
Buyer rejected output because of poor quality	25	27	19	28	42
Lack of buyer caused losses to producer	26	31	20	14	42

Source: Rosset and Remes (1993).

Notes: a. Micro: area of melons cultivated is < 3.5 mz; small: 3.5 mz ≤ Area < 12 mz; medium: 12 mz ≤ Area ≤ 30 mz; and large: Area > 30 mz.

b. These and all following data given as means.

c. Honduran producers excluded.

d. Manzana (mz) = 0.7 ha.

e. Costa Rican producers excluded.

f. Percentages over different loan sources do not add up because some producers received loans from multiple sources.

Table A.2   Average Melon Producers in Central America by Country, 1991 (surveyed in Guatemala, El Salvador, Honduras, and Costa Rica)

	Guatemala	El Salvador	Honduras	Costa Rica
General characteristics				
Number of observations	45	74	49	24
Member of a cooperative (%)[a]	0	92	41	13
Age	40	40	39	38
Years of education	6.3	2.4	n.a.	7.9
Mean experience in melon production (years)	7.8	7.0	7.0	3.1
Yield (boxes per mz)	352.2	415.7	254.2	360.8
Extension of melons cultivated (mz)	6.9	19.3	10.1	18.4
Percentage of land in melon production	61	84	78	n.a.
Access to technical assistance (% of all producers)				
Received technical assistance	91	93	65	83
From a state extension agent	38	15	20	42
From a cooperative	4	1	55	0
From a distributor of agricultural inputs	31	9	4	4
From a buyer of harvest	87	74	18	83
Access to credit (% of all producers)				
Received formal credit	56	86	88	13
From a private bank	0	39	4	0
From a public bank or program	47	20	27	13
From a cooperative	4	9	59	0
From another source	4	19	8	88
Received input credit	49	76	45	88
From a public program	0	24	2	0
From a distributor of agricultural inputs	2	11	4	8
From a cooperative	4	16	33	83
From a buyer of harvest	42	5	31	0
From other source	0	20	2	0
Main buyer of product (% of all producers)				
Private national company	2	55	2	0
Private foreign company	93	43	22	0
Cooperative	2	0	69	100
Other marketing characteristics (% of all producers)				
Sold part of output in a local market	80	16	82	0
Buyer rejected output because of poor quality	16	12	18	100
Producer suffered losses because of lack of buyer	18	36	22	17

Source: Rosset and Remes (1993).
Note: a. All following figures are means.

Table A.3   Average Broccoli Producers by Size Class, 1991 (surveyed in Pixabaj, Sololá, Guatemala)

	All	Micro[a]	Small[a]	Medium[a]
General characteristics				
Number of observations	52	4	37	11
Age[b]	44	40	42	53
Years of education	1.9	2	1.5	3.5
At least one child of producer				
participates in production (%)	69	25	68	91
Experience in broccoli production				
(years)	2	2.3	2	2.1
Percentage of land in broccoli				
production	11	21	11	9
Percentage of land irrigated	11	n.a.	12	11
Access to technical assistance **(% of all producers)**				
Received technical assistance	100	100	100	100
From a buyer of harvest	100	100	100	100
From other sources	0	0	0	0
Main buyer of product **(% of all producers)**				
Private national company	100	100	100	100
Other	0	0	0	0
Sold part of output in a local				
market	0	0	0	0
Buyer rejected output because of				
poor quality	100	100	100	100
Producer suffered losses because				
of lack of buyer	94	100	97	82

Source: Rosset and Remes (1993).

Notes: a. Size = micro if extension of broccoli cultivated is area < 1 mz (= 0.7 ha.); small if 1 mz ≤ area < 2 mz, and medium if 2 mz ≤ area.

b. All following figures are means.

Table A.4   Average Melon and Broccoli Producers, Guatemala, 1991 (melon in
El Valle de la Fragua, Zacapa; broccoli in Pixabaj, Sololá)

	Melon Producers	Broccoli Producers
General Characteristics		
Number of observations	45	52
Age[a]	40	44
Years of education	6.3	1.9
At least one child of producer participates in production (%)	29	69
Mean experience in melon or broccoli production (years)	7.8	2.0
Total land used by producer (mz)	14.8	1.2
Percentage of land in melon or broccoli production	61	11
Percentage of land irrigated	95	12
Previous land use (% of land in melon or broccoli cultivation)		
Forested or mountain land	2	0
Cattle pasture	6	0
Basic grain production	50	100
Fallow	7	0
Other agriculture	35	0
Received technical assistance (% of all producers)	91	100
From a state extension agent	38	0
From a cooperative	4	0
From a distributor of agricultural products	31	0
From a buyer of harvest	87	100
Main buyer of product (% of all producers)		
Private national company	2	100
Private foreign company	93	0
Cooperative	2	0
Sold part of output in a local market	80	0
Buyer rejected output because of poor quality	16	100
Producer suffered losses because of lack of buyer	18	94

Source: Rosset and Remes (1993).
Note: a. All following figures are means.

Acronyms

▼▼▼▼▼▼▼▼

ACCCR	Asociación de Carreteras y Caminos de Costa Rica (Costa Rican Association for Roads and Highways)
ALCOSA	Alimentos Congelados, S.A. (Frozen Foods, Inc.) (Guatemala)
ARENA	Aliaza Republicana Nacional (National Republican Alliance) (El Salvador)
ATO	alternative trade organization
AVANSCO	Asociación para el Avance de las Ciencias Sociales (Association for the Advancement of the Social Sciences) (Guatemala)
BANDESA	Banco Nacional de Desarrollo (National Development Bank) (Guatemala)
CAAP	Consejo Agropecuario Agroindustrial Privado (Private Sector Agricultural and Agroindustrial Council) (Costa Rica)
CACM	Central American Common Market
CATIE	Centro Agronómico Tropical de Investigación y Enseñanza (Tropical Center for Agricultural Research and Education) (Costa Rica)
CCAD	Comisión Centroamericana de Ambiente y Desarrollo (Central American Commission on Development and the Environment)
CCCR	Cámara de Comercio de Costa Rica (Costa Rican Chamber of Commerce)
CECADE	Centro de Capacitación para el Desarrollo (Development Training Center) (Costa Rica)
CENPRO	Centro de Promoción de las Exportaciones (Center for the Promotion of Exports) (Costa Rica)
CINDE	Coalición de Iniciativas de Desarrollo (Coalition for Development Initiatives) (Costa Rica)
CIPRES	Centro para la Investigación, la Promoción y el Desarrollo

185

	Rural y Social (Center for Research and Promotion of Rural and Social Development) (Nicaragua)
CNP	Consejo Nacional de Producción (National Production Council) (Costa Rica)
CODESA	Corporación Costarricence de Desarrollo, S.A. (Costa Rican Development Corporation, Inc.)
COFIDESA	Corporación Financiera del Desarrollo, S.A. (Development Finance Corporation, Inc.)
CRESUHL	Cooperativa Regional de Horticultores Sureños Limitada (Southern Regional Cooperative of Vegetable Growers, Ltd.) (Honduras)
EARTH	Escuela de Agricultura de la Región Tropical Húmeda (Regional Agricultural School for the Humid Tropics) (Costa Rica)
ECLAC	Economic Commission for Latin America and the Caribbean
EPA	Environmental Protection Agency
ESF	economic support funds
FDA	Food and Drug Administration
FLMN	Frente Farabundo Martí de Liberación Nacional (Farabundo Martí National Liberation Front) (El Salvador)
FSLN	Frente Sandinista de Liberación Nacional (Sandinista Front for National Liberation) (Nicaragua)
FUSADES	Fundación Salvadoreña para el Desarrollo Económico y Social (Salvadoran Foundation for Economic and Social Development)
GATT	General Agreement on Tariffs and Trade
GDP	gross domestic product
GIFAP	Groupement International des Associations Nationales de Fabricants de Produits Agrochemiques (International Group of National Associations of Agrochemical Producers) (France)
ICADS	Institute for Central American Development Studies (Costa Rica)
ICES	Instituto Costarricence de Estudios Sociales (Institute for Social Studies) (Costa Rica)
IDB	Inter-American Development Bank
IICA	Inter-American Institute for Cooperation on Agriculture
IMF	International Monetary Fund
IPM	integrated pest management
MAG	Ministry of Agriculture
NTAE	nontraditional agricultural export
OCIA	Organic Crop Improvement Association

PACCA	Policy Alternatives for the Caribbean and Central America
PATSA	Productos Acuáticos y Terrestres, S.A. (Sea and Land Products, Inc.) (Honduras)
PLN	Partido de Liberación Nacional (Party of National Liberation) (Costa Rica)
PMA	pesticide management activity
POSCAE	Posgrado Centroamericano en Economía y Planificación (Central American Post-Graduate Program in Economics and Planning) (Honduras)
PREIS	Programa Regional de Investigación sobre El Salvador (Regional Research Program on El Salvador)
PROEXAG	Nontraditional Agricultural Export Support Project (USAID)
SEA	Secretaria del Estado de Agricultura (Ministry of Agriculture) (Dominican Republic)
USAID	United States Agency for International Development
USDA	United States Department of Agriculture
WHO	World Health Organization

REFERENCES

▼▼▼▼▼▼▼

"AID Provides $140 Million." 1987. *Tico Times* (Costa Rica), April 4.

Altieri, Miguel A., and Susanna B. Hecht. 1990. *Agroecology and Small Farm Development.* Boca Raton: CRC Press.

Anderson, L. 1991. "Mixed Blessings: Disruption and Organization Among Peasant Unions in Costa Rica." *Latin American Research Review* 26(1):111–143.

Andow, David A., and Peter M. Rosset. 1990. "Integrated Pest Management." In C. R. Carroll, J. H. Vandermeer, and P. M. Rosset, eds., *Agroecology.* New York: McGraw-Hill.

Appel, Judith, Flor de María Matus, Inge Maria Beck, Tania García, Otilio Gonzales, and Jurrie Reiding. 1991. *Uso, Manejo y Riesgos Asociados a Plaguicidas en Nicaragua.* Managua: Confederación Superior Universitaria Centroamericana (CSUCA).

AVANCSO/PACCA. 1992. *Growing Dilemmas: Guatemala, the Environment, and the Global Economy.* Washington, D.C.: Policy Alternatives for the Caribbean and Central America.

Avery, D. T. 1985. "Central America: Agriculture, Technology, and Unrest." *Department of State Bulletin* 85(2094):70–74.

Ayala Rivera, Mario, and John H. Young. 1990. *Cooperativa Agrícola Integral Unión de Cuatro Pinos.* Guatemala: Agencia para el Desarrollo International de los E.U.A. (USAID).

Banco Central de Costa Rica. 1988. "Mecanismo para la Autorización de Divisas para la Importación de Materias Primas a Exportadores de Productos No Tradicionales a Mercados fuera de Centroamérica y Panamá." Paid advertisement. *La Nación* (Costa Rica), February 20.

Banco de Guatemala. 1986. *Informe Económico, Año XXXIII.* October–December.

Barham, Bradford, Michael Carter, and Wayne Sigelko. 1992. "Adoption and Accumulation Patterns in Guatemala's Latest Agro-Export Boom." Social Systems Research Institute Working Paper no. 9216, University of Wisconsin.

Barham, Bradford, Mary Clark, Elizabeth Katz, and Rachel Schurman. 1993. "Non-Traditional Agricultural Exports in Latin America: Toward an Appraisal." *Latin American Research Review* 27(2):43–82.

Barletta, Héctor, and Alfredo Rueda. 1991. "MIP en melones de exportación." *Agricultura de las Américas* November–December:22–27.

Barry, Tom. 1987. *Roots of Rebellion: Land and Hunger in Central America.* Boston: South End Press.

Berman, Daniel M. 1978. *Death on the Job: Occupational Health and Safety Struggles in the United States.* New York: Monthly Review Press.

Bezmalinovic, Bea, Lori Bollin, Lucy Morse, Julie Smith, and Tom Thacher. 1987.

"Agricultura de Cambio: Mad About Macadamia?" ACM Working Paper. Costa Rica: Associated Colleges of the Midwest.

Biderman, Jaime M. 1982. "Class Structure, the State and Capitalist Development in Nicaraguan Agriculture." Ph.D. diss., University of California at Berkeley.

Biehl, John. 1988. "No Me Sentí Extranjero en Costa Rica." *La Nación* (Costa Rica), June 17.

Blumberg, Rao Lesser. 1985. "Following Up a Guatemalan 'Natural Experiment on Women in Development': Gender and the Alcosa Agribusiness Project in 1985 vs 1980." Report of the University of California, San Diego, to the U.S. Agency for International Development, Bureau for Latin America and the Caribbean.

Bolton, William E., and Harry Manion. 1989. *Evaluation of USAID/Costa Rica Nontraditional Agricultural Export Strategy* (Contract No. 515–0000-C–00–9035–00). Washington, D.C.: Checchi and Co. Consulting, Inc. and ATMA International, Inc.

Brockett, Charles D. 1988. *Land, Power, and Poverty: Agrarian Transformation and Political Conflict in Central America*. Boston: Unwin Hyman.

Brumback, Nancy. 1990. "Organically Grown Produce: How to Tell If It's the Real Thing." *Produce Business,* May:38–43.

Bulmer-Thomas, Victor. 1987. *The Political Economy of Central America since 1920.* Cambridge: Cambridge University Press.

Burbach, R., and P. Flynn. 1980. *Agribusiness in the Americas.* New York: Monthly Review Press.

Burnett, Tammy. 1990. "Organics Group Optimistic for the '90s." *The Packer,* January 27.

Byrnes, Kerry J. 1992. *A Cross-Cutting Analysis of Agricultural Research, Extension, and Education (AGREE) in AID-Assisted Countries.* Washington, D.C.: Agricultural and Rural Development Technical Services Project, AID/LAC/DR/RD, Chemonics International, U.S. Dept. of Agriculture.

————. 1991. *From Melon Patch to Market Place: How They Learned to Export a Non-traditional Crop.* Revised version. Washington, D.C.: Chemonics International, Latin American and Caribbean Agriculture and Rural Development Technical Services Project.

————. 1989. "From Melon Patch to Market Place: How They Learned to Export a Non-traditional Crop." Paper prepared for AID/LAC/CDIE Trade and Investment Workshop, Alexandria, Virginia, November 13–14.

Calva, José Luis, et al. 1992. *La Agricultura Mexicana Frente al Tratado Trilateral de Libre Comercio.* Mexico: CIESTAAM.

Carroll, C. R., J. H. Vandermeer, and P. M. Rosset, eds. 1990. *Agroecology.* New York: McGraw-Hill.

Carvajal, María Elena, 1988a. "Bank Tries to Calm Panic." *Tico Times* (Costa Rica), February 12.

————. 1988b. "Central Bank Chief: Politicking Will Overshadow Economic Reform Effort." *Tico Times* (Costa Rica), May 6.

————. 1988c. "CINDE Will Answer Deputies' Questions About Use of AID Funds." *Tico Times* (Costa Rica), April 29.

————. 1988d. "Who Owns ¢14 Billion Fund?" *Tico Times* (Costa Rica), April 8.

————. 1987. "Government Turns to AID in Search for Cash." *Tico Times* (Costa Rica), December 11.

————. 1986. "Nation in the Eye of an Economic Hurricane." *Tico Times* (Costa Rica), December 5.

Castillo, Luisa E., and Catharina Wesseling H. 1987. *Diagnóstico de la Problemática de los Plaguicidas en Costa Rica.* Heredia: Universidad Nacional.

CEDOPEX. 1987. *Boletín Estadístico.* Santo Domingo: Centro Dominicano de Promoción de Exportaciones.

CENAP, CEPAS, Justicia y Paz, y Extensión ESEUNA. 1988. *Lucha Campesina en Costa Rica: No Hay Paz sin Alimentos.* San José: CENAP.

Chambers, Robert. 1990. "Farmer-First: A Practical Paradigm for the Third Agriculture." In Miguel A. Altieri and Susanna B. Hecht, eds., *Agroecology and Small Farm Development.* Boca Raton: CRC Press.

CICP. 1988. *Environmental Assessment of the Highlands Agricultural Development Project.* College Park, Md.: Consortium for International Crop Protection.

Clarke, Margie. 1995. *Fact Sheet and Market Analysis of the Organic Foods Market, and Advantages for Central American Farmers Entering the International Organic Foods Market.* Oakland: EarthTrade, Inc.

Cleaver, H. M. 1972. "The Contradictions of the Green Revolution." *American Economic Review* 72:177–188.

Codas F., Roberto. 1991. *Exportaciones Agrícolas No Tradicionales de El Salvador: Producción de Melón de Exportación.* San Salvador: PREIS.

Cole, Donald C., Rob McConnell, Douglas L. Murray, and Feliciano Pacheco Anton. 1988. "Pesticide Illness Surveillance: The Nicaraguan Experience." *Bulletin of the Pan American Health Organization* 22(2):119–132.

Conroy, Michael E. 1990. "The Political Economy of the 1990 Nicaraguan Elections." *International Journal of Political Economy* 20(3):5–33.

―――. 1989. "The Diversification of Central American Exports: Chimera or Reality?" Paper presented at the fifteenth International Congress of the Latin American Studies Association, December.

Contreras, Mario. 1990. *Situation, Perspective and Strategies for the Use of Pesticides in Central America.* Guatemala: USAID Regional Office for Central American Programs (ROCAP).

Cook, R. L. 1990. "An Overview of the Dynamic Fresh Produce Industry." In A. A. Kader and F. G. Mitchell, eds., *Post Harvest Technology of Horticultural Crops.* Berkeley: University of California Press.

Cook, Roberta, Kim Norris, and Carolyn Pickel. 1989. "Does Organic Mean Big Paper? or Economic Comparison of Organic and Conventional Production." *Coastal Grower,* Fall:12–16.

Costa Rica. Ministerio de Agricultura y Ganadería (MAG). 1988. "Incorpórese a la Agricultura de Cambio: El Cambio que Todos Necesitamos." Paid advertisement, *La Nación* (Costa Rica), May 19.

Crosby, Benjamín L. 1987. "Fragmentación y Realineamiento: Respuesta Política a la Crisis Económica." *Revista-INCAE* (Costa Rica) 1(1):7–14.

Curtis, Jennifer, with Lawrie Mott and Tom Kuhnle. 1991. *Harvest of Hope: The Potential of Alternative Agriculture to Reduce Pesticide Use.* Washington, D.C.: Natural Resources Defense Council.

DANIDA. 1992. *Environmental Sector Support: Strategic Framework, Control of Pesticide Use, Central America, First Draft.* Copenhagen: Danish International Development Agency (DANIDA).

de Campos, Marit. 1987. "Problemas Asociados con el Uso de Plaguicidas en Guatemala." In *Seminario sobre los Problemas Asociados con el Uso de Plaguicidas en Centroamérica y Panamá.* San José, Costa Rica.

de Janvry, Alain. 1981. *The Agrarian Question and Reformism in Latin America.* Baltimore: Johns Hopkins University Press.

de Janvry, Alain, R. Marsh, D. Runsten, E. Sadoulet, and C. Zabin. 1989. "Rural Development in Latin America: An Evaluation and a Proposal." Program Papers Series no. 12. Inter-American Institute for Cooperation on Agriculture.

de Janvry, Alain, E. Sadoulet, F. Rello, S. Varese, R. Irigoyen, J. Secco, A. Hintermeister, T. van der Pluijm, G. Howe, A. Monares, M. Chiriboga, H. Colmenares, P. Verteeg, B. Caas, M. Velásquez, D. Myfre, and R. García. 1992. "Agricultural Sector Reforms and the Peasantry in Mexico. Summary and Conclusions." IFAD's Special Programming Mission to Mexico: May–June, 1992. United Nations, International Fund for Agricultural Development, Geneva. Unpublished paper.

de la Ossa, A., and E. Alonso. 1990. *Exportaciones No Tradicionales en Centroamérica.* Costa Rica: FLACSO.

Deo, S. D., and L. E. Swanson. 1990. "Structure of Agricultural Research in the Third World." In C. R. Carroll, J. H. Vandermeer, and P. M. Rosset, eds., *Agroecology.* New York: McGraw-Hill.

Dornbusch, Rudiger. 1990. "Latin American Trade Misinvoicing as an Instrument of Capital Flight and Duty Evasion." IDB Occasional Papers no. 3. Washington, D.C.: Inter-American Development Bank.

Durham, W. H. 1979. *Scarcity and Survival in Central America: Ecological Origins of the Soccer War.* Stanford: Stanford University Press.

Dyer, Richard. 1988a. "Audit Memos Charge AID Favoritism Here." *Tico Times* (Costa Rica), February 19.

————. 1988b. "Explanation Asked of AID." *Tico Times* (Costa Rica), January 29.

ECLAC. 1992. *Preliminary Overview of the Latin American and Caribbean Economy. Notas sobre la Economía y el Desarrollo.* Santiago, Chile: United Nations Economic Commission for Latin America.

————. 1983. *Preliminary Overview of the Latin American Economy. Notas sobre la Economía y el Desarrollo.* Santiago, Chile: United Nations Economic Commission for Latin America.

Edelman, Marc, and Joanne Kenan, eds. 1989. *The Costa Rica Reader.* New York: Grove Press.

Escoto, Jorge, and Manfredo Marroquín. 1992. *La AID en Guatemala: Poder y Sector Empresarial.* Managua: CRIES/AVANCSO.

Fagen, Richard. 1987. *Forging Peace: The Challenge of Central America.* New York: Blackwell/PACCA.

FAO. Various years. *FAO Production Yearbook.* Rome: Food and Agriculture Organization of the United Nations.

————. 1990. *Centroamérica: Estudio Regional del Algodón.* Rome: Food and Agriculture Organization of the United Nations.

FDA. Various years. Files of the National Import Detention System. Washington, D.C.

————. 1989. *World Wide Import Detention Summary (Fiscal Year 1989).* Washington, D.C.: Department of Health and Human Services, Food and Drug Administration.

————. 1988. *Residues in Food—1988.* Washington, D.C.: Department of Health and Human Services, Food and Drug Administration.

Flora, Jan L. 1987. "Roots of Insurgency in Central America." *Latin America Issues* 5:1–46.

Flores, Edmundo. 1965. "La Alianza para el Progreso y la Reforma Agraria." In Oscar Delgado, ed., *Reformas Agrarias en la América Latina: Procesos y Perspectivas.* Mexico: Fondo de Cultura Económica.

FPX. 1990. *Plan de Desarrollo de Producto: Melón, 1990/1991.* San Pedro Sula: Federación de Productores y Exportadores Agropecuarios y Agroindustriales de Honduras.

Friedland, William. 1984. "Commodity Systems Analysis." *Research in Rural Sociology* 1:221–235.

Gereffi, Gary. 1994. "The Organization of Buyer-Driven Global Commodity Chains: How U.S. Retailers Shape Overseas Production Networks." In Gary Gereffi and Miguel Korzeniewicz, eds., *Commodity Chains and Global Capitalism*. Westport, Conn.: Praeger.

Gereffi, Gary, and R. S. Newfarmer. 1985. "International Oligopoly and Uneven Development: Some Lessons from Industrial Case Studies." In R. Newfarmer, ed., *Profits, Progress and Poverty*. Notre Dame: University of Notre Dame Press.

Glade, W. P. 1969. *The Latin American Economies: A Study of Their Institutional Evolution*. New York: American Books.

Glover, David, and Ken Kusterer. 1990. *Small Farmers and Big Business: Contract Farming and Rural Development*. New York: St. Martin's Press.

Goldsmith, Arthur. 1985. "The Private Sector and Rural Development: Can Agribusiness Help the Small Farmer?" *World Development* 13(10/11):1125–1138.

Grynspan, Devora. 1988. "Central America: Development Options for a Region in Crisis." Paper presented at the Annual Meetings of the Latin American Studies Association, New Orleans, March.

Hansen-Kuhn, Karen. 1993. *Structural Adjustment in Central America: The Case of Costa Rica*. Washington, D.C.: The Development GAP.

Hayami, Y., and V. W. Ruttan. 1985. *Agricultural Development*. Baltimore: Johns Hopkins Press.

Honey, Martha. 1994. *Hostile Acts: U.S. Policy in Costa Rica in the 1980s*. Gainesville: University Press of Florida.

Hoppin, Polly. 1991. "Pesticide Use on Four Non-Traditional Crops in Guatemala: Program and Policy Implications." Ph.D. diss., Johns Hopkins University, Baltimore, Md.

———. 1989. "Pesticide Use in Four Non-Traditional Crops in Guatemala: Implications for Residues." Report of the Center for International Crop Protection, Washington, D.C., June 16.

How, R. Brian. 1991. *Marketing Fresh Fruits and Vegetables*. New York: Van Nostrand Reinhold.

ICAITI. 1977. *An Environmental and Economic Study of the Consequences of Pesticide Use in Central American Cotton Production*. Guatemala: Instituto Centroamericano de Investigación y Tecnología Industrial.

ICCARD. 1989. *Poverty, Conflict, and Hope: A Turning Point in Central America*. Durham, N.C.: International Commission on Central American Reconstruction and Development, Duke University Center for International Development Research.

ICES (Instituto Costarricense de Estudios Sociales). 1987. "Costa Rica es el Nombre del Juego." Working paper, CRIES, Nicaragua, Series 14:37–90.

IDB. 1990. *Economic and Social Progress in Latin America. 1990 Report*. Washington, D.C.: Inter-American Development Bank Social Progress Trust Fund.

———. 1989. *IDB Notes*. Washington, D.C.: Inter-American Development Bank.

———. 1987. *Economic and Social Progress in Latin America. 1987 Report*. Washington, D.C.: Inter-American Development Bank Social Progress Trust Fund.

IFPRI (International Food Policy Research Institute), Institute of Nutrition of

Central America and Panama, Unión de Cuatro Pinos Cooperative, Ileana Pinto, et al. 1992. *Nontraditional Export Crops Among Smallholder Farmers and Production, Income, Nutrition and Quality of Life Effects: A Comparative Analysis 1985–1991.* Washington, D.C.: IFPRI.

"IMF Okays Contingency Loan for Costa Rica." 1987. *Tico Times* (Costa Rica), October 30.

Jeyaratnam, J. 1990. "Pesticide Poisoning: A Major Global Health Problem." *World Health Statistics Quarterly* 43:139–144.

Kaimowitz, David. 1991. "Cambio Tecnológico y la Promoción de Exportaciones Agrícolas No Tradicionales en América Central." San José: IICA (photocopy).

Keifer, Matthew C. 1991. "Protective Effect on Cholinesterase Levels of an Integrated Pest Management Program in Nicaraguan Basic Grain Farmers." Managua: CARE/MINSA.

Keifer, Matthew C., and Feliciano Pacheco. 1991. "Reporte de Encuesta de Subregistro de Intoxicaciones con Plaguicidas Sobre el Año 1989, Región II, León, Nicaragua." Managua: CARE International.

Kissinger Commission. 1984. *Report of the National Bipartisan Commission on Central America.* Washington, D.C.: United States National Bipartisan Commission on Central America.

Knirsch, Jurgen. 1991. "Pesticides in the Global Marketplace." *Global Pesticide Monitor* 1(3):1–7.

Korten, Alicia. 1995. "A Bitter Pill: Structural Adjustment in Costa Rica." Institute for Food and Development Policy (Food First) Development Report no. 7.

———. 1993. "Central American Farmers on Free Trade." *IEEE Newsletter* (July):9–11.

———. 1992. "Structural Adjustment, the Environment and the Poor: The Case Study of Costa Rica." Senior Honors thesis, Latin American Studies Department, Brown University, Providence, R.I.

Krueger, Chris. 1989. "Development and Politics in Rural Guatemala." *Bulletin of the Institute for Development Anthropology* 7(1):1–6.

La Nación. 1988. "CNP Inició Distribución de Frijoles Importados." *La Nación* (Costa Rica), January 10.

Lack, Stephen, C. Kenneth Laurent, Conchita Espinoza, Arden Christiansen, and Donald Calvert. 1989. *Final Evaluation Report: Agricultural Crop Diversification/Export Promotion Cross-Cutting Evaluation.* Washington, D.C.: Experience, Inc.

Levine, R. S. 1985. "Informal Consultation on Planning Strategy for the Prevention of Pesticide Poisoning" (unpublished document). Geneva: World Health Organization.

Lindarte, Eduardo. 1990. "Technological Institutions in the Region: Evolution and Current State." Paper prepared for Conference on the Transfer and Utilization of Agricultural Technology in Central America, sponsored by the Inter-American Institute for Cooperation on Agriculture (IICA) and USAID-ROCAP, San José, Costa Rica, March 12–18.

López, Gilberto, and Eduardo Ramírez. 1988. "Entrevista a John Biehl." *Semanario Universidad* (Costa Rica), June 24.

López, José Gabriel. 1990. "Agrarian Transformation and the Political, Ideological and Cultural Responses from the Base: A Case Study from Western Mexico." Ph.D. diss., University of Texas, Austin.

López, Mario R., and Irene Guevara O. 1991. *Los Productos Agrícolas No Tradicionales en Nicaragua: Un Perfil de Productores de Melón y Piña.* Managua, Nicaragua: CIES, November.

Lordan, Betsy. 1986. "Lizano Urges 'Realism' in Meetings with IMF." *Tico Times* (Costa Rica), September 26.

MacVean, Charles, Ronaldo Pérez, and Helda Morales. 1993. "Impacto Ecológico de Cultivos Hortícolas No-tradicionales en el Altiplano de Guatemala." *Revista de la Universidad del Valle de Guatemala* 3:14–22.

Marenco, Roberto. 1990. *Informe Preliminar de Actividades del Departmento de Protección Vegetal de la Escuela Agrícola Panamericana en el Programa de Manejo Integrado de Plagas de Cucúrbitas en el Sur de Honduras.* El Zamorano, Honduras: Escuela Agrícola Panamericana.

Mathieson, John A. 1988. "Dominican Republic." In Eva Paus, ed., *Struggle Against Dependency: Nontraditional Export Growth in Central America and the Caribbean.* Boulder, Colo.: Westview Press.

McConnell, Rob. 1988. "Epidemiology and Occupational Health in Developing Countries: Pesticides in Nicaragua." In C. Hogstedt and C. Reuterwall, eds., *Progress in Occupational Epidemiology.* Uppsala: Elsevier Science Publisher.

McConnell, Rob, Matthew Keifer, and Linda Rosenstock. 1994. "Elevated Tactile Vibration Threshold Among Workers Previously Poisoned with Methamidophos." *American Journal of Industrial Medicine* 25(3):325–334.

McConnell, Rob, Feliciano Pacheco, Nestor Castro, and Matthew Keifer. 1990. "Poisoning Epidemics and Preventative Health Care." *Global Pesticide Monitor* 1(2):10–11.

Mendes, Rene. 1977. *Informe sobre Salud Ocupacional de Trabajadores Agricolas en Centro América y Panamá.* Washington, D.C.: Pan-American Health Organization.

Mendizábal, Ana Beatríz, and Jürgen Weller. 1992. *Exportaciones Agrícolas No Tradicionales: ¿Promesa o Espejismo?* Panama: Unidad de Publicaciones de CADESCA.

Miller, Valerie. 1992. *High Hopes, Harsh Realities: The Challenge of Development in Central America.* Cambridge, Mass.: Unitarian Universalist Service Committee.

MIS, Inc. 1993. *HealthFocus.* Marketing Intelligence Services, Inc., September.

Morales, Helda, Ronaldo Pérez, and Charles MacVean. 1993. *Impacto Ambiental de Cultivos No-tradicionales en el Altiplano de Guatemala. Reporte Final Presentado a la Asociación para el Avance de las Ciencias Sociales en Guatemala (AVANCSO).* Guatemala: Universidad del Valle, Instituto de Investigaciones.

Morgan, Jennifer, et al. 1990. "Expanding the Organic Produce Niche: Issues and Obstacles." USDA-ERS Report no. 20816.

Mott, Lawrie, and Karen Snyder. 1988. *Pesticide Alert: A Guide to Pesticides in Fruits and Vegetables.* New York: Sierra Books.

Murray, Douglas L. 1994. *Cultivating Crisis: The Human Cost of Pesticides in Latin America.* Austin: University of Texas Press.

———. 1992. *Informe de Viaje a Zacapa, 18–22 Mayo.* Guatemala: Asociación para el Avance de las Ciencias Sociales (AVANCSO).

———. 1991. "Export Agriculture, Ecological Disruption, and Inequitable Development: Some Effects of Pesticides in Southern Honduras." *Agriculture and Human Values* 8(4):19–29.

———. 1989. *Developing Integrated Pest Management in the Dominican Republic: A Five Year Plan.* Stamford, Conn.: IRI Research Institute.

Murray, Douglas L., Michael Giuliano, and S. Anwar Rizvi. 1989. *Dominican Republic: The Agricultural Exports Protection Report.* Washington, D.C.: Development Alternatives Incorporated.

Murray, Douglas L., and Polly Hoppin. 1992. "Recurring Contradictions in Agrarian Development: Pesticide Problems in Caribbean Basin Nontraditional Agriculture." *World Development* 20(4):597–608.

Murray, Douglas L., and Rob McConnell. 1987. *Pesticide Problems Among Small Farmers in Costa Rica: An Evaluation and Recommendations for CARE Costa Rica.* New York: CARE International.

Nathan Associates, Inc., and Louis Berger International, Inc. 1990. "Export Promotion and Investment Promotion: Sustainability and Effective Service Delivery." Report to the Agency for International Development under Contract No. PDC–0095–1–9096–00.

National Research Council. 1993. *Pesticides in the Diets of Infants and Children.* Washington, D.C.: National Academy Press.

Nelson, Kristen C. 1994. "Participation and Empowerment: A Comparative Study of IPM Technology Generation in Nicaragua." Ph.D. diss., University of Michigan, Ann Arbor.

Nelson, Lisa K. 1988. *The Burden of Development: The Effects of Agricultura de Cambio on the Small Farmer in Costa Rica.* San José: Associated Colleges of the Midwest.

Núñez Soto, Orlando. 1978. *El Somocismo y el Modelo Agro-Exportador.* Managua: UNAN.

Organic Times. 1993. *Natural Foods Merchandiser's 1993 Organic Times.* Boulder, Colo.: New Hope Communications.

Paige, J. M. 1984. "Cotton and Revolution in Nicaragua." Center for Research on Social Organization Working Paper no. 319. University of Michigan.

PANUPS. 1995. "U.S. Organic Sales Top $2 Billion." Pesticide Action Network North America Updates Service no. 21, pp. 4–5, August.

Perdomo, Rodulio, and Hugo Noé Pino. 1992. "El Impacto de las Exportaciones No Tradicionales sobre Pequeños Productores en Honduras: El Caso del Melón." In Ana Beatríz Mendizábal P. and Jürgen Weller, eds., *Exportaciones Agrícolas No Tradicionales: ¿Promesa o Espejismo? Su Análisis y Evaluación en el Istmo Centroamericano.* Panama: CADESCA/PREALC/OIT.

———. 1991. *Impacto de las Políticas de Fomento a las Exportaciones No Tradicionales Sobre Pequeños y Medianos Productores. Casos de los Cultivos del Melón y Camarón, Informe Final.* Tegucigalpa: Posgrado Centroamericano en Economía y Planificación del Desarollo.

Perelman, M. 1977. *Farming for Profit in a Hungry World: Capital and the Crisis in Agriculture.* Totowa, N.J.: Allanheld, Osmun.

Pérez-Brignoli, Héctor. 1989. *A Brief History of Central America.* Berkeley: University of California Press.

Perkins, John H. 1982. *Insects, Experts, and the Insecticide Crisis: The Quest for New Pest Management Strategies.* New York: Plenum Press.

Pimentel, David. 1991. "Environmental and Economic Impacts of Reducing U.S. Agricultural Pesticide Use." In *CRC Handbook of Pest Management in Agriculture.* 2d ed., Vol. 1. Boston: CRC Press.

PROEXAG. 1989. Memorandum from John Lamb to PROEXAG Team, C.A. USAID Missions, and others.

Raynolds, Laura T. 1994. "The Restructuring of Third World Agro-Exports: Changing Production in the Dominican Republic." In Philip McMichael ed., *The Global Restructuring of Agro-Food Systems.* Ithaca, N.Y.: Cornell University Press.

———. 1992. "The Restructuring of Export Agriculture in the Dominican Republic:

Changing Agrarian Production Relations and the State." Ph.D. diss. Cornell University, Ithaca, N.Y.

Reich, Robert B. 1992. *The Work of Nations*. New York: Vintage Books.

Repetto, Robert. 1985. *Paying the Price: Pesticide Subsidies in Developing Countries*. Washington, D.C.: World Resource Institute.

Reuben Soto, Sergio. 1988. *Ajuste Estructural en Costa Rica*. Costa Rica: Editorial Porvenir.

Reuben Soto, William. 1989. "El Potencial de la Economía Campesina en la Reactivación Económica y el Desarrollo de Costa Rica: Contribución a una Estrategía de Ajuste Democrático." In *Los Campesinos Frente a la Nueva Década: Ajuste Estructural y Pequeña Producción Agropecuaria en Costa Rica*. Costa Rica: Editorial Porvenir.

Rivas Villatoro, Alvaro. 1991. "Las Exportaciones Agrícolas No Tradicionales Costarricenses, 1989–1990." Final investigative report, Regional Project, University of Texas, Austin. San José, Costa Rica: CECADE.

Rosa, Herman. 1993. *AID y las Transformaciones Globales en El Slavador*. Managua: CRIES.

Rosenstock, Linda, Matthew Keifer, William E. Daniell, Rob McConnell, and Keith Claypoole. 1991. "Chronic Central Nervous System Effects of Acute Organophosphate Pesticide Intoxication." *The Lancet,* July 26.

Rosset, Peter. 1994. "Eye-Opening Notes from Central America." *Food First News and Views* 16(54):2–4.

———. 1992a. "¿Es Factible el Manejo Integrado de Plagas en el Contexto de la Producción Campesina de los Cultivos No Tradicionales de Agroexportación?" *CEIBA* (Honduras) 33(1A):75–90.

———. 1992b. *Informe de Visita a Guatemala, 16-20 Mayo*. Guatemala: Asociación para el Avance de las Ciencias Sociales (AVANCSO).

———. 1991a. "Non-Traditional Export Agriculture in Central America: Impact on Peasant Farmers." Working paper prepared for the Workshop on the Globalization of the Fresh Fruit and Vegetable System, University of California at Santa Cruz, December 6–9.

———. 1991b. "Sustainability, Economies of Scale and Social Instability: Achilles Heel of Non-traditional Export Agriculture?" *Agriculture and Human Values* 8(4):30–37.

———. 1987. "Precios, Subvenciones y Los Niveles de Daño Económico." *Manejo Integrado de Plagas* (Costa Rica) 6:27–35.

Rosset, Peter, John Gershman, Shea Cunningham, and Marilyn Borchardt. 1994. "Myths and Root Causes: Hunger, Population and Development." *Institute for Food and Development Policy (Food First) Backgrounder* 1:1–8.

Rosset, Peter, and Jaana Remes. 1993. *Informe de Consultoría: Análisis de Encuestas Aplicadas a Pequeños Productores en Guatemala durante 1991*. Guatemala: AVANCSO.

Rosset, Peter M., and E. Secaira. 1989. "Cultivos Hortícolas." In Keith L. Andrews and J. R. Quezada, eds., *Manejo Integrado de Plagas Insectiles en la Agricultura: Estado Actual y Futuro*. El Zamorano, Honduras: Escuela Agrícola Panamericana.

Rosset, Peter, and John Vandermeer. 1986a. "The Confrontation Between Processors and Farmworkers in the Midwest Tomato Industry and the Role of the Agricultural Research and Extension Establishment." *Agriculture and Human Values* 3(3):26–32.

———, eds. 1986b. *Nicaragua: Unfinished Revolution*. New York: Grove Press.

Rostow, W. W. 1960. *The Stages of Economic Growth: A Non-Communist Manifesto.* 2d ed. Cambridge: Cambridge University Press.

Roy, E. P. 1972. *Contract Farming and Economic Integration.* Danville, Ill.: Interstate.

Sabel, Charles. 1993. *Stories, Strategies, Structures: Rethinking Historical Alternatives to Mass Production.* New York: Columbia University Center for Law and Economic Studies.

Sachs, J. D. 1987. "Trade and Exchange Rate Policies in Growth-Oriented Adjustment Programs." In *Symposium on Growth-Oriented Adjustment Programs.* Washington, D.C.: World Bank and International Monetary Fund.

Saldomando, Ángel. 1992. *El Retorno de la AID. El Caso de Nicaragua: Condicionalidad y Restructuración Conservadora.* Managua: CRIES.

Sanford Commission. 1989. *Poverty, Conflict, and Hope: A Turning Point in Central America.* Report of the International Commission for Central American Recovery and Development. Durham, N.C.: Duke University.

Seligson, M. 1980. *Peasants of Costa Rica and the Development of Agrarian Capitalism.* Madison: University of Wisconsin Press.

Shallat, Lezak. 1989. "AID and the Secret Parallel State." In Marc Edelman and Joanne Kenan, eds., *The Costa Rica Reader.* New York: Grove Press.

———. 1988. "AID Building—Monument to Policy Paradoxes." *Tico Times* (Costa Rica), December 2.

SIECA (Secretaria para la Integración Económica Centroamericana). 1988. *Plan de Acción Inmediata.* Guatemala: Government of Guatemala.

Sobhan, Rehman. 1993. *Agrarian Reform and Social Transformation.* London: Zed Books.

Sojo, Carlos. 1992. *La Mano Visible del Mercado: La Asistencia de Estados Unidos al Sector Privado Costarricense en la Década de los Ochenta.* Managua: CRIES.

———. 1991. *La Utopía del Estado Mínimo: La Influencia de AID en las Transformaciones Funcionales e Institucionales del Estado Costarricense en los Años Ochenta.* Managua: CRIES.

Soule, James. 1990. "Transportation. Tropical Horticultural Crop Development for Export Marketing." Special Insert in *HortScience* 25(1):33–35.

Stonich, Susan C., Douglas L. Murray, and Peter M. Rosset. 1994. "Enduring Crises: The Human and Environmental Consequences of Nontraditional Export Growth in Central America." *Research in Economic Anthropology* 15:239–274.

Swezey, Sean L., Douglas L. Murray, and Rainer G. Daxl. 1986. "Nicaragua's Revolution in Pesticide Policy." *Environment* 28(1):6–9, 29–36.

Talekar, N. S., and T. D. Griggs, eds. 1986. *Diamondback Moth Management: Proceedings of the First International Workshop.* Taiwan: AVRDC.

Tapia, Humberto. 1984. *Manejo Integrado del Frijol.* Managua: Instituto Superior de Ciencias Agropecuarias.

Thacher, T. A. 1990. "The Role of Foreign Investment: An Obstacle to National Participation in the Export Sectors of Ornamental Plants, Flowers, and Foliage." Senior report. Northfield, Minn.: Carleton College.

Thrupp, Lori Ann. 1989. "Legitimizing Local Knowledge: From Displacement to Empowerment for Third World People." *Agriculture and Human Values* 6(3):13–24.

Thrupp, Lori Ann, Gilles Bergeron, and William F. Waters. 1995. *Bittersweet Harvests for Global Supermarkets: Challenges in Latin America's Agricultural Export Boom.* Washington, D.C.: World Resources Institute.

Trivelato, Maria D., and Catharina Wesseling. 1991. *El Uso de los Plaguicidas en Costa Rica y Sus Consecuencias.* Heredia: Universidad Nacional de Costa Rica.

UN, CEPAL. 1990. *El Choque Petrolero de 1990 y la Economía Centroamericana: Documento Preliminar, Datos Básicos y Algunas Recomendaciones.* Mexico City: Comisión Económica para América Latina y el Caribe.

United Nations. 1988. "Plan Especial de Cooperación Económica para Centroamérica." New York, March 15.

"US AID Controversy: Arias Advisor Speaks His Mind." 1988. *Latin American Monitor* 5(6):559.

USAID. 1991. "Latin American Exports to the United States: 1991 Projections." PROEXAG.

———. 1990. "Promoting Trade and Investment in Constrained Environments: A.I.D. Experience in Latin America and the Caribbean." Report prepared by The Development Economics Group of Louis Berger International, Inc. U.S. Agency for International Development Evaluation Special Study No. 69.

———. 1987. *Annual Budget Submission FY 1989 Costa Rica.* Washington, D.C.: U.S. Agency for International Development

———. 1982. *Annual Budget Submission FY 1984 Costa Rica.* Washington, D.C.: U.S. Agency for International Development.

———. 1972. *Development Assistance Program FY 1974.* Central America. Washington, D.C.: U.S. Agency for International Development.

USAID/Costa Rica. 1989. *Action Plan FY 1991–1992.* Costa Rica: U.S. Agency for International Development.

———. 1986. *Action Plan FY 1988–1989.* Costa Rica: U.S. Agency for International Development.

———. 1976. *Development Assistance Program.* Costa Rica: U.S. Agency for International Development.

USAID/Honduras. 1990. *Agricultural Sector Strategy Paper.* Tegucigalpa, Honduras: Office of Agricultural and Rural Development.

USAID/LAC. 1984. *Costa Rica Project Paper: Economic Stabilization and Recovery III, AID/LAC/P–173.* Washington, D.C.: U.S. Agency for International Development.

USDA. 1992. *World Agricultural Trade Indicators.* Washington, D.C.: U.S. Department of Agriculture.

USDA Market Research Service. 1991. *Annual Summary of Fresh Fruit and Vegetable Shipments.* Beltsville, Md.: U.S. Department of Agriculture, Market Research Service.

van Gillst, Erik. 1994. "Café Orgánico y Nicaragua: Producción, Comercialización y Rentabilidad." *Revista de Economía Agrícola* (Nicaragua) 7:3–16.

Vandermeer, John, and Ivette Perfecto. 1995. *Breakfast of Biodiversity: The Truth about Rain Forest Destruction.* Oakland, Calif.: Food First Books.

Vaughn, M., and G. Leon. 1977. "Pesticide Management in a Major Crop with Severe Resistance Problems." In *XV International Congress of Entomology.* Washington, D.C.

"'Vendetta' Charged in AID Affair." 1988. *Tico Times* (Costa Rica), February 5.

Vermeer, René. 1989. "La Política Agraria de la Adminsitración Arias en el Marco del Ajuste Estructural." In William Reuben Soto, ed., *Los Campesinos Frente a la Nueva Década: Ajuste Estructural y Pequeña Producción Agropecuaria en Costa Rica.* Costa Rica: Editorial Porvenir.

von Braun, J., D. Hotchkiss, and M. Immink. 1989. "Nontraditional Export Crops in Guatemala: Effects on Production, Income, and Nutrition." International Food Policy Research Institute Research Report No. 73.

Vunderink, Gregg L. 1990–1991. "Peasant Participation and Mobilization during Economic Crisis: The Case of Costa Rica." *Studies in Comparative International Development* 25:3–24.

Watts, Michael. 1990. "Peasants Under Contract." In B. Crow, H. Bernstein, and M. Mackintosh, eds., *The Food Question.* London: Earthscan.

Weir, David, and Mark Shapiro. 1981. *Circle of Poison: Pesticides and People in a Hungry World.* San Francisco: Institute for Food and Development Policy.

Weller, Jürgen. 1992. "Las Exportaciones Agrícolas No Tradicionales y sus Efectos en el Empleo y los Ingresos." In A. B. Mendizábal P. and J. Weller, eds., *Exportaciones Agrícolas No Tradicionales: ¿Promesa o Espejismo?* Panama: CADESCA.

WHO. 1989. *Public Health Impact of Pesticides Used in Agriculture.* Geneva: World Health Organization.

———. 1973. *Safe Use of Pesticides.* Geneva: World Health Organization.

Williams, Robert G. 1986. *Export Agriculture and the Crisis in Central America.* Chapel Hill: University of North Carolina Press.

Williams, S., and R. Karen. 1985. *Agribusiness and the Small Scale Farmer.* Boulder: Westview Press.

Wolff, Mary S., Paolo G. Toniolo, Eric W. Lee, Marilyn Rivera, and Neil Dubin. 1993. "Blood Levels of Organochlorine Residues and Risk of Breast Cancer." *Journal of the National Cancer Institute* 85(8):648–652.

World Bank. Various years. *World Tables: World Bank Data on Diskette.* Washington, D.C.: World Bank.

Wright, Angus. 1986. "Rethinking the Circle of Poison: The Politics of Pesticide Poisoning among Mexican Farm Workers." *Latin American Perspectives* 13(4):26–59.

Zind, Tom. 1990. "Pretto Lures U.S. Melon Business." *The Packer* March 10.

Zuvekas, Clarence, Jr. 1988. "Central America's Foreign Trade and Balance of Payments: The Outlook for 1988–2000." Paper presented at the University of Texas in April 1988.

INDEX

▼▼▼▼▼▼▼

ABOUT THE INSTITUTE FOR FOOD AND DEVELOPMENT POLICY (FOOD FIRST)

▼▼▼▼▼▼▼

Food First is a nonprofit research and education-for-action center. We work to identify the root causes of hunger and poverty in the United States and around the world, and to educate the public as well as policymakers about these problems.

The world has never produced so much food as it does today—more than enough to feed every child, woman, and man. Yet hunger is on the rise, with more than one billion people around the world going without enough to eat.

Food First research has demonstrated that hunger and poverty are not inevitable. Our publications reveal how scarcity and overpopulation, long believed to be the causes of hunger, are instead symptoms—symptoms of an ever-increasing concentration of control over food-producing resources in the hands of a few, depriving so many people of the power to feed themselves. In fifty-five countries and twenty languages, Food First materials and activism are freeing people from the grip of despair and laying the groundwork—in ideas and action—for a more democratically controlled food system that will meet the needs of all.

▼ An Invitation to Join Us

Private contributions and membership dues form Food First's financial base. Because we are not tied to any government, corporation, or university, we can speak with strong independent voices, free of ideological formulas. The success of our programs depends not only on dedicated volunteers and staff, but on financial activists as well. All our efforts toward ending hunger are made possible by membership dues or gifts from individuals, small foundations, and religious organizations.

Each new and continuing member strengthens our effort to change a hungry world. We'd like to invite you to join in this effort. As a member you will receive a 20 percent discount on all Food First books. You will also receive our quarterly publication, *Food First News and Views,* and our timely *Backgrounders,* which provide information and suggestions for action on current food and hunger crises in the United States and around the world.

All contributions to Food First are tax deductible. To join us in putting food first, please call or write us for more information.

Institute for Food and Development Policy/Food First
398 60th Street, Oakland, CA 94618
(510) 654-4400
foodfirst@igc.apc.org

Research internship opportunities are also available.

ABOUT THE BOOK AND AUTHORS

▼▼▼▼▼▼▼▼

Neither structural adjustment policies, nor industrialization, nor traditional agricultural exports have led to sustained economic growth and social equity in Central America. Seeking to reinvigorate the region's struggling economies, U.S. AID—supported by the World Bank and the IMF—designed a new development policy, one based on nontraditional agricultural exports. Crops ranging from passion fruit and broccoli to macadamia nuts and melons have been vigorously promoted through massive foreign aid and fierce pressure on local governments.

This book dissects the varied impacts of a decade of this central AID policy—impacts on the environment, on the livelihoods of thousands of small farmers, and on the sovereignty of elected governments. An anatomy of failure, of a policy gamble run amuck, the book is a cautionary tale that is must reading for scholars, practitioners, policymakers, and students of international development and U.S. foreign policy.

Michael E. Conroy, director of the Latin American Economic Studies Program at the University of Texas at Austin, is currently on leave serving as program officer in the Environment and Development Area for the Ford Foundation's Office for Mexico and Central America. **Douglas L. Murray** is assistant professor of sociology at Colorado State University. **Peter M. Rosset** is executive director of the Institute for Food and Development Policy (Food First) in Oakland, California.